T0309818

From Aristotle to Thomas Aquinas

Other Books of Interest from St. Augustine's Press

From Aristotle to Thomas Aquinas
Natural Law, Practical Knowledge, and the Person

FULVIO DI BLASI

ST. AUGUSTINE'S PRESS

South Bend, Indiana

Manufactured in the United States of America.

1 2 3 4 5 6   26 25 24 23 22 21

Library of Congress Cataloging in Publication Data
Names: Di Blasi, Fulvio, author.
Title: From Aristotle to Thomas Aquinas : natural law, practical knowledge, and the person / Fulvio Di Blasi.
Description: 1st [edition].
South Bend, Indiana : St. Augustines Press, Inc., 2016.
Includes bibliographical references and index.
Identifiers: LCCN 2016033731
ISBN 9781587312731 (hardcover : alk. paper)
Subjects: LCSH: Thomas, Aquinas, Saint, 1225?-1274.
Aristotle--Influence.
Classification: LCC B765.T54 D4833 2016
DDC 171/.2092--dc23 LC
record available at https://lccn.loc.gov/2016033731

∞ The paper used in this publication meets the minimum requirements of the American National Standard for Information Sciences – Permanence of Paper for Printed Materials, ANSI Z39.48-1984.

St. Augustine's Press
www.staugustine.net

TABLE OF CONTENTS

INTRODUCTION

This book collects some of the essays that I have written between the years 2000 and 2006, which I consider a significant expression of the research and personal reflection that follow my book *God and the Natural Law* (Pisa, Italy, 1999; South Bend, IN, 2003). This research concerns chiefly the human being as an ethical agent and the knowledge of the good. My focus is above all on Aristotle and Thomas Aquinas. My reading of these authors is always done in the light of the contemporary philosophical debate as well as the questions raised by modernity and the post-modernity crisis. Rediscovering the beauty and richness of classical thought is not meant to create new epochal contrasts, like the one between modern and medieval times, but rather to look for new syntheses that are less ideological and more useful to the paths on which we continue to walk in history.

My interests lie preferentially in practical philosophy (ethics, politics, and law), and its relationship with metaphysics. The issues and subject matters I address in each chapter benefit from the courses in philosophy that I taught both in the United States and in Italy. Here and there I added some outlines and slides that I used in class in order to make it easier to grasp key arguments and conceptual analysis. This is a two-edged sword. On the one hand, it helps the reader better understand my line of reasoning. On the other hand, it exposes me to sharper and more effective criticism. I hope that, through those slides, readers will appreciate even more the love of the truth that should ground philosophical research. I came to the conclusion over the years that friendship is authentic and flourishes only when it is also a common search for the truth. I am convinced that the particular type of friendship that *ought to* exist in the academic community depends on a difficult but fascinating mixture of charity, detachment, and courage. Truth emerges more from dialectic (in the Greek sense) and from criticism, rather than from obscure writings and obsequious compliments. I consider a good friend whoever takes what I write seriously enough that he does not hesitate to point out to me possible mistakes I may make, or to criticize me strongly and publicly if necessary. "*Si quidam vero contra haec rescribere voluerint, mihi acceptissimum erit. Nullo enim modo melius quam contradicentibus resistendo, aperuit veritas et falsitas confutatur*" (Thomas Aquinas, *De Perfectione Spiritualis Vitae*).

The main topic in the book is the knowledge of the good, which is strictly connected to the concepts of practical reason and practical reasoning. This is the issue that probably caught my attention the most in the years following *God and the Natural Law*, which was highly dependent on the remarkable recovery in the contemporary debate of the concept of practical rationality and of the distinction between practical knowledge and theoretical or speculative knowledge. My impression from reading the classical authors is that concepts that they had already to some extent distinguished from one another appear today as undistinguished; as if, with the passing of the years, we had lost several nuances and ironed out many strategic concepts. Today, for example, it is quite common to use terms like "knowledge of the good," "practical knowledge," and "practical reason" as if they were synonyms, while for the Aristotelian Thomas Aquinas they referred to things that are connected, of course, but very different from one another. I had the same impression of "ironed-out meanings" with other important concepts like person, self, human nature, will, and natural inclination.

The first three chapters are meant primarily to clarify, from an Aristotelian-Thomistic point of view, the exact meanings of "knowledge of the good," "practical knowledge," and "practical reason." They are arranged in a sort of ascending order that reaches its most precise definition in Chapter III, "Law as 'Act of Reason' and 'Command.'" It might appear odd that my most precise definition of practical knowledge is to be found, among all the chapters, in the one most directly and technically devoted the concept of law. However, we should not forget that, for Aquinas law is a concept analogically applied to specific acts of both human and divine reason. If law involves an act of practical knowledge, and if such an act can be referred to God's action as well as to human action, analogical predication has to be suitable to lead us to the perfect meaning (*res significata*) of "practical knowledge" in God. Therefore, the precision of my methodology (assuming that my conclusions are correct) depends on the attempt to consistently apply analogy as an interpretative tool for Thomistic concepts. I explain these implications of the concept of analogy especially in the first section of Chapter III.

The first chapter, "Knowledge of the Good as Participation in God's Love," is perhaps the most metaphysical in the entire book. It aims at reaching the core of Aquinas' concept of good and its intrinsic relationship with the question of God. The most important concept that I use and explain to this purpose is participation, which is in my opinion an extraordinary example of how Aquinas was able to harmoniously merge the apex of Plato's thought and the most refined metaphysics of Aristotle. This chapter is the most suitable introduction to the main themes of the book. Chapter II, on the other hand, "Practical Syllogism, *Proairesis*, and the Virtues: Toward a Reconciliation of Virtue Ethics and Natural Law Ethics," is crucial to understanding my way of interpreting the relationship between Aristotle's ethics and Aquinas' natural law theory. It also explains what kind of knowledge is used in our moral action, and in what sense this knowledge can be called "scientific". In many respects, including the analysis of Aristotle's concept of *proairesis*, it is a very technical chapter that some readers may want to skip. Still, it is an ideal follow-up to the first, and it conceptually grounds what follows.

Natural law is knowledge of the good and knowledge of the truth, which, long before Aquinas goes back to Socrates' teaching that morality is nothing other than acting according to the truth. If I am right about my reading of the ethical tradition that runs from Socrates to Aquinas, natural law is possible in us because of the spiritual nature that makes us persons, and that makes it possible for us to know the truth. This is why one of the key concepts in my natural law approach is precisely the concept of person, which in turn grounds everything more specific that remains to be said about natural law.

In Chapter IV, "Spirit or Digital Self? The Concept of Person in Philosophy and Contemporary Science," I try to recover a more metaphysical and less, so to speak, emotional concept of person, which involves something that we may as well call spirit or soul. Today everybody likes to talk about the dignity of the person and about inviolable human rights, but few are willing to go deeper to the metaphysical grounds of that dignity and alleged inviolability. As a result, "person" easily becomes everything that people emotionally like; and when they don't like it, of course, it "must not" be a person. I try to show how the concept of person was implicitly born in Greek philosophy, and technically discovered and explained in Medieval Christian thought, and arrives at the detailed analysis offered by Aquinas. Despite many superficial references to Aquinas' "metaphysical" approach in recent debates, the core of his definition of the person is ethical and so "modern" that both Rousseau and Kant would have rejoiced in it had only they known. I address the concept of person first by engaging contemporary science and the concept of artificial intelligence. In fact, I believe that due in part also to so many (and fascinating) sci-fi movies today science offers a wonderful battleground for anybody like me who claims that there is something more to the person than just digital codes, neuronal electrical impulses, or a sequence of nucleotides or genetic code.

If natural law relates to an agent—the person—whose nature goes beyond the borders of the material world, the overall point or meaning or end of this agent should not be limited to, or by, the world as we see it in this life. Even from this viewpoint, it makes a lot of sense to me that Aquinas raised Aristotle's concept of ultimate end—the grounding concept of his ethics—to the level of our beatitude, the vision of God. Our transcendental nature as spiritual beings together with a sound concept of the person and his capacity to know the truth shed a lot of light on the meaning of the human being as an ethical subject or agent. To the concept of ultimate end and beatitude is committed chapter V, "Ultimate End, Human Freedom, and Beatitude: A Critique of Germain Grisez", which was originally presented a the 2001 *Natural Law Conference* organized by the *Natural Law Institute* of the Notre Dame Law School. This conference focused on a lecture given by Germain Grisez on "Natural Law, God, Religion, and Human Fulfillment," to which the other speakers were invited to reply. The articles that appeared in the proceedings of the conference in the *American Journal of Jurisprudence*, 46 (2001) are very different from the papers that were originally given. I have always preferred my original paper because, I think, it is clearer, more concise, and truer. I had never published it in English until now.

Since my book *God and the Natural Law*, I have always claimed that several modern and contemporary natural law theories—especially today the so called new natural law theory developed by John Finnis, Germain

Grisez, and others—even when trying to recover Aquinas' approach, have been missing both "nature" and the "legislator", so practically nullifying the very term "natural law". In Chapter IX, I will go back from slightly different angles, on the way in which modern natural law theories have slowly pushed God out of the picture. However, what I had not done at all in *God and the Natural Law* was to show how these misunderstandings of the concept of nature can damage natural law reasoning in approaching specific moral issues. This is what I try to do in Chapter VI, "What Nature? Whose Nature? Reflecting on Some Recent Arguments in Natural Law Ethics." I do so by going through some arguments on contraception and marriage as developed by the new natural law theorists and by Martin Rhonheimer. While criticizing them, I also try to show how, in my opinion, a sound ethical reasoning grounded on the knowledge of nature should work.

Chapter VII, "Natural Law as Inclination to God," is the closest in time to *God and the Natural Law*, which was originally published in Italian in 1999 (ETS, Pisa). "Natural Law as Inclination to God," too goes back to 1999, when it was presented at a conference in Spain. However, at the moment of publishing it I received strong criticism from a blind reviewer and I ended up taking it out of the book in which it was supposed to appear. Later, I changed and rewrote it many times, and presented at other conferences, until I published an entirely new version in 2006 in Italian and in 2009 in English. The same version is now embodied in Chapter VII. The main criticism raised by the reviewer concerned the relationship between the concepts of command and inclination, on the one hand, and of reason on the other. I cannot talk about them because the exchange was "blind," but what I can say is that I have never changed the main theses the reviewer criticized. I was only forced to work much more on them. I believe that a long and modern voluntaristic tradition has made it very difficult for many authors to think of the concept of command in terms that are not opposed to the concept of the act of reason. Moreover, the concept of inclination is thought of as if it could only refer to an irrational sphere of human nature, and not to the very act of practical knowledge. This criticism that I received has been a good reminder in my subsequent research of what I must deepen and explain better, especially concerning the knowledge of the good as "inclined knowledge," about the law as an act of reason, and about natural law as the rule of our moral action. Both because of chronological reasons and because of its structure, this chapter could have been an excellent introduction to the main themes of this book. On the other hand, it offers a synthesis and an overall view that may be of a greater benefit to those who have already dealt with the previous chapters.

As John Paul II reminds us, natural law—the truth of our moral action—is also about self-giving. We are "ethical" when we love the truth more than we love ourselves, when we are willing to sacrifice our own things for the sake of what is good and needs to be done. The most vivid and profound passage from Aquinas that embodies this truth is, in my opinion, *Summa Theologiae*, I, question 60, article 5, where he says that by nature we love God before ourselves and "with a greater love," otherwise our "natural love would be perverse" and "not perfected, but destroyed by charity." Self-giving is crucial to moral action and to the knowledge of the good, and since Greek philosophy it has been embodied in the concept of friendship. Friendship is what makes other people important to us. In Greek culture, however, it was very difficult to separate the concept of friendship from some kind of selfishness—that is, from our *need* for friends. Even in Aristotle it seems that ultimately we love our friends *just* as a way to love ourselves. This is partly true, and indeed there are many dimensions of friendship. However, friendship's highest dimension of pure love of self-giving had to wait for the Christian concept of charity and for the higher dimension of the love of God and the common good. Friendship is a key concept for natural law theory. We are made to be together, to live with others and for others, to know that we are important for someone—ultimately for God. My studies of friendship have been intrinsically linked to my studies of the concept of person, and I believe that they ground a sound understanding of political theory. There is a weakness in contemporary human rights culture as it looks too much at the concept of equality and too little at the concepts of friendship and the person. This is what I try to show in Chapter VIII, "Friendship or Equality? Notes towards an Ideal of Political Personalism."

Chapter VIII and Chapter IX, "Natural Law, Democracy, and the Crisis of Authority," directly address the contemporary debate in political philosophy. Chapter IX focuses on the subtle and insidious ideology that in modern and contemporary political thought tries to ground liberal democracy not on fundamental truths about the human being—not on nature, that is—but on some kind of moderate relativism, which undermines both the concept of authority and the concept of natural law. It was written in the context of a debate on pluralism and relativism and this provides a background for its analyses.

Acknowledgments

As to acknowledgments, my thoughts go first, as in my previous book, to God, because I hope that there is something good in what I write, and God is the first person to thank for anything good that we may do in our lives. Moreover, I do not feel like I am always that good in making Him happy in my private life, so I hope that if I am not ashamed of Him in public, He too will not be ashamed of me, and when the time comes, He will welcome me as a *friend*. After God, my thought goes immediately to my wife Francesca, my parents Francesco and Loredana, and my brothers Riccardo and Giulio.

A special thank goes to Ralph McInerny, not just for his comments and corrections, but above all for his encouragement and example. He was a good friend. The void he left has not yet been filled.

I am grateful to Becket Gremmels for his precious editorial suggestions.

"Knowledge of the Good as Participation in God's Love" was published the first time in *Giornale di Metafisica* 2 (2005), and then in F. Di Blasi, J. Hochschild, J. Langan (eds.), *Ethics Without God? The Divine in Contemporary Moral and Political Thought* (St. Augustine's Press, South Bend: 2008). An Italian version was included in F. Di Blasi, *Conoscenza pratica, teoria dell'azione e bene politico* [*CP 2006*] (Rubbettino, Soveria Mannelli: 2006). "Practical Syllogism, *Proairesis*, and the Virtues: Toward a Reconciliation of Virtue Ethics and Natural Law Ethics" was published in English in *New Things & Old Things* 1 (2004), and in Italian in *CP 2006*, with the title "Il sillogismo pratico, la proáiresis e le virtù: verso una riconciliazione tra l'etica delle virtù e l'etica della legge naturale." "Law as 'Act of Reason' and 'Command'" was published in English in *New Things and Old Things*, 3 (2006), and in Italian in *Aquinas* 3 (2006) with the title "La Legge come atto della ragione e come comando." It was also included in *CP 2006*. "Spirit or Digital Self? The Concept of Person in Philosophy and Contemporary Science" was published in Italian with the title "Il concetto di persona tra filosofia e scienza contemporanea," in *Aquinas* 1(2006). It was then included in *CP 2006*. The present version has been slightly revised. "Ultimate End, Human Freedom, and Beatitude: A Critique of Germain Grisez" has never been published in English, but an Italian version of it was included in *CP 2006*. A very different (and longer) version of it appeared in the *American Journal of Jurisprudence*, 46 (2001). "What Nature? Whose Nature? Reflecting on Some Recent Arguments in Natural Law Ethics" was included in 2002 in the volume edited by Michael Waddell, *Reclaiming Nature: Essays in Thomistic Philosophy and Theology* (St. Augustine's Press, South Bend, IN), which is forthcoming. The essay was then published in Italian in *CP 2006*, and in *Aquinas* 2 (2006) with the title "Quale natura? Natura di cosa? Riflessioni su alcune recenti questioni di etica della legge naturale." "Natural Law as Inclination to God" was originally written in English but first published in Italian, with the title "Legge naturale come inclinazione a Dio," in *CP 2006*. It appeared later in English in *New Things and Old Things*, 2 (2009). "Friendship or Equality? Notes towards an Ideal of Political Personalism" was published for the first time in Italian with the title "Amicizia o eguaglianza? Riflessioni sul fondamento della comunità politica," in F. Viola (ed.), *Forme della cooperazione: pratiche, regole, valori* (Il Mulino: Bologna, 2004); and then republished in *CP 2006*. "Natural Law, Democracy, and the Crisis of Authority" was first published in Italian with the title "Democrazia, crisi dell'autorità e legge naturale," in R. Di Ceglie (ed.), *Pluralismo contro relativismo. Filosofia, religione, politica* (Edizioni Ares, Milano, 2004); and then republished in *CP 2006*.

ABBREVIATIONS

CG   Thomas Aquinas, *Summa Contra Gentiles*. Translations are by Anton C. Pegis for book 1, by James F. Anderson for book 2, and by Vernon J. Bourke for book 3 (Notre Dame, IN: University of Notre Dame Press, 1975).

OS   Aristotle, *On the Soul*. Translations from Aristotle are from *The Revised Oxford Translation*, ed. Jonathan Barnes (Princeton: Princeton University Press, 1995).

DV   Thomas Aquinas, *Quaestiones Disputatae De Veritate - Truth* (Chicago: Henry Regnery Company, 1952) Volume I, questions i-ix, trans. Robert W. Mulligan, S.J., and Volume III, questions xxi-xxix, trans. Robert W. Schmidt, S.J.

In Eth.   Thomas Aquinas, *Commentary on Aristotle's Nicomachean Ethics*, trans. by C. I. Litzinger, O.P. (Notre Dame, Ind.: Dumb Ox Books, 1993).

In An.   Thomas Aquinas, *Commentary on Aristotle's De Anima*, trans. K. Foster, O.P. and S. Humphries, O.P. (Notre Dame, IN: Dumb Ox Books, 1994).

MA   Aristotle, *Movement of Animals*. *The Revised Oxford Translation*.

MP   Aristotle, *Metaphysics*. *The Revised Oxford Translation*.

NE   Aristotle, *Nicomachean Ethics*. *The Revised Oxford Translation*.

Pol.   Aristotle, *Politics*. *The Revised Oxford Translation* (unless otherwise indicated).

ST   Thomas Aquinas, *Summa Theologiae*. Translations are by the Fathers of the English Dominican Province (New York: Benzinger, 1947).

1

KNOWLEDGE OF THE GOOD
AS PARTICIPATION IN GOD'S LOVE

Thomas Aquinas often suggests not only that every creature naturally loves God above all things and more than itself, but also that our knowledge of the good essentially involves knowledge and love of God. Let us read, for example, the following passages:

> Because nothing is good except insofar as it is a likeness and participation of the highest good, the highest good itself is in some way desired in every particular good.[1]

> Every movement of a will whereby powers are applied to operation is reduced to God, as a first object of appetite [*primum appetibile*] and a first agent of willing [*primum volentem*].[2]

> To know that God exists in a general and confused way is implanted in us by nature, inasmuch as God is man's beatitude. For man naturally desires happiness, and what is naturally desired by man must be naturally known to him. This, however, is not to know absolutely that God exists; just as to know that someone is approaching is not the same as to know that Peter is approaching, even though it is Peter who is approaching; for many there are who imagine that man's perfect good which is happiness, consists in riches, and others in pleasures, and others in something else.[3]

1   *In Eth.*, lect. 1, no. 11.
2   *CG*, Book III, Ch. 67.
3   *ST*, I, q. 2, a. 1 ad 1. See also *CG*, Book I, 10-11; *ST*, I, q. 12; I-II, q. 3, a. 8.

Now, these are difficult words that do not seem to fit common morality, in which apparently God does not play such an important role. Broadly speaking, we face two possibilities: either Aquinas was so immersed in abstract metaphysical reflections that he lost sight of the most ordinary reality, or his metaphysics expresses in the most radical way the deepest meaning of ordinary ethical reality. I pick the second. And this is why I reproduce the third quotation, in which the idea emerges that for many—ordinary—people to know and to love God can just mean to vaguely sense or realize that "someone is approaching."

In my opinion, the key concept in understanding Aquinas' view on this issue is the concept of participation, which I take in this book as a purely philosophical concept. The best approach, accordingly, is to focus first on Aquinas' general thesis that every good of this world is not good "essentially" (*per suam essentiam*) but by participation. This thesis entails that knowledge of created goods provides a mediating knowledge of God as the essential good. The second step is to focus on our act of knowledge of the good. The object of this act is the participated good and, through it, God as the essential good. At the same time, our knowledge of the good is itself a very special kind of participated good. Its goodness consists in a *formal* participation in God's *knowledge* of the good—that is, in his love of himself and of creation in view of himself [See diagram 1 below.] In other words, our act of knowledge of the good has both an objective aspect and a subjective aspect. Objectively, we know the good as participated—and thus as objectively revealing God as the essential good. Subjectively, we are able to know the participated good due to our formal participation in God's love. The third step is to focus on the idea of "someone approaching," which taken alone would deserve more than an essay and here must be limited to a short concluding remark.

Scholars today are very familiar with both a wide revival of the concept of practical knowledge[4] and an intense debate on the concept of ultimate

---

4   The widespread contemporary debate on practical knowledge is closely connected to the strong rediscovery of Aristotle's thought that was started in the second part of the last century by authors like Leo Strauss, Eric Voegelin, and Hannah Arendt. For a bibliographical survey of this phenomenon, see Franco Volpi, "The Rehabilitation of Practical Philosophy and Neo-Aristotelianism,"

end in both Aristotle and Aquinas.[5] I should say immediately that in the present discussion I do not want to focus on "practical knowledge" as such but on "knowledge of the good" generally speaking. The two concepts are

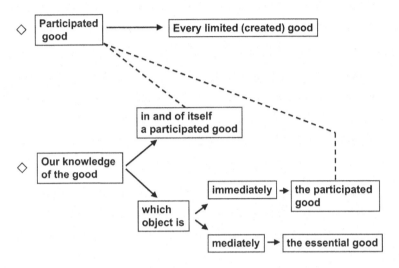

in Robert C. Bartlett and Susan D. Collins (eds.), *Action and Contemplation* (New York: State University of New York Press, 1999), pp. 3–25. In the Anglosaxon analytic world, the renewed attention to practical knowledge is related to the discussion of the "reasons for action" intended as a way to overcome the gaps created by the value-free approach to human action in moral, political, and legal philosophy. A pioneer work in this direction, has certainly been done by Herbert Hart in his *The Concept of Law* (Oxford: Clarendon Press, 1961).

5   The Aristotelian debate on the ultimate end flared up after W. F. R. Hardie in "The Final Good in Aristotle's Ethics," in *Philosophy* 40 (1965): 277–295 suggests the distinction between dominant end and inclusive end. It is worth noticing the critical approach to this issue offered by J. L. Ackrill, "Aristotle on *Eudaimonia*" [1974], in N. Sherman (ed.), *Aristotle's Ethics* (Lanham, Md.: Rowman & Littlefield, 1999), pp. 57–77. Among Thomists, the question is presently highly debated due to the claim that there are not one but many incommensurable ultimate ends of human life made by the so-called "new natural law theorists." The new natural law theory is strongly related to the rehabilitation of practical knowledge, and is initiated by a well-known article written by Germain Grisez in 1965, "The First Principle of Practical Reason: A Commentary on the Summa theologiae, 1-2, Question 94, Article 2," in *Natural Law Forum*, 10 (1965).

often put together as if they were the same thing. This is a mistake. Practical knowledge, at least in Aquinas, is a secondary and specific instance of knowledge of the good that involves a means-end relationship in which the end, being actually wanted or desired, makes the means desirable (*dilectio electiva*) and becomes action. Knowledge of the good, simply speaking, is not practical but speculative.[6] Moreover, the current debate on the ultimate end appears to be too narrowly centered on the arguments from intentionality and from the natural desire given by Aquinas especially in *ST*, I-II, q. 1, a. 4 (Is there an ultimate end for human life?) and q. 3, a. 8 (Does the happiness of man consist in the vision of the divine essence?). The present discussion does not focus on these arguments, either. There are deeper metaphysical principles at the root of Aquinas' view on the ultimate end and these principles are presently my main concern.

In what follows, I will first offer a short introduction to the concepts of good and of participation (Section 1). These concepts will be then better elucidated as the chapter progresses. In Section 2, I will address Aquinas' general thesis of the created good as participated. Then, in section 3, I will move toward the analysis of our act of knowledge of the good. Finally, in section 4, I will return briefly to the last passage quoted above regarding our necessary—but general and confused—knowledge of God.

1. Introducing the Concepts of Good and Participation

Good (*bonum*) is, for Aquinas, a transcendental concept because it signifies exactly the same reality as being (*ens*). Yet, the term "good" makes conceptually explicit something that in the use of *ens* remains implicit. This is why Aquinas says that "good" adds something to the *understanding* of *ens* (*super intellectum entis*): something that is not in the thing (*in rerum natura*) but only in reason (*in ratione tantum*). Specifically, "good" adds to *ens* a conceptual reference to the fact that the *ens' esse*[7] is an act, which gives existence

---

6   See, for example, *ST*, I-II, q. 3, a. 5, where Aquinas explains that "happiness [beatitude] consists in activity of the speculative intellect rather than the practical."

7   I use the Latin *ens* and *esse* to avoid ambiguity, as in English they are both translated with "being."

and *perfection* to the *ens*, and which is therefore what the *ens* itself tends toward. The concept of good, in other words, contains a conceptual reference to the actual—or existing—*ens* as it is always an end and an object of an appetite: "*et inde est quod omnes recte diffinientes bonum ponunt in ratione eius aliquid quod pertinet ad habitudinem finis.*"[8]

This short but rather technical account reveals an important metaphysical view of reality. For Aquinas, an existing being is dynamic: i.e., it is simultaneously an action and completion. The existing being tends not only toward other things but also toward its own act. This is why it preserves itself and remains in existence instead of falling back into nothingness. Consequently, when we know the existing being we know it also as good—namely, as an end and the object of an appetite. Its being good, however, is nothing else than its *esse*. To know the good is nothing other than to know the way in which things exist, or to know their *act(s)*— whether substantial or accidental. This is why Aquinas writes that "to be in act [...] constitutes the nature of the good [*esse igitur actu boni rationem constituit*]," or that "by nature, the good of each thing is its act and perfection [*naturaliter enim bonum uniuscuiusque est actus et perfectio eius*]."[9] This is what we should keep in mind for the purposes of the present discussion: to look for "the nature of the good [*boni rationem*]" is to look for the "act" and "perfection" of things.

The concept of participation refers to a specific kind of causality— namely, the causality that is simultaneously required for the effect to exist. An example is my hand holding a book: in this case, when my hand ceases to act as a cause the book falls down. Another example is light shining on the book: when the light ceases to act the book is invisible.[10]

---

8   For all the quotations in this paragraph see *DV*, q. 21, a. 1.

9   *CG*, Book I, Ch 37. See also, *DV*, q. 21, a. 2 c.: "Existence itself, therefore, has the essential note of goodness. Just as it is impossible, then, for anything to be a being which does not have existence, so too it is necessary that every being be good by the very fact of its having existence [*Ipsum igitur esse habet rationem boni. Unde sicut impossibile est quod sit aliquid ens quod non habeat esse, necesse est ut omne ens sit bonum ex hoc ipso quod esse habet*]."

10   See the famous passage in Aquinas on the *per se* series of efficient causes: "In efficient causes it is impossible to proceed to infinity *per se*—thus, there cannot be an infinite number of causes that are 'per se' required for a certain effect;

Whenever something is acting in a way that cannot be caused by its own nature, we must logically refer its action to an external cause that is able to cause it by its essence, and we say that the relevant object *participates* in that cause. The suspended book participates in the power of my hand, and the visible book participates in the power of a luminous object. Participation, thus, is something real in things, and it means a simultaneous and external causal dependence of their actions or properties. This causal relation has two important characteristics: (1) that the action (whatever it is) of the participating object follows the actual direction given to it by the cause (the suspended book stays exactly where the hand holds it, and the visible book is visible according to the kind of light that is acting upon it); (2) that the action of the participating object makes it similar to the cause (the suspended book *as suspended* reveals something of the power of the hand, and the visible book *as visible* is similar to the light-source affecting it). This can be summarized by saying that, in participation, the effect *as effect* is similar to the cause *as cause* and obeys its teleology.

As soon as we focus on the fact that, for Aquinas, the very *esse* of things is participated, we can see why the concept of participation is so important in his metaphysics. For Aquinas, all things are actually dependent on God as their efficient, final, and exemplary cause—including rational agents' act of knowledge of the good, an act which is an accidental perfection of their being. Hence, the thesis that our act of knowledge of the good is

for instance, that a stone be moved by a stick, the stick by the hand, and so on to infinity. But it is not impossible to proceed to infinity 'accidentally' as regards efficient causes; for instance, if all the causes thus infinitely multiplied should have the order of only one cause, their multiplication being accidental, as an artificer acts by means of many hammers accidentally, because one after the other may be broken. It is accidental, therefore, that one particular hammer acts after the action of another; and likewise it is accidental to this particular man as generator to be generated by another man; for he generates as a man, and not as the son of another man. For all men generating hold one grade in efficient causes—viz. the grade of a particular generator. Hence it is not impossible for a man to be generated by man to infinity; but such a thing would be impossible if the generation of this man depended upon this man, and on an elementary body, and on the sun, and so on to infinity" (*ST*, I, q. 46, a. 2 ad 7).

participated entails: [1] that God simultaneously causes it as knowledge of the good (participation in God as efficient cause); [2] that our act involves love of the same ultimate end that God loves in causing it (participation in God as final cause); and [3] that our knowledge of the good is similar to God's own knowledge of the good (participation in God as exemplary cause).[11]

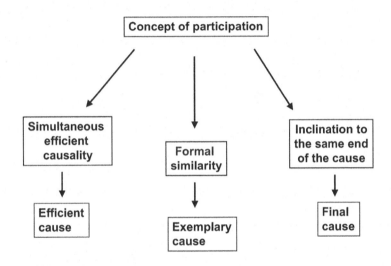

2. Created Good as Participated

In *De Veritate*, q. 21, a. 5, Aquinas following "Augustinum, Boetium et auctorem libri De Causis" explains that the created good is said to be participated in a threefold way: as to the accidental good; as to the essential or substantial good; and as to the ordering to the first cause (*secundum ordinem ad causam primam*). Aquinas puts the accidental good first because, for him, something is said to be good absolutely speaking not due to its substantial being but to its accidental being. For my purposes, however, it is better to follow an ontological order and start with the essential or substantial good.

11 See, *ST*, I, q. 6, a. 4: "[E]ach thing is called 'good' by the divine goodness, as by the first exemplar, efficient, and final principle of goodness in its entirety."

2.1. Substantial Good as Participated

The essential good of something is the act, or *esse*, that makes it existent according to its nature (man, tree, etc.). The essential principles of each *ens*, explains Aquinas, are what make it perfect in order for it to exist—"*In se ipso autem aliquid perficitur ut subsistat per essentialia principia.*" As I just mentioned, Aquinas adds that as far as these principles are concerned something is good only *secundum quid* because a creature, in order to be good absolutely speaking, must be good (or *in act*) according to both the essential and the accidental principles. [An existing human being, for example, is certainly good according to the act of existence of his nature but can still be either morally good or morally evil. When we say, "This is a good man," we refer, simply speaking, to his moral personality.] Yet my focus is not this, rather participation. Why is the creature's essential good participated? The answer to this question is that, except in the case of God, the essence of things does not logically include existence. Otherwise their natures could give existence to themselves and they would never die or be corrupted. It is logically possible to think of a man as not existent. Thus, when a man exists, it means that his *esse* participates in what possesses *esse* by essence, and this can only be God.[12] The *esse* of limited beings is like the visibility of the book: if God ceases to create the book *disappears*. The *esse* of limited beings as the result of God's creative action is both similar to God's *esse* and ordered to the end for the sake of which God creates.

2.2. Accidental Good as Participated

More difficult is the question of the accidental good, because accidents by definition exist not in themselves but in the substance's act. In point of fact, to say that the accident's good participates in the substance's good—which is in turn participated—does not seem very interesting, and Aquinas' discussion in *De Veritate*, q. 21, a. 5 seems to be no more than homage paid to a statement made by Augustine. However, the same thesis is strongly restated in *ST*, I, q. 6, a. 3 and without any explicit reference to Augustine. This fact calls for more attention to the relevant text in *De Veritate*, q. 21, a. 5, particularly where Aquinas writes,

12 See, *ST*, I, q. 44, a. 1.

Now it is by its essential principles that a thing is fully constituted [*perficitur*] in itself so that it subsists; but it is not so perfectly constituted as to stand as it should in relation to everything outside itself [*ut debito modo se habeat ad omnia quae sunt extra ipsium*] except by means of accidents added to the essence, because the operations by which one thing is in some sense joined to another proceed from the essence through powers distinct from it. Consequently nothing achieves goodness absolutely unless it is complete in both its essential and its accidental principles.

Aquinas sees accidents as the metaphysical principles that relate the *ens* to the other things external to it (*ad omnia quae sunt extra ipsum*). Movement, for example, is always an interaction. But we might also think of color as the relation between the visible objects and the sense of sight, or of mass as the attractive relation of material bodies with each other, or even of our intelligence as the relation of our mind with every other reality (including ourselves as reflexively known). Now, a principle connecting the *existence* of two or more things with each other—i.e., making them *co-exist* in the same universe—cannot come from one of them unless this one is the creator of the other(s). So, the fact that limited things interact with each other due to their accidents calls for a transcendent cause in which they participate *as interacting with each other*—that is to say, according to their accidents. If I understand Aquinas correctly on this point, the metaphysical principle grounding his idea of the accidental good as participated coincides with his key idea that there is *order* in nature: namely, that things act naturally in a way that is at the same time intelligible and harmonious. Aquinas always explains this point by referring to the notions of part and whole. His point is very refined because to say that there is order means exactly to say that there is a whole in which things make sense as parts. And this, in turn, means, not only that the good of the whole as such is the ultimate meaning of the good of the parts as parts, but also that every part must be inclined to the good of the whole before and more than to its own good as part. After all, this is the reason for the existence of the specific movement of each *part*: to contribute to the existence of the whole. If this were not so, the order itself (the whole) could not exist.

Whatever we might think of this argument, Aquinas takes it very seriously. This is why he states that all creatures, including man and angels, love God before themselves and with a greater love.

> Not only man, so long as his nature remains unimpaired [*in suae integritate naturae*], loves God above all things and more than himself, but also every single creature, each in its own way, i.e. either by an intellectual, or by a rational, or by an animal, or at least by a natural love, as stones do, for instance, and other things bereft of knowledge, because each part naturally loves the common good of the whole more than its own particular good. This is evidenced by its operation, since the principal inclination of each part is toward common action conducive to the good of the whole. It may also be seen in civic virtues whereby sometimes the citizens suffer damage even to their own property and persons for the sake of the common good.[13]

In *ST*, I, q. 60, a. 5, more or less with the same words, the same principle is specifically applied to the natural inclination, or natural love, of the will of both man and angels: "Consequently, since God is the universal good, and under this good both man and angel and all creatures are comprised, because every creature in regard to its entire being naturally belongs to God, it follows that from natural love angel and man alike love God before themselves and with a greater love."[14] It might be helpful to recall that the

---

13 *ST*, II-II, q. 26, a. 3 c.

14 This is the whole relevant passage: "Now, in natural things, everything which, as such, naturally belongs to another, is principally, and more strongly inclined to that other to which it belongs, than toward itself. Such a natural tendency is evidenced from things which are moved according to nature: because 'according as a thing is moved naturally, it has an inborn aptitude to be thus moved,' as stated in *Phys.* ii, text. 78. For we observe that the part naturally exposes itself in order to safeguard the whole; as, for instance, the hand is without deliberation exposed to the blow for the whole body's safety. And since reason copies nature, we find the same inclination among the social virtues; for it behooves the virtuous citizen to expose himself to the danger of death for the public weal of the state; and if man were a natural part of the

existence of a natural order is also the starting point of the fifth way to prove the existence of God—which, in turn, coincides with the philosophical proofs given by Aquinas for the existence of providence and of the eternal law.[15]

2.3. *Secundum Ordinem ad Causam Primam*

A still further difference is discovered between the divine goodness and that of creatures. Goodness has the character of a final cause. But God has this, since He is the ultimate end of all beings just as He is their first principle. From this it follows that

city, then such inclination would be natural to him. Consequently, since God is the universal good, and under this good both man and angel and all creatures are comprised, because every creature in regard to its entire being naturally belongs to God, it follows that from natural love angel and man alike love God before themselves and with a greater love [*naturali dilectione etiam Angelus et homo plus et principalius diligat Deum quam seipsum*]. Otherwise, if either of them loved self more than God, it would follow that natural love would be perverse, and that it would not be perfected but destroyed by charity."

15 See, e.g., *CG*, Book III, Ch. 64: "Moreover, that natural bodies are moved and made to operate for an end, even though they do not know their end, was proved by the fact that what happens to them is always, or often, for the best; and, if their workings resulted from art, they would not be done differently. But it is impossible for things that do not know their end to work for that end, and to reach that end in an orderly way, unless they are moved by someone possessing knowledge of the end, as in the case of the arrow directed to the target by the archer. So, the whole working of nature must be ordered by some sort of knowledge. And this, in fact, must lead back to God, either mediately or immediately, since every lower art and type of knowledge must get its principles from a higher one, as we also see in the speculative and operative sciences. Therefore, God governs the world by His providence. Furthermore, things that are different in their natures do not come together into one order unless they are gathered into a unit by one ordering agent. But in the whole of reality things are distinct and possessed of contrary natures; yet all come together in one order, and while some things make use of the actions of others, some are helped or commanded by others. Therefore, there must be one orderer and governor of the whole of things."

any other end has the status or character of an end only in relation to the first cause [*secundum ordinem ad causam primam*],
because a secondary cause does not influence the effect unless
the influence of the first cause is presupposed, as is made clear
in *The Causes*. Hence too, good, having the character of an end,
cannot be said of a creature unless we presuppose the relation
of Creator to creature [*ordine creatoris ad creaturam*].[16]

The key words here are, "because a secondary cause does not influence
the effect unless the influence of the first cause is presupposed." This principle is more explicit in *CG*, Book III, Chapter 17:

Now, the supreme agent does the actions of all inferior agents
by moving them all to their actions and, consequently, to their
ends. Hence, it follows that all the ends of secondary agents are
ordered by the first agent to His own proper end. Of course,
the first agent of all things is God. [...] There is no other end
for His will than His goodness, which is Himself. [...] Therefore, all things [...] are ordered to God as to their end.

In order to understand Aquinas on this point we must remember that
the concept of good involves the appetite for an end. Now, except in the
case of God—in whom there is no real distinction between his appetite
and his being—appetite implies *movement*. And every movement in Aristotle and Aquinas' metaphysics requires participation in a first Unmoved
Mover. It goes without saying that when God moves something, he cannot
but do it according to his end, which is himself. And it goes without saying
that what is at stake here is not the extrinsic movement of things, but the
intrinsic movement of their beings: that is to say, their *natural inclinations*.[17]

16 *DV*, q. 21, a. 5 c.
17 See *DV*, q. 22, a. 1 c.: "What is directed or inclined to something by another
    is inclined to that which is intended by the one inclining or directing it. The
    arrow, for example, is directed to the same target at which the archer aims.
    Consequently, since all natural things have been inclined by a certain natural
    inclination toward their ends by the prime mover, God, that to which every-
    thing is naturally inclined must be what is willed or intended by God."

This same argument is specifically applied by Aquinas also to the human will, which under this respect is not different from any other participated appetite—for "to give natural inclinations is the sole prerogative of Him Who has established the nature. So also, to incline the will to anything is the sole prerogative of Him Who is the cause of the intellectual nature."[18] Therefore, if it is true that our moving world requires an Unmoved Mover, it necessarily follows that every nature—or natural inclination—and every appetite depends on God as "a first agent of willing [*primum volentem*]" (efficient cause) and tends to God "as a first object of appetite [*primum appetibile*]" (final cause).[19]

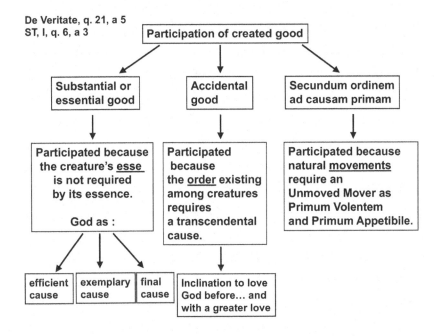

De Veritate, q. 21, a 5
ST, I, q. 6, a 3

Participation of created good

Substantial or essential good — Accidental good — Secundum ordinem ad causam primam

Participated because the creature's <u>esse</u> is not required by its essence.

God as :

Participated because the <u>order</u> existing among creatures requires a transcendental cause.

Participated because natural <u>movements</u> require an Unmoved Mover as Primum Volentem and Primum Appetibile.

efficient cause — exemplary cause — final cause

Inclination to love God before... and with a greater love

---

18 *CG*, Book III, Ch. 88.
19 *CG*, Book III, Ch. 67. Here it might be helpful to recall also *CG*, Book II, Ch. 23, in which Aquinas argues that the first unmoved mover must be a voluntary agent. This thesis complements the first way by qualifying the unmoved mover as a rational agent. Let us read, for example, the following passages from Chapter 23: "[T]hat which acts by itself is prior to that which acts by another [*quod per se agit, prius est eo quod per aliud agit*], for whatever is by another [*per aliud*] must be referred to that which is by itself [*per se*]; otherwise,

3. Our Knowledge of the Good as Participated

Let us shift our focus now to our act of knowledge of the good. On the basis of what was explained above, we should already be able to conclude that as an accidental perfection of our being this act is participation in the order God gave to creation. As such, it tends chiefly to God as to the end of the whole of creation. That is to say, through this act we love God before ourselves and with a greater love. Moreover, as our knowledge of the good involves the movement of an appetite, it requires the creative action of God as Unmoved Mover. Thus, it participates in God as "a first agent of willing" and tends to God "as a first object of appetite."

However, as correct as these conclusions might be theoretically, they do not look very satisfactory when what is at stake is an act as complex as our act of knowledge of the good. Unquestionably, we need a more specific approach to the nature of this act and to the supposed need for it to be participated. And, first of all, we need to focus on what exactly "knowledge of the good" means compared with the concept of good in general.

3.1. "Good" and "Knowledge of the Good"

"Good," as we recalled above, means that the *ens* is always an end and an object of an appetite—without appetite for an end, properly speaking, there is no good. "Knowledge," on the other hand, means for both Aristotle and Aquinas "intentional possession of a form." Knowledge of the good—whether sentient or intellectual—must mean intentional possession of the form of something *as* object of an appetite. But, in turn, since knowledge

---

we fall into an infinite regress. A thing that is not master of its own action, however, does not act by itself; it acts as directed by something else [*ab alio actus*], not as directing itself [*seipsum agens*]. Hence, the first agent mast act as master of His own action. But it is only by will that one is master of his own action. It follows, therefore, that God, who is the first agent, acts by His will [*per voluntatem agere*], not by necessity of His nature [*non per naturae necessitatem*]"; "To the first agent belongs the first action, even as the first motion pertains to the first thing movable. But the will's action is naturally prior to that of nature. For that which is more perfect is prior in nature, though in one and the same particular thing it be temporally posterior."

of the good is an act—and therefore a good—of the knower, it cannot happen but *by way of appetite*. Knowledge of the good, therefore, means to tend toward the *ens* by means of a form (of something *as* object of an appetite) intentionally possessed by the agent. In the knowledge of the good, the possessed form and the inclination of the appetite coincide.[20]

In the case of rational beings, knowledge of the good means simultaneously: (a) to have intellectual knowledge of the *ens* as object of an appetite; and (b) to tend toward it as intellectually known, or to love it by way of what we call "rational appetite." The intellectual knowledge of the good is nothing else than a sort of *inclined knowledge*: that is, an appetite for the *ens* understood as an end. This is why Aquinas seems to suggest that to know the good and to will the good are the same thing: "For, since the understood good [*bonum intellectum*] is the proper object of the will, the understood good is, as such, willed. Now, that which is understood is by reference to one who understands [*intellectum autem dicitur ad intelligentem*]. Hence, he who grasps the good by his intellect [*intelligens bonum*] is, as such, endowed with will [*volens*]."[21]

For my purposes it is important to notice that it is our very act of (intellectual) knowledge of the good—this accidental perfection of our being—that needs to be participated. As the luminous object participates *as luminous* in what possesses the light by essence, and as every created good participates *as appetite for ens* in what is essentially good, so our intellectual knowledge of the good should formally participate *as intellectual knowledge of the good*—that is, as a (rational) appetite for the *ens* known as an end—in God's knowledge as the cause of every good. This means, in turn, that

20 This does not mean that the known good is necessarily practical, but only that it cannot be known *as good* without the inclination of the appetite. This is why animals know as good only the things toward which their sentient appetite tend, whereas we know as good every *ens* insofar as it fits the inclination to the (intelligible) truth that we call will. To *know* a beautiful panorama means to *love* it, even if there is nothing we can do with it (i.e., even if it is not a practical object of our knowledge). God *loves* even non-created worlds because he knows them as something he does not want to create That is to say, he loves these worlds insofar as they are known to him, but he does not love them according to his practical knowledge.

21 *CG*, Book I, Ch. 72.

our participation must formally happen—at the intellectual level—by way of *inclination* to God *known* as the "first agent of willing" and as the ultimate end (*primum appetibile*) of both ourselves and the whole universe, and also as the exemplary cause of everything. But, does Aquinas offer any specific argument in support of these things? The answer is yes—the concept of the active intellect.

3.2. The Need for the Active Intellect

For both Aristotle and Aquinas, knowledge, whether sentient or intellectual, is an actualization of a receiving (or passive), knowing faculty caused by the act of the known object as knowable. For instance, the visible object as visible (in act) causes the act of seeing it in the visual faculty. There are two important principles at stake here: one is that the object known must be in act in order to be known, and the other is that to know is an act of the knowing faculty. We can think of a file (known object) saved on a flash drive (knowing faculty). What we call "file" should exist (be in act) before—and while—being saved, and the saved file is no more than the flash drive configured (actualized) in a particular way. Now, the reason we need the active intellect to know the truth (whether theoretical or practical) is that *the universals* that our (passive) intellect receives when it knows things through the senses do not exist as such—as universals—in the (particular) things known. In other words, the intelligible objects do not exist as intelligible except in the intellect that knows them. Thus, our intellect must be able to abstract them (i.e., to turn them from potentiality into actuality) before receiving them—as if the flash drive had to make the file a file before receiving it into itself as a file. The key point is that our intellect in order to make the intelligible species an intelligible species must already be in act as intellect *before* possessing any actual knowledge at all. I say "as intellect" because this first act of the intellect as a knower must be *similar* to the known object as known—that is, as intelligible. Knowledge is always a question of similarity. Strictly speaking, we can say that the passive intellect does not *exist* without any knowledge making it actual, but that the active intellect is *subsistent*.

This point will be clearer if we focus more closely on the relevant difference between sense knowledge and intellectual knowledge. In the case of sense knowledge, the knowing faculty is actualized by the act of the material thing as perceptible.[22] In the case of intellectual knowledge, there is no act of the material thing as intelligible. If the material individual thing were intelligible in act it would not be individual and it would not be material. Therefore, unlike sense knowledge in the case of intellectual knowledge the act of the intelligible object is caused by the knowing faculty itself. The intellect, in other words, *moves* itself by causing the act of the intelligible object as intelligible in order to receive it as an intelligible species.[23]

3.3. The Participation of the Active Intellect

The reason why our active intellect requires God's causality is that it is a *moved mover* of what is intelligible. The active intellect causes the acts of the intelligible objects as intelligible but does not create their intelligibility. This is why our intellect is still a *receiver* of knowledge and does not already know everything. Rather, "it reaches to the understanding of truth by arguing, with a certain amount of reasoning and movement. Again it has an imperfect understanding; both because it does not understand everything and because, in those things which it does understand, it passes from potentiality to act": the human intellect is "mobile" and "imperfect."[24] As a *moved mover* of what is intelligible that knows according to *degrees of knowledge*, the active intellect fits the rationale of both the first and the fourth ways to prove the existence of God given in *ST*, I, q. 2, a. 3. That is to say, the existence of the active intellect requires: (1) the existence of a first intellect that moves every act of understanding without being moved; and

22 As is well known, for both Aristotle and Aquinas the act of the sentient faculty and the act of the thing perceived are one and the same act. See, *OS*, III, 425b26–426a27; *In An.*, III, 2, 425b22–426a26 (pp. 184–185, n. 592–596).

23 "Since [...] forms existing in matter are not actually intelligible; it follows that the natures of forms of the sensible things which we understand are not actually intelligible. Now nothing is reduced from potentiality to act except by something in act; as the senses are made actual by what is actually sensible. We must therefore assign on the part of the intellect some power to make things actually intelligible, by abstraction of the species from material conditions. And such is the necessity for an active intellect" (*ST*, I, q. 79, a. 3 c).

24 *ST*, I, q. 79, a. 4 c.

(2) of an intellect that possesses what is intelligible at the highest degree, and in which every lower degree of intellectual knowledge participates. This train of reasoning is clear in *ST*, I, q. 79, a. 4, and it is ultimately the reason that Aquinas thinks the active intellect receives its "intellectual light" (its first act) directly from God's intellect—the active intellect makes us able partially to see things as they are in God's mind.[25]

For Aquinas, *ens* is the first notion of intellectual knowledge, and "ens in universali," or "ens universale" (universal being), is the common object of this knowledge.[26] The concept of *ens* and the concept of intelligibility go together. To know something intellectually and to know it *as ens* (being) are the same thing. Everything is intelligible insofar as it *is* (a table, a dog, red, tall, pleasant, Sicilian, etc.). The analogical notion of *ens*—analogical because no specific difference can add something to it as if this something were not *ens*—precedes, therefore, all particular intellectual knowledge and constitutes, so to speak, the glasses through which we see reality *as intelligible*. Hence, to say that our intellect tends to know the truth is equivalent to say that our intellect tends to know the *ens* as *ens* (i.e., the *is* of *being*).

As we saw already, our knowledge of each particular *ens* reveals a real distinction between its *being* (*esse*) and its being *something* (*essence*)—"this is a pencil," but "is" is not only of the pencil. We have already focused on the need for creatures' *esse* to participate in an efficient and final cause that *is* by essence. Now we will focus on the need for the creatures' *esse* to be an imitation of this cause.

Esse is common to everything and indeterminate—i.e., it can exist according to every possible essence. Essence, on the other hand, in a sense limits being to a specific way of being. Every particular knowledge of the *ens* reveals, therefore, a *limitation* of the infinite possibilities of *esse*, but it also reveals a real *imitation* of what possesses *esse through essence*. This corresponds exactly, from the side of our knowledge, to the way in which for Aquinas God knows everything through knowledge of himself:

25 On the participation of the active intellect in God's intellect, besides *ST*, I, q. 79, a. 4, see also q. 84, a. 5, where Aquinas specifies that we receive from God the "intellectual light" but not "the intelligible species, which are derived from things."

26 See *DV*, q. 1, a. 1; and *ST*, I, q. 78, a. 1.

the divine essence comprehends within itself the nobilities of all beings [...] according to the mode of perfection. Now, every form, both proper and common [...] is a certain perfection. [...] The intellect of God therefore, can comprehend in His essence that which is proper to each thing by understanding wherein the divine essence is being imitated and wherein each thing falls short of its perfection. Thus, by understanding His essence as imitable in the mode of life and not of knowledge, God has the proper form of a plant; and if He knows His essence as imitable in the mode of knowledge and not of intellect, God has the proper form of animal, and so forth. Thus, it is clear that, being absolutely perfect, the divine essence can be taken as the proper exemplar of singulars. Through it, therefore, God can have a proper knowledge of all things.[27]

In short, our knowledge of (limited) *entia* (Latin plural of *ens*) reveals its being causally dependent on what has *esse* as its own essence. On the one hand, existence is not logically required by the essence of what is not its own *esse*—the actual existence of limited beings (their *esse*) requires a creative action by what exists by essence. On the other hand, the plurality and gradation of the (common) *esse* in the existing things requires a single, subsistent, and exemplar cause that has *esse* at the highest degree.[28] This is how Aquinas proves creation: "all beings apart from God are not their own being, but are beings by participation. Therefore it must be that all things which are diversified by the diverse participation of being, so as to be more or less perfect, are caused by one First Being, Who possesses being most perfectly."[29]

Our intellectual knowledge is always in tension between the *immediate* knowledge of limited ways of being and the *mediate* knowledge of the Being that has in itself the fullness of being, and that is at the same time (a) the efficient cause, (b) the exemplary cause, and (c) the final cause. Intellectual

---

27 *CG*, Book I, Ch. 54.
28 On this type of causality see also Aquinas, *Quaestio disputata De Potentia*, q. 3, a. 5.
29 *ST*, I, q. 44, a. 1 c.

curiosity tends to go beyond a specific essence toward a fuller understanding of universal being: our constantly fleeing the (limiting) essence.[30] If this is true, Aquinas should have defined intellectual knowledge with reference to God as its ultimate object—namely, as the final cause of the knowledge of truth, or as the end toward which the knowledge of truth ultimately tends. In point of fact, this is exactly what he does. He does it in the treatise on law at the exact moment of indicating the inclination specifically distinguishing man from lower natures: "Thirdly, there is in man an inclination to good, according to the nature of his reason, which nature is proper to him: thus man has a natural inclination to know the truth about God, and to live in society."[31] At first glance, this passage might appear strangely reductive with respect to our inclination to know the truth. However, it is fairly accurate as it refers our inclination to the truth to its ultimate object and to our openness to the *ens in universali.*

3.4. *Ens Universale* and *Bonum Universale*

"For the will must be commensurate with its object. But the object of the will is a good grasped by the intellect [*bonum intellectum*], as stated above. Therefore, it is of the nature of will to reach out to whatever the intellect can propose to it under the aspect of goodness [*sub ratione boni*]."[32] If our intellect knows everything in the light of universal being, and so reaches the knowledge of a first efficient, final, and exemplary cause, Aquinas can legitimately attribute the same scope to our rational appetite. Thus, the *ens universale* corresponds, on the will's side, to the *bonum universale*, which determines the nature and ultimate end of our desire. The passage I quoted at the beginning—"Because nothing is good except insofar as it is a likeness and participation of the highest good, the highest good itself is in some way desired in every particular good"—should now make more sense. Since we know the goods of this earth in the light of the universal good, it is

---

30 See, on this tension in our knowledge, Cornelio Fabro, *Dall'essere all'esistente* (Brescia: Morcelliana, 1965), pp. 60–69.

31 *ST,* I-II, q. 94, a. 2 c. On the rationale of this inclination it is worth reading Lawrence Dewan, "St. Thomas, John Finnis, and the Political Good," in *The Thomist 64* (2000).

32 *CG,* Book II, Ch. 27.

impossible for us to know them without simultaneously knowing and desiring through them their first cause: the highest good itself.

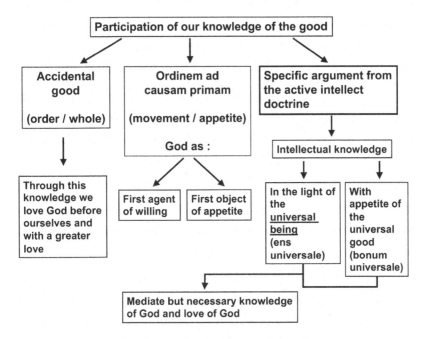

4. "Someone is Approaching"

It is time now to revisit the last passage quoted at the beginning:

> To know that God exists in a general and confused way is implanted in us by nature, inasmuch as God is man's beatitude. For man naturally desires happiness, and what is naturally desired by man must be naturally known to him. This, however, is not to know absolutely that God exists; just as to know that someone is approaching is not the same as to know that Peter is approaching, even though it is Peter who is approaching; for many there are who imagine that man's perfect good which is happiness, consists in riches, and others in pleasures, and others in something else.

It is important to recall what this passage means because otherwise Aquinas' ethical foundation would be, while consistent, a bit odd. It is obvious that not many people think of God when they act morally, and everybody has experience of good people who do not believe in God. What does it mean, therefore, that the very knowledge of the good is knowledge and love of God? As we can see in the passage above, what Aquinas means is much more nuanced than it might appear at a first and superficial glance. What we necessarily need when we know the good is to see that "Someone [the highest good] is approaching." This is a necessary (mediate) knowledge that can be general and confused, and that does not mean to know God absolutely speaking. It does mean, however, that knowledge of the good has an absolute and transcendental character. This thesis corresponds to what Aquinas says in *ST*, I-II, q. 5, a. 8, namely, that "every man necessarily desires happiness" and "according to the general notion of happiness" (*secundum communem rationem beatitudinis*). Yet, with regard to the content of the ultimate end (*secundum specialem rationem quantum ad id in quo beatitudo consistit*), "not all desire happiness." For Aquinas, in order to know and to love God absolutely we cannot do without reasoning and without morally good behavior.

Now, the idea that we know the good only when we know that "the highest good is approaching" is not only extremely interesting, but also very beautiful. After all, what does it mean to act morally—i.e., according to conscience—if not to act on the assumption that what is good transcends both you and me, and so ought to be done? From this viewpoint, the person who tries sincerely to act morally without believing in God even without realizing it is on his or her way toward knowing God absolutely. Whereas the immoral person damages and distorts his or her own intellectual nature by overlapping the vision of the highest good that is approaching with the selfishness of his or her concupiscence, or, in a sense, by putting or forcing down the transcendental character of the good.

Let me conclude by saying that there are many features of moral experience that reveal its transcendental character. After all, moral experience is the paradox of fulfilling oneself by forgetting or sacrificing oneself. It is the desire for *absolute* moral truths, and of an absolute happiness and justice that are not possible in this world. Many people make strong moral decisions only when they get to thinking of God. The so-called "good atheist" ought eventually to find his way to God. Otherwise he cannot be entirely good. He will embrace some kind of idolatry, and he will finally frustrate his nature and the nature of people around him.

II

PRACTICAL SYLLOGISM, *PROAIRESIS*, AND THE VIRTUES: TOWARD A RECONCILIATION OF VIRTUE ETHICS AND NATURAL LAW ETHICS

The contemporary Aristotelian-Thomistic debate in ethics is marked by a strong contrast between natural law and prudence, or between the so-called "natural law ethics" and "virtue ethics." A clear example of this contrast is Daniel Mark Nelson when he writes that, "for Thomas, the moral life as well as reflection on it depend on prudence and not on knowledge of the natural law."[1] Another example is Edward A. Goerner when he refers natural law to "the bad man's view" or the view of a man who obeys general extrinsic rules out of fear of punishment. According to Goerner, the full standard of right/good belongs to "the good man's view," that is to say, the view of those who possess practical wisdom and prudence.[2]

---

1   Daniel Mark Nelson, *The Priority of Prudence: Virtue and Natural Law in Thomas Aquinas and the Implications for Modern Ethics* (University Park, Penn.: The Pennsylvania State University Press, 1992), p. xii.

2   Edward A. Goerner, "On Thomistic Natural Law: The Bad Man's View of Thomistic Natural Right," in *Political Theory* 1 (1979): 101–22; Edward A. Goerner, "Thomistic Natural Right: The Good Man's View of Thomistic Natural Law," in *Political Theory* 3 (1983): 393–18. Goerner's interpretation of Aquinas is not reliable. His legalistic concept of natural law should rather be traced back to the utilitarian natural law theory advanced by John Austin (1790–1859) in *The Province of Jurisprudence Determined and the Uses of the Study of Jurisprudence* (London: Weidenfeld and Nicolson, 1971). But one can also think of ethical (rational) egoism as described (and criticized) by Henry B. Veatch in his *Human Rights: Fact or Fancy?* (Baton Rouge and London: Louisiana State University Press, 1985), pp. 33–48. A good response to

This kind of citation could easily go on,[3] but what is important now is to focus on the theoretical root of the contrast—namely, the difficulty (apparently insurmountable) of joining together the *universal* nature, or character, of law and the *contingent and particular* nature of moral life.[4] Precisely because of its universal character, law allegedly cannot reach the particular and so cannot be a real guide for moral life. The particular has therefore priority, and the nature of the good is "fragile."[5]

Usually, even authors who try to reconcile law and virtue by means of rediscovering the concepts of natural inclinations, first principles of practical reason, etc., accept this dualism. On the one hand, there is the realm of *universality* with natural law, natural inclinations, first precepts (or

Goerner is found in Pamela Hall, "Goerner on Thomistic Natural Law," in *Political Theory* 4 (1990): 638–49; see also her *Narrative and the Natural Law: An Interpretation of Thomistic Ethics* (Notre Dame: University of Notre Dame Press, 1994). Hall's main criticism coincides with the one Veatch addresses to ethical egoism—i.e., the incapacity to go beyond a mere technical rationality and reach the ethical dimension of human life. I am afraid to say that in his "Response to Hall" in *Political Theory* 4 (1990): 650–655 Goerner shows no sign of accepting Hall's invitation to focus on a moral meaning of natural law.

3   In Italy, the most important example would be Giuseppe Abbà: see his *Lex et Virtus: Studi sull'Evoluzione della Dottrina Morale di san Tommaso d'Aquino* (Roma: LAS, 1983); *Felicità, Vita Buona e Virtù: Saggio di Filosofia Morale* (Roma: LAS, 1989); *Quale Impostazione per la Filosofia Morale?* (Roma: LAS, 1996). I criticized Abbà's concept of natural law in my *God and the Natural Law: A Rereading of Thomas Aquinas* [Italian edition: 1999] (South Bend: St. Augustine's Press 2006). Abbà's work is remarkable, though, and deserves close attention.

4   Thomas S. Hibbs focuses correctly on this epistemological problem in his "Principles and Prudence: The Aristotelianism of Thomas's Account of Moral Knowledge," in *The New Scholasticism* 3 (1987): 271–84.

5   I am thinking, of course, of Martha C. Nussbaum, *The Fragility of Goodness: Luck and Ethics in Greek Tragedy and Philosophy* (New York: Cambridge University Press, 1986); and *Love's Knowledge: Essays on Philosophy and Literature* (New York: Oxford University Press, 1990). For a recent criticism of Nussbaum (but also of Nancy Sherman and Sarah Broadie) on "the priority of the particular," see Moira M. Walsh, "The Role of Universal Knowledge in Aristotelian Moral Virtue," in *Ancient Philosophy* 19 (1999): 73–88. Walsh's strongest claim is that every act of *phronêsis* "presupposes at least implicit knowledge of the universal human *telos*."

principles), inclination to happiness, etc. On the other hand, we have the realm of *particularity* with prudence and the virtues.[6] Stanley Hauerwas appropriately talks about a "context versus principle debate."[7]

The opposition between natural law and prudence is also the outcome of the trend that the contemporary rediscovery of practical reason has taken over the last fifty years or so. Especially in the Anglo-Saxon sphere, this rediscovery is marked by a strong cultural reaction to Hume's is-ought question and, more generally, to modern philosophy's approach to ethics.[8] To the Humean idea that moral judgments as such are no more than a matter of feelings or emotions, today philosophers object that there is "the perception that moral reasoning does occur, that there can be logical linkages between various moral judgments of a kind that emotivism itself could not allow for ('therefore' and 'if ... then ...' are obviously not used as expressions of feeling)."[9] This clear perception leads both to the *analysis* of practical reasoning in terms of (objective) *reasons for action,* and to the search for the first value-premises (basic reasons for actions) of moral reasoning. Hart's "internal point of view" played a significant role in this context.[10] The value-character of the good as it exists in practical reasoning cannot simply be deduced from a theoretical is-knowledge; and this insight, claim Grisez, Finnis, etc., is exactly what grounded Aristotle's and Aquinas' ethical theories.

6   See Maria Carl, "Law, Virtue, and Happiness in Aquinas's Moral Theory," in *The Thomist* 61 (1997): 425–448. The best example of this tendency is given by the exponents of the so called neo–classical theory of natural law—namely, Germain Grisez, John Finnis, Joseph Boyle, Robert George, William May, etc. For a basic bibliography on (and criticism of) this school of thought let me refer again to *God and the Natural Law.*

7   Stanley Hauerwas, *Vision and Virtue: Essays in Christian Ethical Reflection* (Notre Dame, IN: University of Notre Dame Press, 1981), p. 49. I found this appropriate expression by Hauerwas while reading Thomas Hibbs, "Principles and Prudence: The Aristotelianism of Thomas's Account of Moral Knowledge," op. cit.

8   The obvious reference is to G.E.M. Anscombe, "Modern Moral Philosophy," in *Philosophy* 33 (1958): 175–95.

9   Alasdair MacIntyre, *After Virtue: A Study in Moral Theory* (Notre Dame, IN: University of Notre Dame Press, 1981), p. 19.

10 See Herbert L.A. Hart, *The Concept of Law* (Oxford: Clarendon Press, 1961).

For my present purposes it is important to stress that this trend, even if valuable under several respects, increases the natural *law versus* prudence debate because it leads to a rediscovery of natural law simply in terms of *universal* moral (or premoral) principles (or values). Practical knowledge is a kind of "value knowledge" but it still belongs to the realm of our *universal* and *abstract* knowledge. Even the natural inclinations in this context seem to aim merely at universal objects—i.e., general human values, rights, etc.[11]

Contemporary interpretations of the practical syllogism also reveal the difficulty of joining together universal (and perhaps theoretical) knowledge and particular, or contingent, moral life. These interpretations tend either to approach action in a metaphorical way or to take syllogism in a metaphorical way. The practical syllogism, in other words, either does not really conclude in the action but in a statement/proposition *peri tas praxeis*—which regards or relates to an action—or is not a proper syllogism at all, "syllogism" being just a non-technical term which refers to the various arguments used by the agent as justifications of his action.[12] In both cases a universal moral law, or universal moral knowledge, could not be really

---

11 Russell Hittinger focuses correctly on this narrow approach typical of contemporary natural law theory in his "Natural Law and Virtue: Theories at Cross Purposes," in *Natural Law Theory: Contemporary Essays*, Robert P. George (ed.) (Oxford: Oxford University Press, 1992), pp. 42–70.

12 For this way of looking at the contemporary debate, see Giuseppe Nicolaci, "Può l'Azione Concludere un Sillogismo? Sulla Teoria Aristotelica del Sillogismo Pratico" (hereafter, "Può l'Azione Concludere un Sillogismo?") [1994], in G. Nicolaci, *Metafisica e metafora: Interpretazioni aristoteliche* (Palermo: L'EPOS Società Editrice, 1999), pp. 95–110. Examples of the first tendency are Anthony Kenny, "Practical Inference," in *Analysis* 26 (1965–66): 65–75; and David Charles, *Aristotle's Philosophy of Action* (Ithaca, NY: Cornell University Press, 1984), pp. 84–96. Examples of the second tendency are G.E.M. Anscombe, *Intention* [1957] (Cambridge: Harvard University Press, 2000), pp. 57–66; G.E.M. Anscombe, "Thought and Action in Aristotle," [1965] in *Aristotle's Ethics: Issues and Interpretations*, James J. Walsh and Henry L. Shapiro (eds.) (Belmon, CA: Wadsworth Publishing Company, Inc., 1967), pp. 56–69; William F.R. Hardie, *Aristotle's Ethical Theory* (Oxford: Oxford University Press, 1968); John M. Cooper, *Reason and Human Good in Aristotle* (Cambridge: Harvard University Press, 1975); and again Kenny, "Practical Inference," op. cit.

practical because there is no logical connection between the universal (knowledge) and the particular (action). If there is still *room for something else* between the end of practical reasoning and the action, then it follows that the real cause, the engine, the final *dominus* of our behavior is not our reason or intellect but *something else* (such as autonomous will, emotion, etc.) On the other hand, it is obvious that non-deductive reasoning cannot be addressed by any conclusive objective moral criticism.

I think there are strong reasons to distrust the relevant terminology and the concepts used in the contemporary debate as misleading with respect to both Aristotle's and Aquinas's ethical theories. Natural law certainly relates, in the first place, to universal principles, but these principles are grasped through induction from experience. They not only can be (better) understood in and through experience of moral action, but are also properly *practical* only when they in turn can reach and guide that experience. Natural law can be a true moral guide only if it is truly able to reach the particular action to be performed here and now. The way in which the concepts universal and particular should be used in natural law theory needs to be revisited. I think this reexamination should be made through Aristotle's concepts of *sullogismos tôn praktôn* (practical syllogism) and *proairesis* (ethical, deliberated choice). My opinion is that Aristotle's theory of practical syllogism is one of the two main paradigms of Aquinas' natural law theory, the other being the Stoics' concept of God's law as developed by Christian philosophy and theology.

To construct a practical syllogism, the agent has to find and formulate the two premises from which the conclusion flows. Practical syllogism is the last step of what we call moral, or practical, reasoning. Here there are two levels of reasoning interacting with each other. The major premise depends on scientific reasoning that starts with the first intellectual apprehension of the universal good(s). The minor premise depends on a prudential reasoning that starts with the apprehension of a particular good. In each case, reasoning is *practical* due to the inclination to, or attraction by, the good to be achieved in action. This means that reasoning is practical due to the work of the appetite toward a particular action, and that moral choice happens when the two interacting reasoning processes match (only) one specific course of action. Being practical relates to action. Practical reason, consequently, is more practical the closer it is to the (particular) action. The same applies to natural law: the more it is practical the more it is the effective source of moral action.

In what follows, I will show that Aristotle's *proairesis* (moral choice) depends firstly on a scientific level of moral reasoning that corresponds to Aquinas' concepts of first notion and first principle of practical reason, first and secondary precepts of natural law, and *synderesis*. And, secondly, relies on a prudential level of practical reasoning that corresponds to Aquinas' concept of prudence. This means that prudence depends on what we would call ethical scientific knowledge. Furthermore, I will show that Aristotle's concept of practical syllogism depends from beginning to end on the interplay between intellect (*nous*) and appetite or inclination (*orexis*), and is supposed to effectively reach and cause the particular action. Surprisingly, as we will see, this corresponds closely to Aquinas' definition of natural law.

More particularly, the first section is meant to correctly frame the theory of practical syllogism in the context of Aristotle's physics. Practical syllogism is supposed to explain how *physical* movements happen—specifically, those movements (ours) of which thought is a cause. But since thought alone does not *move* anything, practical syllogism cannot be reduced to a pure theoretical object—it must be a unity of thought and appetite. In a sense, from this point on, this whole chapter intends to explain exactly *what thought* and *what appetite* compose the practical syllogism. Section two ("What Thought? What Appetite?") identifies them by using the distinction of the parts of the soul that Aristotle gives in the *Nicomachean Ethics*. The most relevant conclusion here is that the thought involved in the practical syllogism cannot be primarily the thought of *phronêsis* but a higher thought that relates to the concept of *nous*. Section three ("Why Nous?") aims at carefully explaining this point. Section four ("Orexis and the Virtues") directly addresses the union between thought and appetite. This union originates the knowledge of the good as such, and explains Aristotle's key concept of the *desiring nous*. At this point we will be able to reach a clear account of the concepts of practical syllogism and *proairesis*. This section will also clarify why moral dispositions affect correct practical reasoning; or, in other words, why evil people, for both Aristotle and Aquinas, do not understand ethics. Finally, the fifth section ("*Debitum Actum et Finem*") summarizes and specifies better the connection between Aristotle's theory of the practical syllogism and Aquinas' concept of natural law.

1. An Inquiry into *Physis*[13]

The key point for a correct understanding of Aristotle's concept of practical syllogism is that it does not relate to an inquiry into *logos* but into *physis*. That is to say, Aristotle approaches the practical syllogism in an effort to figure out how movements happen (or are generated) in material reality, and more particularly, in those animals which move by using their reason: human beings. This means, in turn, that the practical syllogism is supposed to be precisely: (a) what directly causes the action (or what concludes in *acting*); and (b) what causes the action as the conclusion of a real *deductive* rational process (proper syllogism). What Aristotle wonders is "how thought can push us to act or not to act, to move or, according to the circumstances, not to move."[14]

> But how is it that thought is sometimes followed by action, sometimes not; sometimes by movement, sometimes not? What happens seems parallel to the case of thinking and inferring about the immovable objects. There the end is truth seen [*theôrêma*] (for, when one thinks the two propositions, one thinks and puts together the conclusion), but here the two propositions result in a conclusion which is an action.[15]

A syllogism "is a discourse in which, certain things being stated, something other than what is stated follows of necessity from their being so."[16] As Carlo Natali has recently pointed out, it is clear that Aristotle "tries to demonstrate that all deductions made according to [this definition] must

---

13 The argument of this section follows the line taken by Nicolaci, "Può l'Azione Concludere un Sillogismo?" This is the best article I have read so far on Aristotle's ethics and the concept of practical reason. Let me refer to it for a deeper understanding of the subject. I am also indebted to Nicolaci for the clarifying and insightful discussions I had with him while working on this topic.

14 Nicolaci, "Può l'Azione Concludere un Sillogismo?" p. 95.

15 *MA* 7.701a8–12. See also, ibid., line 20: "And the conclusion 'I must make a coat' is an action."

16 Aristotle, *Prior Analytics* 1.24b19–20.

take the form of one of the three types of syllogism"[17] described in the *Prior Analytics*, and *practical* deduction is one of them. That Aristotle thinks this way about the practical syllogism is evident in a key passage of Book VII of the *Nicomachean Ethics*:

> The one opinion is universal, the other is concerned with the particular facts, and here we come to something within the sphere of perception; when a single opinion results from the two, the soul must in one type of case affirm the conclusion, while in the case of opinions concerned with production it must immediately act (e.g., if everything sweet ought to be tasted, and this is sweet, in the sense of being one of the particular sweet things, the man who can act and is not restrained must at the same time actually act accordingly).[18]

It would be misleading to try to formalize this example in an attempt to understand the practical syllogism, for the simple reason that, at least for Aristotle, a practical syllogism could not even be *thought* or *expressed by words*.[19] The attempts, for instance by Anthony Kenny and Elizabeth Anscombe, to prove either logically right or logically wrong the examples

---

17   Carlo Natali, *The Wisdom of Aristotle*, trans. G. Parks (Albany: State University of New York Press, 2001), pp. 64–65.

18   *NE* 7.1147a25–31. For the other famous examples of walking, making a house, and making a coat, see *MA* 7.701a12–24. Charles (*Aristotle's Philosophy of Action*, pp. 91–92) cites *NE* 7.1147a25–31, and other similar passages, as evidence that in Aristotle, "the conclusion of the syllogism is a proposition and not an action." His argument rests on the possibility, admitted by Aristotle, of being restrained from acting. In this case, Charles says, "the action will not follow, although the conclusion may be drawn. Hence the conclusion is not the action." I think Charles confuses the agent's point of view (or internal point of view, from which the practical syllogism must be examined) with an external (third person) point of view. Charles's argument is the same as saying that the action of pressing down on the accelerator does not cause the movement of the car because, for instance, there is a wall preventing it from going forward.

19   On this point, see again Nicolaci, "Può l'Azione Concludere un Sillogismo?" pp. 106–107.

given by Aristotle are already *as attempts* a misinterpretation of Aristotle's concept of the practical syllogism. I hope this point will be a bit clearer later in the chapter. What is important in the above passage is rather that it makes clear that Aristotle was thinking of a real *deduction,* in which a conclusion follows from the connection of a *major* with a *minor* premise. And this fact raises again, and more forcefully, the key question: "How can thought push us to act or not to act?"

The reason why this question is so embarrassing is that, according to Aristotle, "intellect [*dianoia*] itself [...] moves nothing."[20] The faculty of the soul that moves is, rather, *orexis* (appetite).[21] This means in turn that, for the practical syllogism to exist, it should be an intrinsic unity of thought (*nous/dianoia*) and appetite (*orexis*). And this is what "practical" is supposed to mean when it joins the *generic* "syllogism" to indicate the existence of a particular *specific* nature. A practical syllogism is a syllogism in which, from the beginning (major premise) to the end (conclusion), *nous* and *orexis* work together as an intrinsic unity.

This unity may look like a kind of "monster"[22]: reasoning which requires desire for its logical steps and which does not conclude with an object theoretically identifiable. How can thought and appetite be joined together? And what does this mean exactly? The term "monster" fits well. Indeed, I hope the practical syllogism will look more and more monstrous as I go on—otherwise we might miss the point by failing to focus on what is simultaneously rational and appetitive. However, this monster does not seem to me bigger or more threatening than the union of body and spirit (or mind) that we experience daily in the strange creature called human being.

---

20 *NE* 6.1139a35–36. The use of *dianoia* is important because it refers generically to the whole intellectual part of the soul. This means, for example, that not even *phronêsis* in itself can cause the movement. See also, Aristotle, *OS* 3.10.432b26–27, where it is specified that neither the calculative part of the soul nor *nous* can be the cause of movement. The reason given is remarkable, and we must keep it in mind during the present discussion: "[M]ind as speculative [*theoretikos*] never thinks [*theorei*] what is practicable [*prakton*]." That is, *theoretikon* cannot *theorei* the action.

21 *OS* 3.10.433a10–29.

22 See Harold H. Joachim, *Aristotle: The Nicomachean Ethics, A Commentary* (Oxford: Clarendon Press, 1955).

Descartes saw this monster clearly, but when he tried to join *res extensa* and *res cogitans* he unhappily failed. Maybe the attempt itself was his mistake. Spirit and body do exist together: this is the only reasonable starting point in understanding human life. Thought and desire exist together in the acting human being. This is, I think, Aristotle's reasonable starting point.

2. What Thought? What Appetite?

Let us take for granted that according to Aristotle moral action is the outcome of a real deductive (syllogistic) reasoning characterized by an intrinsic unity of thought and appetite. The question now is: "Which thought and which appetite are required exactly?" I am going to answer this question by using the distinction of the parts of the soul which Aristotle outlines in the first and sixth books of the *Nicomachean Ethics*. This distinction is made specifically for ethical purposes and does not perfectly correspond to the distinction between vegetative, sentient, and rational soul of the *De Anima*.[23]

At the end of the first book of the *Nicomachean Ethics* (1102a5–1103a10), Aristotle introduces the study of the ethical virtues by distinguishing three parts of the soul. He says first (1102a27–28) that there are two parts of the soul: one with *logos* (*logon echon*) and one without *logos* (*alogon*). This is usually translated as "rational" part and "irrational" part, which is more or less accurate. However, I need to stress here what the real Greek term is, because *logos* by itself is not the best term to indicate what *we* would call rational part of the soul. We usually refer rational to the whole intellectual activity, and we usually include will (the rational desire) in this. Now *logos*, of course, does not refer to the will—which belongs to the part of the soul without *logos,* as I explain later—but even here it does not refer to the whole intellectual sphere (including also *nous* and *epistêmê*), for which the most appropriate generic term would probably be *dianoia* (which still would not include the will). *Logos* is the word (*verbum*) of the intellectual

---

23   On this point, see the recent work by Sarah Broadie, *Ethics with Aristotle* (Oxford: Oxford University Press, 1991), pp. 61, 118. Broadie refers, in turn, to William W. Fortenbaugh, *Aristotle on Emotion* (New York: Barnes & Noble Books, 1975).

part of the soul. It is thought speaking, and in so doing, being either true or false. *Rule* would be a better translation because Aristotle is focusing here not on the intellectual part of the human being as such, but on the *orthos logos*, or the *right rule* of the moral action. This is what his ethics is all about, and accordingly he draws his first distinction inside the soul, i.e., the part with the rule and the part without it.

Immediately after, he further distinguishes the part of the soul without *logos* into two parts: (a) the vegetative part common to all living beings (1102a32–1102b12); and (b) a part without *logos* but which shares somehow in the *logos* (1102b13–35). This is the appetitive part of the soul, the *epithumêtikon* and in general the *orektikon* (b30). The stress here is on *epithumêtikon* because *epithumia* is the specific kind of *orexis* (desire) having pleasure as its object.[24] This desire is what can divert man from virtuous action—action in conformity with the *orthos logos*—since "it is on account of pleasure that we do bad things, and on account of pain that we abstain from noble ones."[25] An action in conformity with *orthos logos* is an action in which the desire for the good as pleasure (*epithumia*) does not prevail over the desire for the good as noble, or morally beautiful (*boulêsis*). The moral virtues, which Aristotle examines in Books II, III, IV, and V, are precisely the perfections of the appetitive part of the soul rendering human beings able to live in harmony with their desires—in conformity with *orthos logos*—and achieve not only the best moral good but also the highest pleasure. It is very important not to make the mistake of thinking that moral virtues affect just a sort of *animal part* of the soul. The appetitive part includes all the three kinds of *orexis*: *epithumia*, *boulêsis* (the will), and *thumos* (the sanguine desire for the good, one might say). And the moral virtues are supposed to perfect all these tendencies bringing them share in the (*orthos*) *logos*.[26]

24 See, *OS* 3.3.414b5–6.
25 *NE* 2.3.1104b10–11.
26 Even if Aristotle says explicitly that the other animals possess *epithumia* as well, I think there is no reason to restrict the concept of *epithumia*—when applied to human beings—to the animal/sentient pleasures only. *Epithumia* is the desire/attraction for the *good as pleasurable*. In this sense, every sentient being possesses it. But in the human being what is pleasurable comes also from the rational activities. The extremes of the vices are always caused by focusing

In the lines 1103a1–3 Aristotle adds another distinction. He says that the part with *logos* "will be twofold, one subdivision having it in the strict sense and in itself, and the other having a tendency to obey as one does one's father." It is obvious that we do not have here a real fourth part because the second one of this last distinction corresponds to the appetitive part. Aristotle is stressing now the fact that this part is not totally without *logos* because it is supposed to desire in conformity with it. When this happens, the *logos* is somehow also in the appetite. So far, therefore, we have three parts of the soul: the vegetative (without *logos*), the appetitive (sharing in the *logos*), and the one with the *logos* in itself.

Let us go now to the beginning of the sixth book, where Aristotle begins his discussion of the intellectual virtues (*aretai dianoêtikai*). For this purpose he needs an additional distinction, which makes the total four. He says (1139a3–15) that there are two parts of the soul which possess *logos*, "one by which we contemplate the kind of things whose principles cannot be otherwise, and one by which we contemplate variable things." These parts are, respectively, the *epistêmonikon* (scientific) and the *logistikon* (calculative). "We must, then, learn what is the best state [*hexis*] of each of these two parts; for this is the excellence [*aretê*] of each" (a15–17). These *aretai* are *dianoêtikai* because they are "the best state" of *dianoia* (thought). Beginning with line 1139b15, Aristotle initiates his examination of the five "states by virtue of which the soul possesses truth by way of affirmation or denial": *technê* (art); *epistêmê* (scientific, or demonstrative, knowledge); *phronêsis* (practical wisdom, or prudence); *sophia* (wisdom); and *nous* (intellect in the strict sense: the intellectual act by which we grasp the first principles of knowledge).[27]

---

only, or too much, on *epithumia*. This point is clear in Aristotle, and it is true of every ethical virtue. To imagine, for instance, that the moral desire causing injustice is just a kind of *epithumia* we share with other non–rational animals would make unintelligible all the *human* pleasures connected with power, money, pride, envy, etc. For Aquinas it is clear that "intelligible delight is through the will, as sensible delight is through the appetite of concupiscence" (*CG*, Book I, Ch. 72).

27   As it will appear later in the chapter, this first description of *nous* is only a partial description.

It is not perfectly clear whether Aristotle thinks of all these five states in terms of *dianoetical virtues*[28] (I will use this unambiguous Aristotelian term—as we do in Italy—instead of "intellectual virtues"). I believe he does so for two main reasons. The first is Aristotle's constant use of *hexis*, which is the technical term indicating the genus of the virtues.[29] The second is that all those five states seem to admit a better or a worse condition according to their correct exercise, and this is what the term "virtue" basically refers to. So, we have three dianoetical virtues for the *epistêmonikon*—*sophia*, *nous*, and *epistêmê*—and two for the *logistikon*—*phronêsis* and *teknê*. And we have four parts of the soul with respect to *logos*: the vegetative (without *logos*), the *orektikon* (appetitive: sharing in *logos*), the *epistêmonikon* (scientific), and the *logistikon* (calculative).

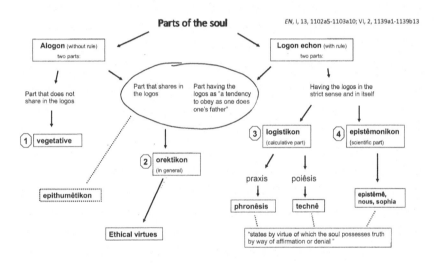

Parts of the soul   EN, I, 13, 1102a5-1103a10; VI, 2, 1139a1-1139b13

28 Marcello Zanatta, recovering an old interpretation advanced by Plutarch, Aspasio, and Alexander of Aphrodisia, argues that the dianoetical virtues for Aristotle are indeed two—*sophía* and *phrónesis*—and that Aristotle's intention in the sixth book is rather to discuss dialectically the traditional five-virtue platonic opinion. See Zanatta's critical edition of the *Nicomachean Ethics* (Milan: Rizzoli, 1986), pp. 902–903.

29 See, *NE* 2.4.1105b19–1106a13. See also, ibid. 1.13.1103a4–6, in which Aristotle lists three examples of dianoetical virtues: *sophia*, *sunesis* (which refers to the *nous*, or knowledge), and *epistêmê*.

Now, whatever the opinion about the exact number of the dianoetical virtues, there is no doubt that *phronêsis* is the virtue of the *logistikon* with respect to *praxis* (moral action). If there is another virtue of the *logistikon*, it cannot be other than *technê*, which deals with *poiêsis* (production). There is also no doubt that ethical virtues are the excellence of the *orektikon* (the appetitive part).

What is striking about all of this is that we now have a clear account, or location in the soul, of both *phronêsis* and the moral virtues, but it is not clear at all how we can get either *proairesis* (deliberated choice: the efficient cause of moral action) or the practical syllogism. Or better, it is perfectly clear that we cannot get either of them by focusing only on *phronêsis* and on the moral virtues.

It is true that in *Nicomachean Ethics* 1139a31–33 Aristotle says that the two principles of *proairesis*, as the efficient cause of moral action, are *orexis* (desire) and *logos* (reasoning with a view to an end). And that is why, in order to have a good (moral) choice, we need a true *logos*—a true calculation of means—and a right desire—*orexin orthen* (1139a23–24). We need, in other words, both *phronêsis*, which makes the calculation of means *true*, and moral virtues, which make the desire *right*. However, Aristotle also says that *proairesis* is not the principle of moral action in terms of final cause (1139a31-32). And he adds that *proairesis* cannot exist without (a) *nous*, (b) *dianoia*, and (c) the ethical virtues (1139a33–34). Now, it is obvious that *nous* cannot be located in the *logistikon* part of the soul. This reference, consequently, moves *proairesis*, much beyond *phronêsis*, to the scientific part of the soul. But it is also curious that Aristotle, immediately after mentioning *logos* and *orexis* as the principles of *proairesis*, uses the generic term *dianoia*. It seems as if he wanted once again to connect *proairesis* to the scientific part of the soul, but with a connotation not already implicit in the term *nous*. In other words, the lines 1139a33–34 add to the *logos-orexis* lines (1139a31–33) both (1) *nous* and *dianoia* as different references to the scientific part of the soul, and (2) *ethical virtues* as the excellence of *orexis*. No word is chosen by chance here but, for my present purposes, I do not need to focus more on the exegesis of these passages.

Rather, I need to recall that when Aristotle starts wondering how it can be that thought causes our actions, both in the *Nicomachean Ethics*

(1139a17–19) and in the *De Anima* (433a9–27), he always uses *nous*, which again is a term that does not fit the *logistikon* part of the soul.[30] Moreover, and most importantly, in the *Nicomachean Ethics* Aristotle defines *proairesis* not only as *orexis bouleutikê* (1139a23)[31]—a term that certainly fits the calculative part of the soul—but also as *orektikos nous* (1139b4)—which does not refer at all to the calculative—and as *orexis dianoêtikê* (1139b5)—which refers above all to the scientific part of the soul. This is certainly a puzzle. But we can already be sure that the solution, whatever it is, does not lie primarily either in *phronêsis* or in the *logistikon*.

3. Why *Nous*?

The crucial question now is, "Why does Aristotle focus on *nous* and not on *logos*?" The first answer is certainly that for the practical syllogism to start it needs (as all demonstrations do) universal principles/knowledge which are not known by way of demonstration. *Nous*, under this respect, is the origin of all human reasoning and in a sense of thought itself. If thought has a role to play in our movements as humans, it should be first of all at the level where its possibility to be (and be true) is generated, hence where all reasoning starts.

However, *nous* is even more. It is the beginning and the end of our intellectual activity. It is the eye of the mind, and its seeing "can never be in error,"[32] whether it sees the first principles of demonstration or a simple apprehension. *Nous* is to thought what *aisthêsis* (perception) is to sense-knowledge. Its object is not the perceptible thing (*to aisthêton*) but the intelligible thing (*to noeton*). *Nous*, in other words, is the direct, immediate, constant, intuitive intellectual knowledge we have of reality while our mind is wandering around using its *logos* (i.e., reasoning). In this sense, *nous* is different from, and constantly grounds and originates, *dianoia* in its more specific meaning(s) as scientific (*epistêmonikos*) and

---

30 See also, *MP* E.1.1025b22.
31 See also, *NE* 3.1113a10–11, where the discussion is focused on *boulêsis* and the process of deliberation.
32 *OS* 3.6.430b26–30.

calculating (*logistikos*) reason. In this sense, *logos*, whether *epistêmonikos* or *logistikos*, always works to achieve a better intellectual sight (*nous*) of reality.[33]

At the level of our universal knowledge of reality *nous* speaks and its words become *scientific dianoia*. In so doing, *nous* can be (not in itself but because of the *logos*) either true or false. That is why, at the highest level where the major premise is generated thought must be both *nous* of the first notions and principles, and scientific *dianoia* of the ethical reality, if it has a part in our movements. *Phronêsis* is not yet in the picture since it belongs to the *logistikon*, and, consequently, it cannot be *epistêmê* (science).[34] Yet *epistêmê* is exactly what we need at this first level of practical activity, and that is why Aristotle talks about *dianoia praktike* and *epistêmê praktike* when he distinguishes human knowledge into the theoretical, the practical, and the productive.[35] As Enrico Berti has forcefully pointed out, the first meaning of "practical reason" in Aristotle belongs to science and not to prudence. And this is what the *Nicomachean Ethics* is supposed to be: a reflexive, scientific treatment of ethical reality able to help the choices of people who want to be good.[36]

The reason why Aristotle wants to ground *proairesis* on *nous* (and *dianoia*), rather than on the *logistikon*, should now be a little clearer, but there is much more to say. *Nous* also grounds intellectual practical activity at the second level where the minor premise is generated when, looking for its completion in the action, it becomes *calculative dianoia*. "The one opinion is universal, the other is concerned with the particular facts, and here we come to something within the sphere of perception [*aisthêsis*]" (*NE* 7,

33   This is also present in Plato's subordination of *diánoia* (mathematical knowledge) to intuitive knowledge (*noêsis*) which takes man to the world of ideas.

34   *NE* 6.5.1140b1–2.

35   *MP* 6.1.1025a25; 2.1026b4–5; Aristotle, *Topics* 6.6.145a15–16; 8.1.157a10–11. *Politiké epistéme* is "science" according to Aristotle because there is demonstrative science, not only of what is necessary, but also of what is "for the most part" (*hos epi to polu*): this is an epistemological trait that ethics shares also with physics. See, Enrico Berti, "Ragione Pratica e Normatività in Aristotele" (hereafter "Ragione Pratica") in *Ragione Pratica, Libertà, Normatività*, M.S. Sorondo (ed.) (Roma: Herder – Università Lateranense, 1991), p. 28.

36   Berti, "Ragione Pratica," op. cit., 27–43.

1147a25–31). Let us try to go deeper into Aristotle's mind's eye. On the one hand, reasoning about particulars requires the universal *nous/dianoia* knowledge that generates the major premise (e.g., "everything sweet ought to be tasted"). On the other hand, it requires "the eye of the intellect" to grasp, through *aisthêsis*, the nature of the particular thing which will be the object of deliberation and which will produce the minor premise (e.g., "this is sweet, in the sense of being one of the particular sweet things").[37] And this explains the famous but difficult passage of *Nicomachean Ethics* VI, 11, 1143a35–1143b6:

> And comprehension [*nous*] is concerned with the ultimates in both directions; for both the primary definitions and the ultimates are objects of comprehension [*nous*] and not of argument [*logos*], and in demonstrations comprehension [*nous*] grasps the unchangeable and primary definitions, while in practical reasoning [*en tais praktikais*] it grasps the last and contingent fact, i.e., the second proposition [*protaseôs*: premise]. For these are the starting-points of that for the sake of which, since the universals are reached from the particulars; of these therefore we must have perception [*aisthêsin*], and this is comprehension [*nous*].

Epistemologically, *nous* grasps the (intelligible) particulars through *aisthêsis* (through induction) before all universal knowledge, but this is not my focus now. Rather, it is important to see that practical reasoning is the gathering together of a universal *nous/dianoia* and of a particular *nous/dianoia* in an *aisthêsis*-experience, each of them trying to focus clearly on their respective objects: the major premise for the former and the minor for the latter. These premises are the conclusions of two different *dianoiai*: the

---

37   An important specification: all this is supposed to be a real rational process; that is, a process that spontaneously happens in ordinary people's minds. Precisely because we are spontaneously rational in this way, we can also *reflexively* focus on our intellectual activity (e.g., writing the *Nicomachean Ethics*) and try to make our rational processes more consistent. In other words, scientific *dianoia*, before being a (reflexive) science, is one of the ways in which our mind constantly, and spontaneously, works.

scientific and the calculative, respectively. They are both grounded on *nous*. They can both be true or false because: (a) *nous* is the objective basis of the truth, and (b) *dianoia* (*logos*) can make mistakes. They both look for their own completion in the same *aisthêsis*-experience and in the context of a dialectical interplay, back and forth from scientific to calculative. Yet "when a single opinion [*doxa*] results from the two, the soul must in one type of case affirm the conclusion, while in the case of opinions concerned with production it must immediately act." If the agent still has a doubt about one of the two premises, or regarding their becoming one, if he still has time to *reflect* on them, the practical syllogism (either true or false) is not concluded.[38]

Now, although all this is very interesting, it does not suffice. For the practical syllogism to start it needs the presence, at its very origin, of the proper principle of movement: *orexis*. If *nous* does not *desire* it will not develop into *dianoia*, it will not descend to the second premise, and it will never become action. For practical reasoning from its very beginning is nothing more than a search for the good to be achieved here and now: a search for the action.

4. *Orexis* and the Virtues

This is the last crucial passage of my discussion. If it is true that Aristotle focuses on *nous* as the source and the leader of the syllogism's steps, it is also true that for him *nous* is still not the cause of our movements. We need therefore another source and another leader—this is *orexis*.

Without *orexis*, *nous* could not start its *dianoetical* movement at the level of the major premise since "everything sweet ought to be tasted" is not just theoretical knowledge; indeed, *nous* could not even say "this is sweet" at the level of the minor premise. Here we really meet the monster because for practical reasoning to exist we need a *desiring nous* at the level of our universal knowledge, a *desiring nous* at the level of our particular (calculative) knowledge, and a *desiring nous* as the conclusion.

---

38 This does not necessarily mean that the agent will not act. It means simply that the agent does not always act on the basis of a practical syllogism—that is, on the basis of a perfect harmony between his thought and his appetite.

I think Aquinas understood very well the concept of *desiring nous* when, while explaining his natural law theory, he wrote that the first notion of practical reason is not *ens* but *bonum*,[39] a term which signifies the relationship between the *ens* known and the will tending toward it. *Bonum* is a primitive concept but still a complex one that depends and is grounded on knowledge of the *ens*.[40] For Aquinas, the first principle of practical reason is *bonum est faciendum et prosequendum, malum vitandum*.[41] This means that, for the *nous* to originate movements it must know reality as attractive (as good) at the very first level in which it is infallibly true. It can only do so if it is informed by, or intrinsically joined to, *orexis*. Building on Aristotle, Aquinas says that "all those things to which man has a natural inclination, are naturally apprehended by reason as being good, and consequently as objects of pursuit." Aquinas calls these kind of *first intellectual apprehensions* first principles of practical reason, or first precepts of natural law. Interestingly enough, they are for him exactly the level of natural law that "cannot be changed" and "cannot be abolished from the heart of man."[42] In other words, for Aquinas practical reasoning could not even start without a *habit* of immediate intellectual knowledge of notions and principles (which includes the *seeds* of the virtues). He calls this habit *synderesis*. Yet, as soon as nous becomes scientific dianoia—which is the process of knowing moral rules and more specific principles of action—natural law (its secondary precepts) can either change or be "blotted out from men's hearts."[43]

Let me go back now to the main question I want to address here: "What is the impact of *orexis* on *nous* in practical knowledge?"

Orexis "arises through perception [*aisthêsis*] or through imagination [*phantasia*] and thought"[44] but, of course, it always relates and tends to particulars. The object of *orexis* is not a "truth seen [*theôrêma*]" and, consequently, properly speaking it cannot be *thought* or *expressed* by words. "Mind as speculative [*theoretikos*] never thinks [*theorei*] what is practicable

39 *ST,* I–II, q. 94, a. 2 c.
40 *DV,* q. 1, a. 1.
41 *ST,* I–II, q. 94, a. 2 c.
42 *ST,* I–II, q. 94, aa. 5–6.
43 Ibid.
44 *MA* 7.701a35–36.

[*praktov*]."[45] *Theoretikon* cannot *theorei orexis*. This is why Aristotle in the *Metaphysics* confronts truth with action when he writes that "philosophy should be called knowledge [*epistêmê*] of the truth. For the end of theoretical knowledge is truth, while that of practical knowledge is action."[46] *Orexis* (and not *phronêsis*, which in itself belongs to *dianoia* and to *theoria*) makes the particular present to, and active in, the *nous*. In so doing it makes *nous* practical. However, the union between *orexis* and *nous* as such is not any more thinkable. Even if this union contains truth it is not, properly speaking, *just* truth because it is not *just* thought. When we try to write either the major or minor premise, or the conclusion of a practical syllogism, we abstractly isolate their theoretical aspects, and thereby miss their real nature. This is also the reason why Aristotle's ethics is intrinsically *dialectical*, because the ethical dialogue requires a common starting point at the practical level of *orexis* (moral desire, or values for those who prefer this term). In other words, the dialogue starts as soon as the interlocutors discover they share at least one love, or value.

Nous is in all cases right but *orexis* is always right only at the very first level of *nous*-knowledge. *Orexis*, then, as well as *logos*, can be either right or wrong. *Orexis* depends on *dianoia*, but a mere mistake in the dianoetical process would not make *orexis* intrinsically wrong. For Aristotle, such a mistake would rather make the action involuntary. The reason why *orexis* can be either right or wrong is that *orexis* is intrinsically complex (*epithumia*, *boulêsis*, *thumos*).[47] In order to work correctly *orexis* requires (the perfection of) the moral virtues. Commenting on Aristotle concerning this point, Aquinas writes that "the rectitude of the appetitive faculty in regard to the end [determined for man by nature: i.e., known by *nous*] is the measure of truth for practical reason."[48] Now, if we focus on the nature of *orexis* as the engine of practical reason—that is, as what leads (practical) thought towards its (particular) object—this fact acquires tremendous importance. It basically means that, developing into *dianoia*, both at the level of the first premise

---

45   *OS* 3.10.432b26–27.

46   *MP* 2.1.993b20–21.

47   In Thomistic philosophy the reason is more complex. I have sketched a more complete account of it in the third chapter of *God and the Natural Law*.

48   *In Eth.*, 6, lect. 2, 1131.

and at the level of the second premise, *nous* depends on the moral dispositions of the agent. Scientific and calculative reasoning follow the directions
and the paths given by the desire. When *nous* does not desire the right way,
its (practical) knowledge will be distorted, misdirected. Above all, the *epistêmonikos logos* will not focus on the right things and will not formulate, or
develop, the right moral rules and principles. As a consequence, the *logistikos
logos* too will be misdirected, and the action will be immoral.

A wrong moral desire impedes correct universal knowledge of what is
good. This is the reason why Aristotle says that neither "the ignorance in
proairesis"—which causes vice—nor "the ignorance of the universal"—
which is a cause for blame—make the action involuntary.[49] This ignorance
is the bad work of *dianoia* both in formulating the major premise and in
calculating the moral choice that is due to an evil moral desire. The thought
is *in itself incorrect* because of a bad moral disposition, but it is nevertheless
correctly following that disposition. As far as *orexis* and the moral intention
are concerned, the action is voluntary and the person evil/vicious. Aristotle
had strong epistemological reasons for saying that ethics is studied in order
to be good, and that evil people cannot understand ethical science.

Our "*proairesis* and practical syllogism" puzzle should by now have been
solved. *Proairesis* is the conclusion of the practical syllogism. As such, it is
a mixture of *nous* and *orexis*. It is at the same time the perfection of the
practical *nous*—which seeks its good in the action—and the efficient cause
of the movement—i.e., what directly and effectively causes it. This perfection is attained both through the scientific *dianoia* and calculative *dianoia*.
Consequently *proairesis* is also the perfection of practical *dianoia*. *Proairesis*
is, therefore, *orektikos nous* and *orexis dianoêtikê*. Furthermore, in the more
specific sense of *dianoia* related to the second premise it is also *orexis bouleutikê*. *Phronêsis* is concerned only with this last sense, whereas the ethical
virtues affect the whole process of the practical syllogism as the excellence
of *orexis*.

Let me now summarize the discussion of practical syllogism as related
specifically not to Aristotle's ethics, but to Aristotle's *physics*. Practical syllogism does not exist if not in the acting rational agent. It is the agent's
first-person knowledge of his action as action. This is Aristotle's conclusion

49 *NE* 3.1.1110b31–35.

about the physics of rational action: it happens due to a combined work of thought and appetite and according to a kind of syllogism. In other words, the rational action happens: (1) when the agent, *for whatever reason,* reaches *right now* the value-conclusion that he should act upon a maxim such as "everything sweet ought to be tasted" (or that "I need a covering," or "I should go to the store," or "I should exercise")—i.e., when this maxim is in this moment what is chiefly moving his rational desire or appetite—and (2) when he reaches the conclusion that "this is sweet" (or that "this cloak is a covering," or "the car downstairs is the best way to go to the store," or "right now soccer is for me the best way to exercise"). When the actual appetite-premise matches the identified (best) means, no other conceptual element is required for the action to happen. If the action does not happen (besides the case of material impediments), it means that the agent is still doubtful, *reasoning* about the right maxim/desire, the best means, or both. The examples of practical syllogisms given by Aristotle appear as perfect examples if we consider: (1) that real examples, for him, cannot be written down, and (2) that every example is supposed to be a way of looking, from the agent's perspective, at the action accomplished. In this sense, we might account for John's action by saying that he tasted the apple pie on the assumption that it was a moral obligation for him to taste everything sweet, and that that apple pie was the sweet thing he saw as available to him at the time he tasted it. That both assumptions might have been wrong, unreasonable, or grounded on other complex reasoning does not change the fact that in the end John acted upon a kind of syllogism.

If we want to help John—that is, if we shift our focus from physics to ethics—we do not have to try to formulate a different syllogism for him to use, but to better form both his scientific moral knowledge and his moral desire. That is to say, we have to: (1) teach him how to focus on better moral concepts, principles, and maxims; and (2) give him a better education in virtue. This is precisely the point of Aristotle's ethics, and this is why he did not think of giving a special place in it to the practical syllogism as such.[50]

50 Even when we can formulate a deductive (syllogistic) argument that is directly applicable to action—for example, (a) abortion is always wrong, (b) this particular medical procedure is an abortion, (c) this particular medical procedure cannot be done—it will be a practical syllogism only for those who will act

Good practical syllogisms will naturally follow from good moral education and good scientific study of ethical reality. Some contemporary interpreters, like Kenny and Anscombe, try to reach a sort of theoretically complete (multiple-step) account of the reasoning behind what I have now identified as the real practical syllogism. They miss the point that the complete syllogism is a conclusion of the agent's discursive (and *desiring*) reasoning, not the reasoning itself. Moreover, they wonder how the syllogism, whatever its formulation, can actually compel the agent to act, overlooking the fact that no third-person formulation of the syllogism can lead anyone to act. We should add that contingent action cannot be reduced to any abstract description. Except for God, who has perfect knowledge of every individual, there is no way to know for sure what the real apprehension of the premises is for the agent. Most of the time, the agent himself has difficulty in reaching an adequate knowledge of why exactly he did what he did. To have a perfect knowledge of a practical syllogism means no more and no less than to have perfect knowledge, with respect to one particular action, of someone's moral conscience—indeed, of the person's complete state of mind.

5. *Debitum Actum et Finem*

The reason why focusing too much on *phronêsis* is misleading when attempting to understand practical reasoning should by now be evident. Practical syllogism is grounded first of all on *nous*, which for Aristotle refers to an intellectual objective knowledge acquired by induction. This knowledge grounds the work of *logos* both at the level of the major premise and at the level of the minor premise. But both the practical character and the correct working of *nous-dianoia* knowledge depend on (the excellence of) the appetite—*orexis*—and always refers to, and finds its completion or perfection in, the concrete action which concludes the syllogism. Practical knowledge is primarily the lived moral knowledge of the rationally acting agent. It is only remotely knowledge—either reflexive or otherwise—of first values or practical principles (major-premise level) and knowledge of suitable means (minor-premise level). Properly speaking, practical knowledge cannot be

upon it; and it will be a better syllogism for those who have a better moral apprehension of its premises.

separated from the (particular and concrete) action. Universal knowledge of the good is practical only *secundum quid*, as far as it is directed to the action. Otherwise, it would be theoretical knowledge, no longer searching for but *contemplating* the good. This is a very important point: for Aquinas the intellectual (*nous*) knowledge of the good is not practical knowledge because what is practical is only what relates to the action, and action relates to the means. If you are already enjoying the end, or the good, your intellectual knowledge of it is theoretical.[51] What about natural law?

I already mentioned some connections between the first two levels of the practical syllogism and some of the main concepts involved in Aquinas's natural law theory: that is, the first notion and the first principle of practical reason, the first and the secondary precepts of natural law, and the habit of *synderesis*. If I am right, this connection is already remarkable because it shows that this natural-law knowledge depends not only on (the intellectual virtue of) prudence—as some contemporary scholars stress—but also and primarily on a *scientific* ethical knowledge and on the ethical virtues. Yet, if I am right, Aquinas should have defined natural law also at the practical level of *proairesis*, that is, with reference to the effective cause of the concrete action to be performed here and now. Does he do this? Actually, in *Summa Theologiae*, I-II, q. 91, a. 2 c., which is the first article devoted to the natural law and where Aquinas addresses the question "Whether there is in us a natural law," we find the following definition:

> it is evident that all things partake somewhat of the eternal law, in so far as, namely, from its being imprinted on them, they derive their respective inclinations to their proper acts and ends. Now among all others, the rational creature is subject to Divine providence in the most excellent way, in so far as it partakes of a share of providence, by being provident both for itself and for others. Wherefore it has a share of the Eternal Reason, whereby it has a natural inclination to its proper act and end [*naturalem inclinationem ad debitum actum et finem*]: and this participation

51 In *ST*, I–II, q. 3, a. 5, Aquinas explains explicitly that happiness or beatitude is not an activity of the practical intellect because practical intellect relates to the means, not to the end alone.

of the eternal law in the rational creature is called the natural law.

This is certainly Aquinas' most precise and technical definition of natural law. Here there is no doubt that this "natural inclination" is a kind of intellectual and rational *orexis,* but what should surprise us is that the definition is all but simple. In fact, it refers both to the inclination to the *proper end* and to the inclination to the *proper* (or *due*) *act.* These two inclinations are not the same thing. The first one refers to the intellectual (theoretical) knowledge of the end as good. The second one refers to the inclination to the concrete action to be performed here and now.[52] This inclination depends on the work of practical reason, which identifies the right action to do (*recta ratio*). The knowledge of the right action as such is practical knowledge, and it closely matches Aristotle's concept of *proairesis.* So, it very much seems that Aquinas, in line with Aristotle's theory of action, conceives of his natural law also as *practical*—namely, as an effective guide of moral action. Such an approach to natural law theory has extraordinary consequences. This point alone is material for another book.

---

52 I explain the logical meaning of law and natural law in Aquinas (also with respect to the concept of inclination) in chapter VII.

III

LAW AS ACT OF REASON AND COMMAND

In this chapter, I focus on the way in which we should interpret Aquinas' thesis that law pertains to reason when we look at it from the viewpoint of the analogical nature of the concept of law. Due to the modern debate on voluntarism, scholars usually frame Aquinas' thesis in the context of stating the primacy of the intellect over the will in the concept of law. There is something true in this approach, but it is nonetheless misleading. To understand Aquinas' statement that law pertains to reason we must analytically divide it into two conceptual elements: act of reason and command. As striking as it might seem, the first one already includes the power of the will and refers to a perfect meaning of practical knowledge that also applies to God. The second, on the other hand, refers practical knowledge to a relation between two or more subjects, and does not include the binding force, which in the complete definition of law comes later, with the concept of authority. In what follows, I will first touch briefly upon the analogical predication of law, and then I will examine in more detail the meaning of law, respectively, as an act of reason and a command.

1. The Analogical Nature of Aquinas' Concept of Law

For the sake of simplicity, I will assume that a purely equivocal predication of law is clearly not what Aquinas has in mind. Also, a univocal predication should be discarded immediately because three out of the four kinds[1] of law listed by Aquinas (eternal, natural, divine, and human) refer to God's action, and "univocal predication is impossible between God and creatures."[2]

---

1   Of course, as the predication is not univocal I use "kind" in a non-technical way.
2   *ST*, I, q. 13, a. 5. See also *CG*, Book I, Ch. 32.

Moreover, there is obviously no specific difference to add to each kind in order to obtain its respective nature—as we should, for example, add "rational" to "animal" in order to obtain human nature. On whichever kind of law we focus, the definition Aquinas gives is supposed to be already complete.

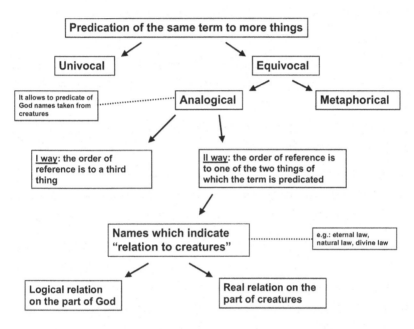

"Law" is used analogically—namely, it is predicated of God's law and man's law "according to proportion" with "something one [*aliquid unum*]," or "according to priority and posteriority" with respect to some one thing.[3] More particularly, it is used analogically according to the second way of analogical predication indicated by Aquinas, namely, the one in which "the order of reference of two things is not to something else but to one of them."[4] Moreover, the terms "eternal law," "natural law," and "divine law" imply relation to creatures. Consequently, they fit what Aquinas says in his *Summa Theologiae*, I, q. 13, a. 7: [1] they are predicated of God *ex tempore*, that is, from our temporal perspective and not by reason of any change in Him; [2] they imply a relation that is real from the side of creatures—as creatures are

3 Ibid. See also *CG*, Book I, Ch. 34.
4 *CG*, Book I, Ch. 34; *ST*, I, q. 13, a. 5 c.

really related to God—and logical from the side of God—since in God there is no real relation to creatures, but a relation only in idea, inasmuch as creatures are referred to Him; and [3] like the terms "Savior" and "Creator," they signify directly the action of God, which is His essence.

The analogical nature of Aquinas' concept of law has many very important consequences which are closely related to one another.

[A] The first consequence flows at once from what we have just said about q. 13, a. 7. When the term "law" refers to God's action it implies *a way to know God* grounded on a real relation to him on the part of creatures. More particularly, when God's law refers to nature, Aquinas' discussion of law overlaps with his philosophical explanation of creation and God's existence and essence. Aquinas' discussion, in other words, depends on what we know about God starting from creatures.[5] On the other hand, when God's action refers to something higher than nature (i.e., grace), Aquinas' discussion of law depends on the knowledge that we have about God that we obtain through revelation. The use of the term law in this case depends on the real relation creatures have to God due to the action of grace.

[B] Second, when the term "law" refers to man's action it involves participation in God's action. That is to say, when we analogically predicate the same term (or perfection) of God and of a creature it means: [B.1.] that the perfection existing in the creature causally depends on God; and [B.2.] that what "*we attribute to creatures, pre-exists in God*, and in a more excellent and higher way."[6] Unjust human law is a perversion ultimately because God's perfection cannot be analogically predicated of what departs from the *imago Dei*.

[C] Third, the meaning of law is prior in God according to reality (*secundum naturam*) but prior in man according to the order of our knowledge (*secundum cognitionem*).[7] This means that when we first call something "law" we do it according to the way (*modus significandi*) in which the human law (which is prior in our knowledge) is law. However, the reality that the term "law" signifies (its *res significata*) belongs primarily to God's

---

5   *ST*, I, q. 13, a. 1 c.
6   *ST*, I, q. 13, a. 2 c. As is well known, Aquinas in this passage uses as an example the term "good."
7   *CG*, Book I, Ch. 34.

action.[8] When Aquinas in *quaestio* 90 begins to define law, he cannot but observe first the nature of law as it exists in human reality.[9] However, the definition of law he elaborates means to reach a level of refinement in which its *res significata* will be perfectly (and first) applied to God's action.

As far as I can tell, the best textual evidence of this is the first objection of *ST*, I-II, q. 90, a. 4 ("Whether promulgation is essential to a law?"), which reads: "It would seem that promulgation is not essential to a law. For the natural law above all has the character of law (*maxime habet rationem legis*). But the natural law needs no promulgation. Therefore it is not essential to a law that it be promulgated." The meaning of this objection is clear: if what *maxime habet rationem legis* does not need promulgation, it follows that this feature is not essential to the concept of law. Aquinas replies: "[T]he natural law is promulgated by the very fact that God instilled it into man's mind so as to be known by him naturally." In this reply, the premise of the objection is confirmed: the perfect *res significata* of what is called "promulgation" belongs indeed to what *maxime habet rationem legis*, that is, to natural law.[10] We might wonder why Aquinas mentions natural law here instead of eternal law, given that the former is not different from the latter[11] although is definitely less comprehensive. There are possibly many reasons for it, but one of them might well be that natural law is, in creatures, the highest level of participation in the eternal law. Natural law, therefore, *maxime habet rationem legis* not only with regard to the human law, but also with regard to all things that are regulated by the eternal law. Probably, at the moment of stating what is essential to the concept of law, Aquinas spontaneously focuses on the highest natural *imago Dei* in creation.[12]

8   *ST*, I, q. 13, a. 6.
9   And even the terminology used—the imposition of names—depends on the way (*modus significandi*) in which "law" is predicated of "human law."
10 *ST*, I, q. 90, a. 4 obj. 1. It is worth noticing that the objection does not refer to any other author. This means that while writing it Aquinas was actually thinking natural law *maxime habet rationem legis*, and that the character of "promulgation" (which is clearly something required for human law to be *just*) should belong to natural law first and in the most excellent way.
11 *ST*, I, q. 91, a. 2 ad 1.
12 It is also possible that Aquinas here uses the term "natural law" in a more general sense, which includes the natural *laws* of both human beings and every

It should be evident at this point what the major difficulty in interpreting Aquinas' concept of law is. Not only the concept as a whole, but
also each term used in defining it, must be analogically applied first (in its
perfect meaning) to God's action and only secondarily to man's action—
even if, as we have said, the first meaning in the order of our knowledge
comes from human reality. But how can a definition made up of genera
and specific differences be applied to God, given that no univocal or
generic predication is possible in the case of God?[13] The answer to this apparent inconsistency lies at the very root of Aquinas' doctrine of the names
of God.

As I mentioned above, "our knowledge of God is derived from the
perfections which flow from Him to creatures, perfections which are in
God in a more eminent way than in creatures."[14] However, the way (*modus
significandi*) in which we know creatures' perfections always depends on
an intellectual process based on genus-specific differences, which ultimately starts with the genus of things (*rerum*).[15] To be alive, for example,
or to be a person, are obtained by adding a specific difference to a certain
genus of existing things: material bodies and individual substances, respectively. It cannot be questioned that every term we use for creature's perfections expresses a specific *quidditas* (*modus significandi*) that as such
cannot be predicated of God. This is why Aquinas to justify his doctrine
on analogy has to make a crucial distinction between names, like "stone"
and names like "living." The former express the perfections flowing from
God's creative act "along with a mode that is proper to a creature."[16] These
names can be predicated of God only metaphorically whereas the latter

other creature, and which refers to the way in which the eternal law exists in
creatures. To reserve the term "natural law" to the case of human nature is a
linguistic convention of which Aquinas should have been well aware.

13   Aquinas himself writes that "nothing is predicated of God as a genus or a difference; and thus neither is anything predicated as a definition, nor likewise
as a species, which is constituted of genus and difference" (*CG*, Book I, Ch.
32).

14   *ST*, I, q. 13, a. 3 c.

15   As *ens* (being) is not a genus: see *CG*, Book I, 25. For the general explanation
of the analogical nature of *ens* see, of course, the first article of *De Veritate*.

16   *CG*, Book I, Ch. 30.

"express these perfections absolutely, without any such mode of participation being part of their signification."[17] In these latter names the *res significata* can be separated from the *modus significandi*, and they can be predicated of God analogically.

For Aquinas, we arrive at every concept by studying the genera and specific differences of the things we know through experience. It is evident that we do not predicate any definition as such of God. At the moment of naming God analogically, we should just be sure that we use concepts that express the perfections of things in a way that is not necessarily limited by their *specific* ways of participating in God's perfection.

2. Law as an Act of Reason

The fact that law is an act of reason does not mean it is discursive knowledge [*scientia discursiva*] because this knowledge is proper to imperfect human intellect[18] but is impossible in God, who "sees all things in one (thing), which is Himself."[19] If by reason we mean "reasoning about something" in the sense that certain knowledge is not immediately available to the intellect, then God's knowledge cannot be called "rational" but only "intellectual." Consequently, God's knowledge of the law must be intellectual knowledge of the means and of the (common) end, both at once. If this is true, the concept of law as such refers neither to prudential reasoning nor to prudence.[20] The fact that humans need prudence should be interpreted

---

17 *ST*, I, q. 13, a. 3 reply to obj. 1.

18 Which "does not simultaneously possess all things capable of being understood, but only a few things from which [it] is moved in a measure to grasp other things" (*ST*, I, q. 60, a. 2 c.).

19 *ST*, I, q. 14, a. 7; *CG*, Book I, Ch. 57,

20 At least, as far as by "prudence" we mean something involving necessarily a reasoning or deliberation process. This is the meaning of prudence most common in the contemporary debate. As I shall mention later, Aquinas sometimes uses a "purified" concept of prudence, which does not involve discursive reason and whose *res significata* can be applied also to God's providence and law. When I say without qualification that the concept of law cannot refer to prudence, I always imply a concept of prudence involving necessarily deliberation and reasoning.

in the sense that our (limited) intellect has to struggle to reach knowledge
(often limited) of the means to the end. However, once the means has been
identified and the law has been passed, there is no proper reason to call our
knowledge of the means-common good (or end of the law) relationship
"prudential" if not in the limited and secondary sense that it is imperfect
knowledge—namely, that most of the time we cannot be sure we have identified the best means to the end.[21]

Act of reason does not mean discursive reason, nor does it mean act of
prudence, but it also cannot mean purely speculative knowledge [*scientia
speculativa*] because law "directs to the end."[22] Aquinas explains that knowledge of the means-end relationship when it is not "ordered to the end of
operation [*ordinatur ad finem operationis*]"[23] is only speculative. In this
sense, both our knowledge of how to build a house that we do not want to
build and God's knowledge of what "He can make, but does not make at
any time" are speculative.[24] However, God has "practical knowledge [*scientia
practica*] of what He makes in some period of time" (i.e., of creation) because "knowledge is called practical from the end."[25] Act of reason in the
definition of law means, therefore, practical knowledge. This knowledge is
called "practical" not because it involves either discursive reason or prudence, and not even because it is knowledge of the means to the end, but
rather because it is knowledge that *tends* towards the end via some means,
that is to say, it is a knowledge that requires the action of the *will*. Aquinas
is extremely clear and consistent on this point. In *ST*, I, q. 14, a. 8 (*videtur*

---

21 As we shall see better a little below, this is true not only of the act of passing
     a law, but of the concept of (free) action itself. For us every action is an act of
     prudence because we need discursive reason to reach the knowledge of the
     means. Prudence, however, cannot be essential to the definition of (free) ac-
     tion; otherwise (free) action could not be predicated of God. This means, in
     turn, that strictly speaking our knowledge of the moral action does not essen-
     tially include the prudential reasoning that is needed in order to figure out
     what the best action to do here and now is.
22 *ST*, I-II, q. 90, a. 1.
23 *ST*, I, q. 14, a. 16.
24 Ibid.
25 Ibid. See also *ST*, I-II, q. 9, a. 1 ad 2: "[T]he speculative intellect is not a
     mover, but the practical intellect is."

quod scientia Dei non sit causa rerum), for example, he clarifies that "the knowledge of God [*scientia Dei*] is the cause of things" insofar as "there is added to it the inclination to an effect, which inclination is through the will." "Now it is manifest that God causes things by His intellect, since His being is His act of understanding; and hence His knowledge must be the cause of things, in so far as His will is joined to it. Hence the knowledge of God as the cause of things is usually called the 'knowledge of approbation' [*scientia approbationis*]."[26]

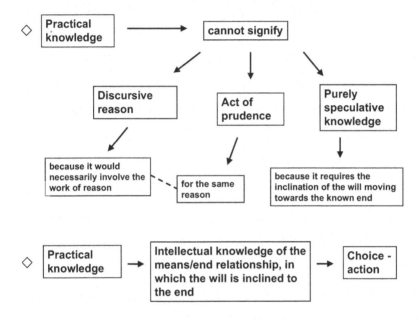

In the order of our knowledge, the analogical meaning of law comes from human law, and due to the limitation of our intellect, human law (like every moral act) requires both discursive reason and prudence. This is why, in the *Prima secundae*, Aquinas uses the term "practical *reason*," which is evidently more appropriate to human reality than to divine reality. However, he is very careful in always considering the *res significata* through practical reason according to its perfect meaning of *scientia practica* that we have just seen in *ST*, I, q. 14, a. 16. This consistency is easy to verify if we just

26 *ST*, I, q. 14, a. 8 c.

focus on the connection that traces *ST*, I-II, q. 90, a. 1 backwards to *ST*, I-II, q. 1, a. 1 [*Videtur quod homini non conveniat agere propter finem*] and furthermore to *ST*, I, q. 19, a. 10 [*Videtur quod Deus non habeat liberum arbitrium*].

In *ST*, I-II, q. 90, a. 1, Aquinas says that law pertains to reason because it is "a rule and measure of acts, whereby man is induced to act or is restrained from acting," and "the rule and measure of human acts is the reason [*ratio*], which is the first principle of human acts, as is evident from what has been stated above, since it belongs to the reason to direct to the end [*rationis enim est ordinare ad finem*], which is the first principle in all matters of action [*in agendi*]." We already catch a glimpse of Aquinas' train of reasoning in that the expression *rationis enim est ordinare ad finem* is virtually equivalent to the expressions used in *ST*, I, q. 14, a. 16 to define divine practical intellect and science. But even before addressing this, we should first discuss the "what has been stated above," which is the way in which he defines *ratio* as the first principle of human acts and as what directs to the end.

ST, I-II, q. 1, a. 1 aims at distinguishing *human* acts as *rational* from the acts of irrational creatures. In short, the difference is that human acts are not the outcome of necessary factors but of "free-will [*liberum arbitrium*]," which is defined as "the faculty of will and reason [*facultas voluntatis et rationis*]." The ratio that directs to the end and is the first principle of human acts must therefore be continuous with the *ratio* of the *liberum arbitrium*. It is important to note that in the definition of *liberum arbitrium* as *facultas voluntatis et rationis* the concept of *liberum arbitrium* depends on the concept of *ratio*, and not vice versa. This is important because *ST*, I, q. 19, a. 10 says that God has *liberum arbitrium* in the same way in which *ST*, I-II, q. 1, a. 1 says that humans have *liberum arbitrium*: "We have free-will with respect to what we will not of necessity, nor by natural instinct. For our will to be happy does not appertain to free-will, but to natural instinct. Hence other animals, that are moved to act by natural instinct, are not said to be moved by free-will. Since then God necessarily wills His own goodness, but other things not necessarily, as shown above, He has free will with respect to what He does not necessarily will."[27]

27 *ST*, I, q. 19, a. 10.

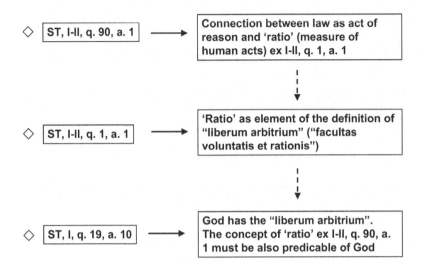

The conclusion is inevitable: if God has *liberum arbitrium*, and *liberum arbitrium* depends on the concept of *ratio*, the concept of *ratio* refers neither to discursive reason nor to prudential knowledge. It is also evident at this point that God has *liberum arbitrium* according to *ST*, I, q. 19, a. 10 exactly as he has *scientia practica* according to *ST*, I, q. 14, a. 16. The only difference being that *scientia practica* does not refer simply to what God does not necessarily will, but also to what he actually freely wants. In other words, as the knowledge of what leads to the end, *ratio* becomes practical knowledge when the end is also wanted by the agent: i.e., when the agent has an active inclination toward it. In this case, the means is loved by the will because of the end (*dilectio electiva*: love of choice)[28] and man is hereby induced to act or is restrained from acting. With this last line, we are back to *ST*, I-II, q. 90, a. 1, and we can confidently assert that Aquinas uses *ratio practica* (or simply *ratio*) in the *Prima secundae* in a way that is consistent with the perfect meaning of *scientia practica* given in *ST*, I, q. 14, a. 16. With this extensive

28 On the concepts of *dilectio naturalis* and *dilectio electiva*, see *ST*, I, q. 60, aa. 1–2.

meaning of *ratio* in mind, Aquinas does not hesitate to apply the term practical reason to God in the treatise on law—as he does in q. 91, a. 1.[29]

This intense discussion has a very relevant conclusion: act of reason, in
the definition of law, does not mean discursive reason or prudence. It also
has two other extremely important consequences. First, it gives us Aquinas'
essential definition of practical knowledge (or practical science). Practical
knowledge is the (intellectual) knowledge of the means-end relationship in
which the will is actually willing the end. This knowledge is already action
because for the agent who is inclined toward the end, the choice of the will
coincides with the identification of the means by the intellect. No other
factor is conceptually required. In God, *scientia practica* is already the choice
and the act of creating.[30] Second, the will is present in the definition of law
from the start as the inclination to the end known by the intellect. The will
makes reason *practical* by providing knowledge with the power to act. *Willing* the common good grounds the choice of the (human or divine) legislator to pursue it via a specific *legal* means. Regardless of what the second
concept of the definition accomplishes, it does not rely on the will.

3. Law as a Command

First of all, we have to dispel any doubt as to whether command is the second conceptual element of law even if it might not clearly appear to be so

29   "*Respondeo dicendum quod, sicut supra dictum est, nihil est aliud lex quam
      quoddam dictamen practicae rationis in principe qui gubernat aliquam commu-
      nitatem perfectam. Manifestum est autem, supposito quod mundus divina prov-
      identia regatur, ut in primo habitum est, quod tota communitas universi
      gubernatur ratione divina. Et ideo ipsa ratio gubernationis rerum in Deo sicut
      in principe universitatis existens, legis habet rationem.*" Actually, Aquinas goes
      so far as to give to prudence the restricted meaning of *scientia practica*, and
      to call God's providence "prudence." He writes: "[I]t belongs to prudence,
      according to the Philosopher, 'to order other things towards an end,' whether
      in regard to oneself [...] or in regard to others subject to him [...]. In this
      way prudence or providence may suitably be attributed to God" (*ST*, I, q.
      22, a. 1 c).
30   There is a striking similarity between Aquinas' concept of practical knowledge
      and Aristotle's idea that practical syllogism concludes with the actual action.

in the famous definition given in *ST*, I-II, q. 90, a. 4 (*quaedam rationis ordinatio ad bonum commune, ab eo qui curam communitatis habet, promulgata*). *Lex* is not just a "dictate of reason [*rationis dictamen*]" but, as *ST*, I-II, q. 92, a. 2 explains, "a dictate of reason *per modum praecipiendi*," that is, by way of (or as a) precept, or command. Command adds a specific nature to the act of reason involved in the concept of law.

Now, the paragraph in which this partial definition—*dictamen rationis per modum praecipiendi*—appears, focuses on distinguishing *lex* from a mere theoretical act of reason, namely, from a "dictate of reason *per modum enuntiandi*." In this sense, the definition could just be referred to the concept of practical knowledge as described in the previous section. However, it is relatively easy to see that *lex est rationis dictamen per modum praecipiendi* means more than that. Specifically, it adds to the concept of act of reason the concept of *imperare* (to command) as described in *ST*, I-II, q. 17. In order to make this point clear, we should first trace the terminology of the treatise on law back to *ST*, I-II, q. 17, and then focus directly on the meaning of *imperare*.

As for the terminology, there is no doubt that "praecipere" and "imperare" are the same kind of action for Aquinas.[31] This clearly appears, both from the overall context of *ST*, I-II, q. 92, a. 2 cited above and from several other passages of the treatise on law. The most important passage for us is none other than the first article of the treatise on law pertaining to reason, and more specifically its *Sed contra*, which reads, "On the contrary, it belongs to the law to command [*praecipere*] and to forbid. But it belongs to reason to command [*imperare*], as stated above (17, 1). Therefore law is something pertaining to reason." In this passage it is unquestionable that *praecipere* and *imperare* are interchangeable, and that Aquinas refers the act of reason that is law to *imperare* as described in *ST*, I-II, q. 17. Therefore, "*[l]ex est rationis dictamen per modum praecipiendi*" is the same as "*lex est rationis dictamen per modum imperandi*" according to the meaning of *imperare* given in *ST*, I-II, q. 17. What then does *imperare* mean in *ST*, I-II, q. 17?

First of all, *imperare* is an act that belongs to the genus of the voluntary

---

31 Except for *secundum quid* predications like the one in *ST*, I-II, q. 92, a. 2, where *imperare* is said to be one of the four acts of law.

acts. Inside this genus, however, it is not voluntary (1) as the acts that proceed from the will without mediation [*ut immediate ipsius voluntatis existentes*], but (2) as the acts that exist as commanded by the will [*qui sunt voluntarii quasi a voluntate imperati*].[32] Not all voluntary acts are strictly speaking acts of the will. For example, *imperare* is technically an act of reason. In any case, it goes without saying that the acts that belong to the second category (like command) must be preceded by acts that belong to the first (like intention and choice).

The distinction between the two categories becomes crucial precisely as soon as we consider that choice (*electio* in Latin; *proairesis* in Greek) belongs to the first category as an act that *materially* pertains to the will and *formally* pertains to reason.[33] This means that since choice is an act following practical knowledge as described in the previous section, and since the acts of the second category follow the acts of the first category, practical knowledge as such does not include the (more specific) meaning of act of reason as command.

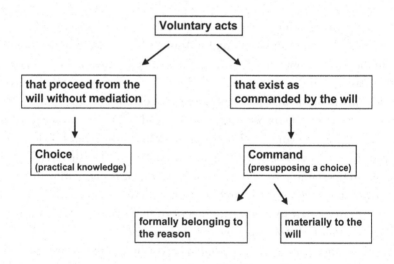

32 See *ST*, I-II, q. 6, prologue.
33 See *ST*, I-II, q. 13, a. 1.

Now, the reason why *imperare* belongs to the second category is that it involves *mediation* between the choice itself and the movement that actually leads from the means to the desired end. In other words, in the case of command we have a second agent responsible for the movement that attains the end chosen by the first agent. "To command [*imperare*] is to move, not anyhow, but by intimating and declaring to another."[34] Again: "To command [*imperare*] is nothing other than to direct someone to do something, by a certain motion or intimation."[35]

As far as the imposition of names is concerned, the term "command" signifies first and foremost the orders given by one human being to another human being. As we have just seen, essential to this is the fracture, so to speak, between the agent who chooses and the agent who performs the movement leading from the means to the end. For example, I want the table to be set for dinner and I tell my child, "Set the table for dinner." The movement leading to the end is performed not by me, but by my child. The command essentially aims at inducing another agent to act in a way that realizes (i.e., makes "real") the means-end connection as known and chosen by the one who commands. It is only by way of an analogical extension that Aquinas uses the term "command" in q. 17 for the command-relations existing between the faculties of the same agent. This is already clear from the fact that in defining command in q. 17 Aquinas uses terminology taken from the relationships humans have with one another: "[…] to direct someone to do something," etc. However, the main evidence is that the inter-faculties meaning could not be predicated of God—whereas command is, for instance, in *ST*, I-II, q. 93, a. 5 c: "God is said to command [*praecipere*] the whole of nature"—because the inter-faculties meaning is inseparable from the way in which our complex and imperfect human nature works.

It is most important to understand why command for Aquinas is an act of reason. This is not easy for us because we are culturally too close to a long voluntaristic tradition that deeply affects both moral thought and legal theory. In a sense, Aquinas' point is extremely simple and reasonable. He says that command is basically what "orders the one commanded [*ordinat eum*

34   *ST*, I-II, q. 17, a. 1 ad 1.
35   *ST*, I-II, q. 17, a. 2 c.

cui imperat]." That is to say, a command is meant to *create an order*—a means-end order—in the action of the one commanded with respect to the end to be achieved through his action. Now, it goes without saying that the act of ordering something (in the sense of putting in order, arranging, etc., which is clearer in Latin) belongs in and of itself to reason. Therefore, the means-end relations that those who command want, so to speak, to transfer to the ones commanded is something essentially rational. At the same time, since the power of the soul that *moves* is never the knowing faculty but always the appetite—which, by definition, is what goes or tends towards the known object—and since command is supposed to induce a movement in the second agent, Aquinas says that command is an act of reason that retains in itself something of an act of the will. "Since therefore the second mover does not move, save in virtue of the first mover [i.e. the will], it follows that the very fact that the reason moves by commanding, is due to the power of the will. Consequently it follows that command is an act of the reason, presupposing an act of the will, in virtue of which the reason, by its command, moves to the execution of the act."[36]

Yet how does command induce the second agent to act? This is a key question because appetite, whether rational or irrational, is an internal principle of movement. The fact that I'm hungry does not make somebody else eat. The simple fact that I want somebody to do something does not make him do it. Certainly, the command should express or convey the will of the one who commands to the one commanded. Precisely in this sense the act of reason retains in itself something of an act of the will. Thus, the execution of the command happens by way of *obeying* and not *just* by way of doing something reasonable. However, even if the one commanded clearly perceives the will of the one who commands, he might remain perfectly indifferent to the command if his internal principle of motion—his appetite, or inclination—were not somehow aroused by the command itself. Therefore, in order for the command to be *effective* the one who commands must have the *power* to cause the movement of—or to *bind*—the internal principle of motion of the one commanded. Without this power, somebody might well command something but no result would follow from it, like shouting a command in a public square. From this point of view, the

36 *ST*, I-II, q. 17, a. 1 c.

conceptual element of the power to move the second agent, or to bind him, does not seem to be logically implicit in the notion of command. I think this is why the concept of law is usually associated with another element called "authority." And this is also why command admits of a reflexive predication, unlike the term "law." Let me explain this better.

In q. 17, a. 6, Aquinas says that it is not inconsistent to say that "reason commands itself" because "reason reflects upon itself, consequently just as it directs [*ordinat*] the acts of other powers, so can it direct [*ordinare*] its own act." On the basis of Aquinas' explanation, we might think of cases in which we tell ourselves something like "Okay, I have to focus on this now," or in a situation that is not perfectly clear, "This is what I have to do because it is clearly the right thing to do." Since to command means to induce a movement according to a rational means-end plan, we can say that we command ourselves when we *reflexively* try to reach the final *assent* to a specific course of action by telling ourselves that it is the most rational course of action to undertake. What we cannot say is that, in these cases, we obligate, or bind, ourselves. And this is why Aquinas consistently writes in the treatise on law that "properly speaking, no one imposes a law on his own actions [*nullus, proprie loquendo, suis actibus legem imponit*]."[37] This is also consistent with the principle, which Aquinas takes from Aristotle, according to which nobody can, properly speaking, do injustice to himself because (1) injustice is something going against the will/freedom of somebody, and (2) nobody, strictly speaking, can voluntarily go against his own will.[38]

Now, providing command does not imply the meaning of the term "to bind," what then does it add exactly to the act of reason in the definition of law? Basically it adds three things: (1) the conceptual element of the relation between two subjects or agents (according to a rational plan—order—envisioned by he who commands); (2) the conceptual element of being an external principle of action; and (3) the conceptual element of involving a formal act of obedience. The first should be already clear from what we have said above. As for the second, it means that command as such is *external* to the (second) agent that moves according to the means-end relation implicated by the command. [This is conceptually true also in the

---

37 *ST*, I-II, q. 93, a. 5 c.
38 See, *In Eth.*, V, 17, 1138b5–14 (p. 351, n. 1107).

case of reason commanding itself because this is exactly what the reflexive intellectual process does: make reason dialogue with itself as if from the outside.] In other words, to command is something external to the actual movement at stake—as when I say "Set the table for dinner" is external to my child setting the table for dinner. This means that strictly speaking, when we have a command the action performed by the second agent must be formally described as an act of obedience. If this were not the case, the use of command (and, accordingly, of law) would only be metaphorical— as when we do what somebody else wants us to do *just* because we recognize that it is the best thing for us to do.

The question now is, "Are these conceptual elements present in the treatise on law?" The answer is as easy as it is surprising. In the entire structure of the *Summa Theologiae*, law is dealt with at the exact moment of approaching the external principles of action: "*Consequenter considerandum est de principiis exterioribus actuum.*"[39] Starting with the first article of the treatise, Aquinas is very clear that law "may be in something in two ways [*dicitur dupliciter esse in aliquo*]. First, as in that which measures and rules [*uno modo, sicut in mensurante et regulante*] [...] Secondly, as in that which is measured and ruled [*alio modo, sicut in regulato et mensurato*]." Finally, the fact that law requires obedience is implicit in every passage related to the binding force of law, for example in *ST*, I-II, q. 96, a. 4 ("Whether human law binds a man in conscience?"). Yet the binding force, as we mentioned, also requires the *power* of the authority, and the analysis of this conceptual element extends beyond the limits of this book. In Chapter VII—"Natural Law as Inclination to God"—I explain in more detail how the conceptual elements of command as explained above apply to the concept of natural law.

---

39   *ST*, I-II, q. 90, prologue.

IV.

Spirit or Digital Self?
The Concept of Person in Philosophy and
Contemporary Science

In the contemporary debate on artificial intelligence it is common to refer to the digital self as if it means the same thing as person. The underlying idea is that the human body is like a computer's hardware, whereas the mind is like software. Many assume that there is no qualitative difference between ourselves and a digital machine. In the near future computers will be built that will be able to think and act as human beings, or so the theory goes.

The famous science-fiction movie, *The Matrix*—the first of its kind—portrays this concept well. In *The Matrix*, people grow up and live their lives in virtual reality—a huge and highly sophisticated software program—precisely because their personalities (their selves) are digital and, consequently, can be separated from the lives of their bodies. Learning is regulated by algorithms: the better the algorithms, the faster the learning process. For those who have seen the movie, one recalls when Trinity learns how to fly a helicopter, or when Neo starts learning martial arts. The learners are simply hooked up to a computer and new software is uploaded, which quickly and easily imparts the desired knowledge. The comical remark made by Neo's computer-expert trainer is revealing, "He is a machine!"

Throughout the movie algorithms do everything, even predict the future. The theme of the movie is clear: in this virtual world, there is no necessary link between body and spirit. Neo could have been born a woman or a dwarf. Personality is merely a question of software.

This theme unwittingly entails an unspoken, perhaps even unintended, message about prejudice, bigotry, and bias. Humans try to free themselves from intelligent and sensitive machines, which in turn had been used and controlled by humans for a long time. As both machines and humans have digital personalities, there is no real reason to identify with or support the humans in the movie. We do so *just* because *we ourselves are* humans and because machines are depicted as the antagonists. If we ignore these two elements for a moment, it is easy to see that the only difference between the humans and machines is in the hardware: in the case of humans, the hardware is biological. I agree with Roger Penrose that this fact in and of itself could not make any relevant difference.[1]

The Matrix instantiates a strong artificial intelligence (AI) theory that raises the ultimate moral question about human dignity. This question is not, "Why shouldn't we give absolute respect to every digital machine?" Rather, "Why should we give absolute respect to anyone, given that ultimately he, she, or *it* is *just* a machine?"

In this chapter, I argue that the idea of the digital self, and other similar ideas connected to AI theories, are neither right nor false. They are, rather, strictly speaking "senseless." If my argument works, it follows that physics, mathematics, and other similar sciences are intrinsically inadequate to approach the concept of person and other related concepts like personality and consciousness. Instead, a correct understanding of the concept of person requires a specific philosophical approach that was initiated by Socrates, has been developed through Greek and medieval thought, and reached its most refined definition with the famous definition offered by Boethius and defended by Thomas Aquinas: *rationalis naturae individua substantia*. Accordingly, the chapter is divided into two parts. The first (*Determinism, Chance, and Freedom*) relates mostly to philosophy of science, and offers a formal criticism of the idea of the digital self. The discussion is centered on the radical difference between the way in which algorithms (and therefore computers) work, on the one hand, and the nature of human free and true judgments, on the other. I also offer a criticism of the so-called Turing Test, which is the most famous thought experiment meant to understand whether or not a machine's intelligence is equivalent to that of a human, and therefore whether there is a substantial difference between men and machines. In the second part of the chapter ("Discovering the Concept of Person"), I focus on the concept of person as it was understood and developed in both Greek and medieval philosophy.

1   Roger Penrose, *The Emperor's New Mind: Concerning Computers, Minds, and the Laws of Physics* (New York: Oxford University Press, 1990), p. 29.

1. Determinism, Chance, and Freedom

I would like to start by focusing on the meaning of a hypothetical statement that might be expressed in the following way: "Every event in nature is caused either by chance or by a strictly deterministic series of previous events." This statement expresses an alleged simple truth that we can easily and often find, or detect, in contemporary discussions about science and nature. For my purposes, I need to analyze this statement by referring to the concepts of determinism, chaos, and freedom. Thus, I will immediately (and briefly) clarify what we usually mean by these three concepts.

1.1. Conceptual and Terminological Clarifications

Determinism, at least in the present context, refers to a philosophical theory according to which every event in nature is the necessary and mechanistic outcome of a sequence of previous events. Chance, on the other hand, is a cause that cannot be traced back to any reasonable or predictable series of events.

Sometimes we call "chance" what we do not (yet) know or understand—perhaps, this is the case with non-linear and chaotic events, which, as unpredictable as they appear, might later be discovered to be *univocally* determined by previous related events. Conceptually, however, chance is opposed to determinism in that it indicates something that, before it happens, could occur in several different ways, whereas determinism indicates something that, given a particular series of events, necessarily happens the way it happens.[2] Chance, in other words, means contingency. Therefore, if there is *real* chance in nature, determinism as a strong philosophical theory is false.

From a different viewpoint, determinism and chance go together as they both involve blind causality. That is to say, whether an event is caused randomly or deterministically, it is not caused by an intelligent agent. From

---

2   Historically, the strongest example of determinism is the Stoic theory of the cyclical universe, a kind of big bang theory in which the universe expands and restricts every time exactly the same way. Of course, in a cyclical universe there is no room for freedom because even what we call "choices" happen again and again the same way in each universe due to the same overall deterministic sequence. As is obvious, without freedom there is no room for ethics and moral responsibility.

the viewpoint of its random or deterministic cause, such an event cannot be said to be rational: it does not happen *rationally*, it just *happens*. If we do call such an event rational, we implicitly refer it to an *external* intelligent being, who either created the event's (random or deterministic) cause or interprets it according to a conventional meaning.[3]

Let me give some examples to explain this point better. As examples of the first case (that of creation), we can think of the event given by the result of an algorithm—which is rational from the viewpoint of the person who makes the algorithm, and this example should be clearer later on in the chapter. Or, we can think of the digestive system, which would not be a digestive system without a *teleological* (rational) meaning intrinsic to it, a meaning that the digestive system obviously does not give to itself. As an example of the second case (that of the interpretative/conventional), we can think of a chair-shaped object erupted by a volcano. Obviously, such an object is not a chair. It can be called a chair only according to the conventional meaning that we give to similar artifacts due to the particular use we make of them (*telos*). The rationality of the concept of chair comes from the *telos*, or function, that we attach to it. If we did not exist, there would be no chairs. This is true not because we would not be around to produce chairs, but because we would not be around to think of something as a chair.

Chance, insofar as it means contingency, is consistent with freedom because both chance and freedom indicate events that, before they happen, could truly occur in several different ways. Yet inasmuch as chance means blind causality it is as opposed to freedom as is determinism. In fact, freedom requires an intentional choice, which makes the caused event a *wanted* event according to a particular *sense* or *meaning*, that is to say, wanted according to an intelligent plan. This meaning is what the agent pursues by means of his choice and what grounds his rational decision process, which is a means-end decision process. From this viewpoint, "*casu enim esse dicimus quae praeter intentionem agentis sunt* (we use the word 'random' to name things that fall [or happen] outside the agents' intention)."[4]

---

3   By "conventional meaning" I intend a meaning that does not belong as such to the event; or, in other words, a meaning that is not intrinsic to the event.

4   *CG*, II, 39. Incidentally, what makes many evolutionary theories very ambiguous is that they want to be teleology-free theories, but they cannot but use a

1.2. Algorithms and Truth

Returning to the hypothetical statement mentioned above, let us imagine two different algorithms. The first causes a computer to necessarily conclude its sequence by stating, or articulating, the sentence, "Every event in nature is caused either by chance or by a strictly deterministic series of previous events." And the second causes a computer to perform a random sequence, which concludes by stating, or articulating, the sentence, "Every event in nature is caused either by chance or by a strictly deterministic series of previous events."[5]

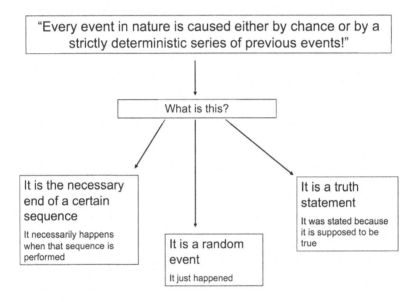

concept—evolution—that is not teleology-free. If there is evolution in nature, there is an intelligent plan too, which transcends the evolutionary process and controls—or directs or guides—it for the best. It is interesting, from this viewpoint, to read Etienne Gilson's humorous criticism of Julian Huxley's (the famous zoologist) teleology-free theory. See, Gilson, *God and Philosophy* (New Haven and London: Yale University Press, 1941), pp. 127–136.

5   The term "random sequence" is inaccurate. To make the argument simpler, I am talking as if deterministic series of events and chance were applicable in the same way to the physical world and to the computer world. This is not the case, though. When we say that a computer performs a random sequence

At first glance, one might think that both sentences are contradictory because if they were true what they state would not be stated due to the truth they convey. As far as algorithms are concerned, the sentences could have stated the exact opposite and this would not have made any relevant difference. The result of an algorithm can only be said to be "true" when it is the correct last step of an operational sequence correctly performed. So, if the software programmer makes its computer say something contradictory, it will still be true from the viewpoint of the algorithm.

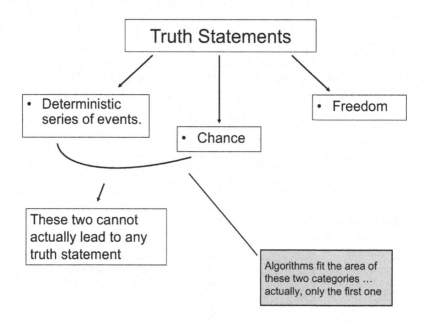

However, upon closer examination, it should be easy to see that the terms "true," "false," or "contradictory," are just *not applicable* to the case at hand. In fact, the sentence is not contradictory but meaningless because it is not stated due to the intrinsic truth of its contents but due to the blind

or produces a random result, we speak metaphorically because computers can "choose" (here is another metaphorical term) between A and B only due to a very precise algorithm making A different than B to the effect of the computer's random choice. A true random event in the computer world is impossible unless the computer is using data from real random events taken from outside, like the time in which we press keys on our keyboards.

outcome of a sequence—whether univocal or random—which is indifferent to the truth-content of its last step.[6] The sentence is actually as meaningless as the chair-like object erupted by the volcano.

What we have here is a formal and conceptual difference between stating something *as true* and stating something as the outcome of a random or deterministic sequence. In the second case, the term "stating something" is actually metaphorical because the sequence does not "state" anything—it just ends with a certain event.[7] Truth-judgment conceptually transcends any given sequence—even the sequence that leads reason to draw a conclusion from a given set of premises. Truth always needs to freely judge sequences *from the outside*.

If truth involves freedom—specifically, the freedom to state something *because it is true*, and not because it is the outcome of a sequence—and if the physical world involves material sequences, then truth appears to be something that goes conceptually beyond the physical world. In other words, if there is truth there is something not physical about it. Yet, if there is no truth we cannot presently be discussing it. In fact, we are not even reading: our eyes are just receiving meaningless photons that reflect meaningless ink blotches resulting from some sequences, which started maybe at the time of the Big Bang.

When Aristotle specifically asks about thought, he writes something truly astonishing: "*nous* can have no nature of its own." He also writes that "before it thinks" thought cannot be "any real thing," or that "it cannot reasonably be regarded as blended with the body."[8] Aristotle was focusing on the fact that thought must be, so to speak, *transparent* to everything precisely in order to be able to receive every possible object in itself (knowledge is some kind of possession) and judge it *for what it is*. If thought were already *configured* according to a particular nature—say, the nature of an algorithm—it would see everything according to numbers and numerical sequences.

---

6 I am using "last step" instead of "result" to emphasize the blindness of the sequence. "Result" is a rational interpretative concept external to the algorithm. An algorithm as such does not know how to have a "result" precisely because it is formally indifferent to it.

7 Strictly speaking, we could not even say that the sequence "ends" because this would be an external rational interpretation of it. If there is no someone looking at the sequence *from the outside* as a rational unity, there is no beginning of it and no end. As a matter of fact, there is not even *a* sequence.

8 *OS*, III, 429a10 ff.

Like the algorithms, thought would not be able to stop its sequence for a non-algorithmic reason. Just as a hand cannot not feel cold while feeling hot in the same location, thought could not simultaneously understand contraries and non-thought natures if it had a nature of its own. However, thought *can* think of everything, including, at the same time, natures opposed to one another: number and non-number, cold and hot, algorithm and non-algorithm, even thought and non-thought. Consequently, thought cannot be in and of itself any specific nature, "other than that of having a certain capacity."[9] Since bodily, or physical, reality is always *configured* in a particular way, "thought," concludes Aristotle, "cannot reasonably be regarded as blended with the body."

It seems to me that Aristotle's conclusion that thought can have no nature of its own is similar to saying that truth involves freedom and must therefore transcend physical reality. It might be helpful to recall that the traditional definition of truth is not conformity between two things but conformity between intellect, or thought, and reality (*adaequatio rei et intellectus*). In this sense, truth is a spiritual viewpoint on reality: it is thought looking freely— from the outside—at reality and judging that things are what they really are.

1.3. Turing's Test

As is well known to scholars who work on AI theories, in 1950 Alan Turing proposed a test to understand whether computers think.[10] The test was grounded on the idea "that the computer *thinks* provided that it *acts* indistinguishably from the way that a person acts when thinking."[11] If an observer gives questions to both a computer and a human being—without knowing whom or which he is addressing—and he cannot distinguish the computer's answers from the human being's answers, Turing argues that this computer can think. Of course, this test presupposes very sophisticated algorithms making the computer answer appropriately even absurd or ironical questions.

9   Ibid.
10   Alan M. Turing, "Computing Machinery and Intelligence," in *Mind* 59 (1950).
11   Penrose, *The Emperor's New Mind*, op. cit., p. 7.

In my opinion, what is most striking about Turing's test is that it focuses on the material result of the algorithm. For example, if asked a hypothetical question like "How are natural events caused?" the computer might answer, "Every event in nature is caused either by chance or by a strictly deterministic series of previous events." Yet, this focus completely neglects the formal nature of the cause that makes this result either true/false or meaningless. Apparently, Turing does not wonder at all about the kind of cause we need in order to obtain the effect of having truth statements.

Penrose underlines that the test is "quite unfair on the computer" as it requires the computer to pretend to be a human, and not the reverse. As is obvious, humans could not perform "some very complicated arithmetical calculation" as computers easily do, and they would be by far recognized as humans if questioned about such calculation.[12] However, Penrose reminds us that the test requires that questions and answers "are all transmitted in an impersonal fashion, say typed on a keyboard and displayed on a screen."[13] This is surprising and quite revealing. If we agree that the central formal feature of human truth-discourse is the capacity to transcend necessary sequences—to be free from them—this premise of Turing's test is not just unfair to humans but manifestly mistaken. The impersonal fashion hides the fact that the answer might come not from a true/false reasoning but from a blind mechanical sequence. On the other hand, even ignoring or laughing at a question are accurate signs of true (free) thought. It is also interesting that we humans calculate or work much faster when we either use special *mental techniques* or when we do not *reflect much* on what we are doing. In other words, our minds work faster when we, so to speak, enter the computer's area by using technical sequences. It is *reflection*—contemplation of the truth—that takes time. Computers can go their way without bothering about it. This is probably why we have kids who are mathematical geniuses, but not kids who are philosophical geniuses, for example, or literary critics. Or why some people with autism manifest exceptional skills with numbers and numerical sequences, and yet do not relate correctly with others and themselves.

I wonder whether mathematicians have ever tried to solve the "halting

12 Ibid, p. 8–9.
13 Ibid.

problem" by asking The Universal Turing Machine[14] to stop working with numbers and to forget about acting upon numbers. Of course not. This is how one day *I* stopped reading *The Emperor's New Mind* and started (again) *Herry Potter and the Order of the Phoenix*. Yet, unlike me, the Universal Turing Machine cannot exit its own operative system: as every good digital machine, it is slave of numbers and numerical sequences.

Penrose while slightly criticizing Searle's Chinese Room[15] writes, "But it is not inconceivable to me that there might be some 'critical' amount of complication in an algorithm which it is necessary to achieve in order that the algorithm exhibit mental qualities."[16] This seems contradictory to me. In fact, if truth, freedom, and mental qualities go together, that statement might be correctly rewritten as follows, "There might be some 'critical' amount of complication in an algorithm which it is necessary to achieve in order that the algorithm transcend (free itself from) numbers and numerical instructions, thus exhibiting non-algorithmic qualities." This is like saying, "There might be some 'critical' amount of complication in a circle, which is necessary to

14   The Turing Machine is the first theoretical representation of our modern computers: a machine able to solve mathematical problems by means of mechanical, or algorithmic, sequences. The Universal Turing Machine is the ideal of a Turing Machine able to solve *every* mathematical problem. AI theorists have been very fond of this ideal because it incorporates a strong concept of (virtually omnipotent) algorithms. If such a machine existed, it would be able *to stop*—reaching the correct result—every time it performed a specific algorithmic sequence. This is why the question of the existence of Universal Turing Machine depends on showing that this machine would always be able *to stop* its sequence. This is called "the halting problem," and, as is well known, it has been mathematically solved negatively: the Universal Turing Machine cannot exist.

15   Searle's Chinese Room is a thought experiment meant to show that computers (or software) do not have self-consciousness. Basically, Searle imagines himsellf performing the English instructions of a special software able to offer correct "Yes" or "No" answers to some questions asked in Chinese. Searle, in other words, imagines playing the part of the hardware. If the software instructions are correctly performed, the final answers should be correct, even if Searle himself does not know what the Chinese questions actually meant. Searle refined the Chinese room experiment, but this is not relevant to the purpose of our current discussion.

16   Penrose, *The Emperor's New Mind*, op. cit., p. 25.

achieve in order that the circle exhibit non-circular (for example, triangular) qualities." It is the term "complication" that is ambiguous here because it designates something that is still itself (just more complicated), whereas the case at hand involves a radical change in nature: from algorithm to not-algorithm, from circle to triangle, and the like. After all, no matter how complicated it becomes, an algorithm is still a sequence of numbers and numerical instructions. The difference between a simple algorithm and a complicated one is always a difference in degree. It can never be a difference in kind.

2. Discovering the Concept of Person

I would like now to walk a different path, namely, the path that began with Greek philosophy, travelled through medieval thought and led to the concepts of person and personal acts as we know them today. I believe this path is methodologically necessary because what we are wondering at present is whether a highly sophisticated algorithm—the digital self—is a person, and vice versa, whether a person is a highly sophisticated algorithm. AI theories usually have an excellent awareness of the history and concept of algorithm, and of the sciences (mathematics, physics, etc.) which study them. However, they take too often for granted the concept of person, as if it were so obvious that we do not need to specifically focus on it. This attitude easily leads one to underestimate, or even completely neglect, one or more central features of the person without realizing it.

2.1. From Philosophy of Nature to Moral Philosophy

Philosophy was born in Greece as *philosophy of nature* when some brilliant thinkers in the seventh century before Christ began to search for a principle of intelligible unity in the variety of physical phenomena. These thinkers realized that no change, or becoming, could ever happen without the simultaneous presence of something that does not change or become. It was a logical insight: if something moves from position A to position B, from moment A to moment B, or from situation A to situation B, that something as the subject of the movement should necessarily be *the same thing* in both positions A and B, and the movement should be accidental to it. Every movement, in other words, is always predicated of the same subject.

Change – Becoming - Movement

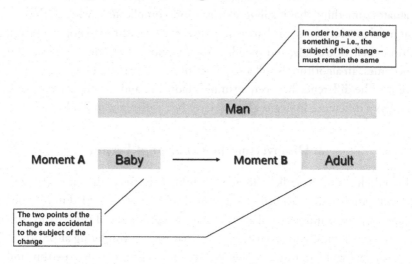

In order to have a change something – i.e., the subject of the change – must remain the same

Man

Moment A   Baby   ⟶   Moment B   Adult

The two points of the change are accidental to the subject of the change

If we want to talk logically about change in the case of substantial movement, for example the death of a man, we have to predicate change either of the soul (which changes from existing with the body to begin existing separately) or of the matter (once used to *compose* the body and now is *decomposing* into something else). The concept opposite to change is creation. In the case of creation there are indeed different subjects in the two moments A and B, but, in fact, talking about two different moments is logically incorrect because two moments must necessarily belong to the same unity. It is for this reason that Thomas Aquinas vigorously states that creation is not a movement, because there is absolutely nothing before creation: nothing that can change, nothing that can remain the same, nothing that can pass from moment A to moment B.[17]

By observing movements in a natural world in which it seems that everything can change into everything else, pre-Socratic philosophers began to wonder about the first subject of those movements, or, that is to say, about their substratum or cause. They started to look for the principle of unity that makes all changes possible by always remaining the same. Their

17   *ST*, I, q. 45, a. 1–5.

insights soon moved from the idea of a simple material principle to one that is also efficient, formal, and final. In fact, the efficient cause must also transcend the single movement because the efficient cause is the cause that leads A to B, and that consequently cannot be limited to either. The form, or nature, must transcend each movement as well, otherwise there would be no proportion between A and B, and everything could become everything else without continuity: one cannot move from being a human baby to an adult horse, etc. Finally, the same transcendence must hold for the end, which is understood as the conclusion of the movement determined by—or already inscribed in—the form of the subject. Thus, being adult must be already present in the baby's nature as the termination of the movement.[18]

This insight into the existence of an intelligible unity behind the diversity and plurality of changes was certainly easier in the case of purely physical phenomena than of human phenomena, in which freedom comes into play. In a sense, it was normal for philosophy to start as philosophy of nature. In order for moral philosophy to begin, we have to wait until Socrates in the fifth century before Christ.[19]

At first glance, one might think that the primordial insight of moral philosophy is about the existence of universal values understood as first principles of intelligibility in the plurality and variety of human choices. These values would be what remains unchanged behind every human choice.[20] For example, it would be impossible to explain the existence of many different kinds of games if playing was not already attractive (valuable) to human beings *before* any choice that has a particular game or sport as its object. Soccer and tennis are conventional instances—they are the outcome of historically determined choices. There was a time in which these specific sports did not exist. However, the *purely* conventional could not exist, either. Even in the

18 *MP,* book 1.

19 See G. Reale, *A History of Ancient Philosophy*, vol. 1 (Albany: State University of New York Press, 1987), pp.137–138. The English translation of this history of philosophy, unfortunately, is not very reliable.

20 This is the path followed, for example, by Finnis and Strauss. See, especially, J. Finnis, *Natural Law and Natural Rights* (Oxford: Oxford University Press, 1980), Ch. IV; and L. Strauss, *Natural Rights and History* (Chicago: The University of Chicago Press, 1950), Ch. I.

case of sports there must be an unchanged unity behind the differences. I will call it, along with authors like John Finnis, "value play" even though the name is not important. What is important is to see that no *choice* can choose its own primordial attraction. To use another example, it is only because we are *already* attracted by the other sex that we are then free to choose this or that partner, this or that sexual behavior, or to remain single. The primordial horizon of meaning in human action cannot be an undifferentiated plain (a sexless being, or a being without inclination to play): some hills or mountains already exist. We can call them "values" or "fundamental goods." We can call them "nature." This too would be a mere terminological question. The important thing is the philosophical insight, that if choice were entirely *free* there would be no choice and no freedom.[21] Even God is not free to love Himself, and for this reason He can then love every other thing.[22]

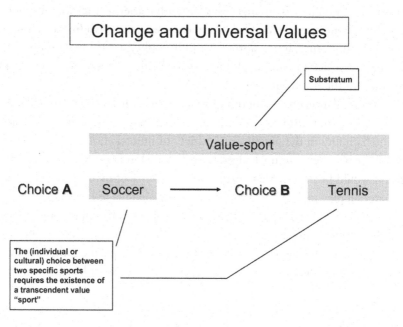

---

21   I do not need to focus here on the further epistemological need for an ultimate value, or good or end. I will approach this need in the next chapter. See also my "Ultimate End, Human Freedom, and Beatitude: A Critique of Germain Grisez," in *The American Journal of Jurisprudence*, 46 (2001): pp. 113–135.
22   *ST*, I, q. 19, a. 3.

As I mentioned above, one might think that this passage from the plurality of human choices and conventions to the unity of some basic (and natural) practical principles, or values, is the first insight that historically determined the birth of moral philosophy. This would be a mistake. The first insight is about freedom, not about necessity. It is the insight of the substratum, or subject, of the free changes that happen in the world. Socrates was searching for the principle of intelligible unity in *human* actions, and he located it in the conscious self which is understood as the center of moral self-decision and self-determination. Man is the only being whose action depends on knowledge of the truth and not on the necessitating work of nature (inclinations, instincts, passions—even universal values). Man is the substratum that remains unchanged behind the variety of free choices as their unique principle, namely as a principle that is not *determined* by the flattening universality of nature. It is understandable that Socrates will say that *man is his soul* because what pertains to the physical realm—to the body—is necessity. Moreover, it is understandable that, in the end, he would center his ethics on knowledge, on the one hand, and on self-control, interior liberty, and autonomy, on the other.

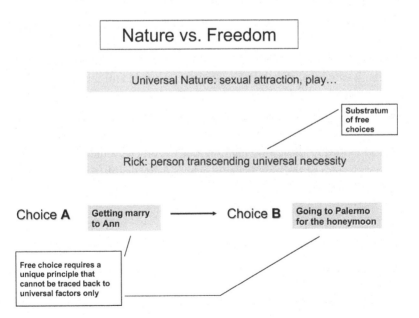

I do not wish to dwell on Socratic intellectualism. Rather, I would like to call attention to the origins of the philosophical insight which I already discussed above and which connects freedom to rationality: being free to know and state the truth. Socrates understood that if truth and contradiction exist, the freedom to see them as such and to state them must exist as well. For him, the full realization of man consists precisely in acting on the basis of his own truth-judgments, namely in being a *subject that transcends the world of the objects* or, again, in being free.

It is interesting that when Thomas Aquinas approaches the question of whether man is free (whether he has free will, *liberum arbitrium*), he explains that since the judgment of reason does not come from natural instinct it is a free judgment, and as such it can spawn different and opposed courses of action.[23] For Thomas rationality and freedom are two sides of the same coin. Kant did not invent anything new when he tried to prove *a priori* the existence of freedom as a necessary condition of rationality. His argument perfectly follows the lines already drawn by both Greek and medieval thinkers.[24]

The importance of self-control (*enkrateia*) and autonomy (*autarkeia*) in Socrates' ethics should now be clearer. Man is the being who raises himself above the forces of nature, who is master and not slave, who has power over his own states of pleasure and pain, and whose moral realization cannot depend on any exterior force. Such a being experiences and interiorly enjoys his own freedom (*eleutheria*) in rationally controlling the impulses of his nature.[25]

The goodness of this moral experience is radical and self-evident. After Socrates, when Aristotle addresses the life of pleasure and enjoyment as a kind of life in which human happiness cannot reside, he simply writes that such a life is "slavish" and "suitable to beasts."[26] This criticism might appear weak or underdeveloped to those who fail to notice the crucial value of freedom as a defining element of the human being, which Aristotle inherits from Socrates and Plato. For Aristotle, a slavish life—a life without freedom—is not even

---

23 *ST*, I, q. 83, a. 1.
24 See, for example, Kant, *Ethical Philosophy* (Indianapolis, IN: Hackett, 1994), pp. 50–51.
25 See G. Reale, *A History of Ancient Philosophy*, vol. 1, pp. 321–326.
26 *NE*, I, 1095b14–22.

worthy of special theoretical attention. Under this respect, the whole of Aristotelian ethics should be seen as an ethics of freedom. It is an ethics in which the moral agent raises himself above the realm of necessity and develops his own personal subjectivity, by living the virtues, and consequently by acting not in the power of passions and pleasures but according to a truth-knowledge of nature (i.e., according to right reason). Those who think that there is no room for freedom in Aristotle's ethics have probably, accidentally missed the most important and grounding feature of his ethics.[27]

2.2. From Freedom to Person

The attention given to human subjectivity by Greek thought is already quite strong, both theoretically and ethically, it can be compared to Augustinian thought and the Cartesian *cogito*. Yet, if I am right, the insight in Greek philosophy that grounds the importance of human subjectivity is the same insight that grounds and determines the development of the concept of person in western Christian tradition.

In Chapter 113 of the third part of the *Summa Contra Gentiles*, Aquinas wonders whether "the rational creature is directed by God to his actions not only by an ordering of the species, but also according to what befits the individual."[28] This chapter is characterized by a strong conceptual contrast between universal nature and human, free individuality. Aquinas wants to say that from the point of view of God, who governs the universe, "the natural inclinations common to the species" are the mechanism by virtue of which individuals act according to Providence's design in particular circumstances and situations. In other words, this design consists exactly of the individuals acting according to those inclinations.

Now, as far as the inclinations common to the species are concerned, God's attention is not for the individual as such, but for the universal nature of the species, namely for the proper movement of the (common) inclinations. If God were a computer scientist, this would be like saying that his

---

27 Germain Grisez seems to make this mistake. See his "Natural Law, God, Religion, and Human Fulfillment", in *The American Journal of Jurisprudence*, 46 (2001): p. 19.

28 *CG*, vol. 3, II.

attention goes entirely either to programming new software or to creating innovative hardware, but not to one of the individual computers that will instantiate both.

This kind of attention would not be enough in the case of human actions, however, because human actions cannot simply derive from a *common* inclination as they are *free* actions. An action is free if, and only if, the principle that causes it is *unique and singular*.

"Many actions are evident, in the case of rational creatures," Thomas writes, "for which the inclination of the species is not enough. The mark of this is that such actions are not alike in all, but differ in various cases. Therefore, the rational creature must be directed by God in his acts, not only specifically, but also individually."[29] Aquinas invites us *to observe* freedom in the fact that there are many human actions that do not depend simply on the common inclination to play—or to pair off and form a family—but on me being Matt Anthony and not Joseph Kolf or Andrew Syski. Regarding these actions, if God wants to help me and guide me, he has to account not just for my (universal) human nature (my instincts, basic values, etc.)[30] but also for the principle of uniqueness that is only mine and that makes me a free being. For Thomas, these actions are what make the difference between man and the other (material) creatures. Apart from the Christian theological context of his writings, the only relevant difference between him and the Greek philosophers is that he knowingly and repeatedly calls these actions "personal acts," which are acts that do not depend on nature but on the person. Let's see now if this concept coincides with his technical definition of person.

2.3. The Definition of Person

As is well known, Aquinas explains and defends Boethius' definition of person as "individual substance of rational nature [*rationalis naturae individua*

---

29 Ibid.
30 For example, by arranging all the surrounding events in such a way that my instincts will be led to react in a particular way and in view of a particular goal. This is something that even man, notwithstanding his limited viewpoint and action, can easily do even with the most "intelligent" animals.

substantia]."[31] This definition depends on the concepts of [1] subsistence, [2] individuality, and [3] rationality in the sense that each of them provides respectively the *ratio* of the three logical passages—according to genus and specific difference—on which the definition is based.

[1] The first relevant difference is that one—in the genus of things (*rerum*)[32]—between substances and accidents. "The substance is a thing to which it belongs to be not in a subject."[33] It is the substratum of the accidental changes (the stone that moves from being white to black, or the giraffe that changes from being small and becomes big). Thus, to be subsistent indicates the specific difference—and therefore the proper nature—of the substance.[34]

[2] Both substances and accidents can be thought of either as individual or as universal. The universal substance or "second substance" (for example, human nature or the essence of man) and the universal accident (for example, whiteness) are logical entities, or entities *di ragione* (if I am permitted to use here this excellent Italian term), in the sense that they do not exist in and of themselves but only as *individualized* in a first substance (or *suppositum*, or *hypostasis*). Individuality is therefore the specific difference and proper nature of the first substance, namely of the real individual that belongs to a certain nature. Here Aquinas states clearly that there is a real difference between nature and *suppositum*. The accidents and the individuating principles do not belong to nature. That is to say, nature is not predicated of the *suppositum*: I am not my nature; I am not my humanity (as also a dog is not its dog-ness, or a tree its tree-ness). Rather, it is the *suppositum* that, like a whole, possesses its nature as the formal and perfective part of itself (*suppositum significatur ut totum, habens naturam sicut partem formalem et perfectivam sui*).[35]

---

31 See, especially, *ST*, I, q. 29, aa. 1–2.

32 *CG*, I, ch. 25.

33 Ibid.

34 Note that to say that "the essence or nature of the substance requires to be subsistent" is very different than saying that "the essence of the substance requires to exist" (this is true only of the essence of God). To be subsistent—understood as the essential character of the substance—means only that, if the substance (a man, for example) exists, it exists by virtue of its proper act, whereas the existence of an accident (for example, to be white) depends on the existence of the substance.

35 See *ST*, III, q. 2, a. 2.

[3] Thus, we have the technical meaning of "individual substance." At this point, Thomas says that a further specific difference is needed, this time in the genus of first substances. The reason for this additional step is truly interesting because it refers to the experiential datum of human freedom— a datum that in and of itself is primordial and cannot be demonstrated (even here Kant and Aquinas would have agreed). Thomas explains that *rational* first substances possess a *degree of individuality* so high that it originates not just a quantitative, but a qualitative difference. He justifies the use of the specific term "person" for these substances. This higher individuality comes from having power over one's own actions, from being subject and not object—that is, from being free. "Further still, in a more special and perfect way, the particular and the individual are found in the rational substances which have dominion over their own actions; and which are not only made to act, like others; but which can act of themselves [*non solum aguntur, sicut alia, sed per se agunt*]; for actions belong to singulars. Therefore also the individuals of the rational nature [*singularia rationalis naturae*] have a special name even among other substances; and this name is 'person.'"[36] Rationality is therefore the specific difference and the proper nature of the individual that, in this account, we say "of rational nature." Such rationality means freedom and means person.[37] Since every definition implies a *generic*

---

36 Ibid., I, q. 29 a. 1 c.

37 Today, there is great emphasis on "self-giving" and "accepting the other [*accoglienza dell'alterità*]" as distinctive characteristics of the person. See, for example, F. Viola, *Dalla natura ai diritti* (Roma-Bari: Laterza, 1997), p. 333. I too believe that the ethical concepts of "self-giving" and *accoglienza* [acceptance, welcome] are probably the most important ones on which we should work today in order to deeply understand the meaning of human freedom. However, I think that Aquinas was right when he did not technically place the *specific nature* of the personal being in those concepts. Self-giving and *accoglienza*, as such, are present also in other animals. Consequently, they could not provide the definition of person with its specific difference. Think of a female cat that looks after and defends her young, or of a bee that lives entirely for the good of the hive. In the case of human beings, what gives a different color to those inclinations, and makes them human and *personal*, are rationality and freedom. In Aquinas' philosophy, furthermore, every being has an inclination to the common good (or to the whole) that is stronger than the inclination to its own being. This is why the order in the things of nature is

predication, it is obvious that person, being a singular reality, cannot strictly speaking be defined. Consequently, Aquinas says that the definition of person as "individual substance of rational nature" indicates only "what belongs to the general idea of singularity [*id quod pertinet ad communem rationem singularitatis*]."[38]

Note that this is an ontological way of reaching the concept of person. As such, it is different than the type of reflection, typically phenomenological, that is found in contemporary philosophies of the self.[39] Both Greek philosophy and Aquinas end up suggesting the existence of an ontological principle of free action that cannot be the mere *manifestation* of generic characteristics of human nature (both corporeal and spiritual). If the principle of Mario's and Antonio's free actions did not exist in a way that is ontologically independent of the universal nature of their species, their freedom would be mere appearance. The manifestation of a *personal* individuality—a *self*—in the body, the states of consciousness, the choices and intentions, sensations, beliefs, desires, pains, etc., would only be phantasms

preserved. And, in this sense, every being *loves* its species and *loves* God before itself and with a greater love. Even the love of God, as such, does not provide a specific difference to the personal being. Man, though, is the only being that is called to formulate a *truth* judgment [*giudizio veritativo*] about God, and to make a *truth* choice [*scelta veritativa*] of his love for Him. Even here, the specific difference is given by rationality and freedom, or—if one prefers to put it this way—by a free love. See, for example, the following passage from Aquinas: "[N]ot only man, so long as his nature remains unimpaired [*in suae integritate naturae*], loves God above all things and more than himself, but also every single creature, each in its own way, i.e. either by an intellectual, or by a rational, or by an animal, or at least by a natural love, as stones do, for instance, and other things bereft of knowledge, because each part naturally loves the common good of the whole more than its own particular good. This is evidenced by its operation, since the principal inclination of each part is towards common action conducive to the good of the whole. It may also be seen in civic virtues whereby sometimes the citizens suffer damage even to their own property and persons for the sake of the common good" (*ST*, II-II, q. 26, a. 3 c).

38 Ibid., I, q. 29 a. 1 ad 1.

39 Think, for example, of the approaches (very different from one another) to the problem of identity elaborated by P. Strawson in *Individuals* (Methuen: London and New York, 1964) and C. Taylor in *Sources of the Self*.

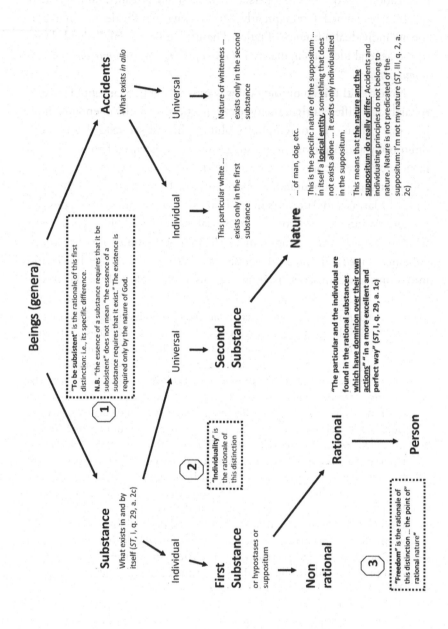

Beings (genera)

Accidents
What exists *in alio*

Substance
What exists in and by itself (*ST*, I, q. 29, a. 2c)

1 — "To be subsistent" is the rationale of this first distinction: i.e., its specific difference.

N.B. "the essence of a substance requires that it be subsistent" does not mean "the essence of a substance requires that it exist." The existence is required only by the nature of God.

Universal

Individual

Universal

Nature of whiteness … exists only in the second substance

Individual

This particular white … exists only in the first substance

Second Substance

2 — "Individuality" is the rationale of this distinction

First Substance
or hypostases or suppositum

Individual

Non rational

Rational

Nature
… of man, dog, etc.

This is the specific nature of the suppositum … in itself a **logical entity**, something that does not exists alone … it exists only individualized in the suppositum.

This means that **the nature and the suppositum do really differ**. Accidents and individuating principles do not belong to nature. Nature is not predicated of the suppositum: I'm not my nature (*ST*, III, q. 2, a. 2c)

"The particular and the individual are found in the rational substances **which have dominion over their own actions**" " in a more excellent and perfect way" (*ST*, I, q. 29, a. 1c)

Person

3 — "Freedom" is the rationale of this distinction … the point of" rational nature"

created by our imagination. In reality, we would have just the mechanistic effect (certainly of individual nature, but not personal) given by the interaction of certain universal inclinations of nature with a particular context, which includes a determinate body, a determinate society, a determinate culture, etc. It is an effect which is quantitatively, but not qualitatively, dissimilar from the one easily observable in the individual existence of an animal, or a software.

It should not come as a surprise that the contemporary phenomenological approach often finds it difficult to distinguish between human beings and animals in moral philosophy,[40] and between human beings and computers in philosophy of science. Contemporary phenomenology focuses on criteria by which *to observe* personal identity. Classical philosophy is concerned with *making personal identity possible*. For Aquinas, if freedom exists there must also be an ontological principle from which freedom originates. This principle cannot coincide with the principle that determines the nature of the species. It either exists from the beginning or it does not exist at all because it is the cause, not the effect, of the manifestations of freedom in the lives of the human beings. Every nature, human or otherwise, is shaped or molded by the individual existence of the *suppositum*. However, only human nature is also shaped by a unique principle of freedom. Such a principle is what Thomas, along with Boethius, called "person."

The attention that Greek philosophers and Aquinas give to the subject and to his freedom looks very modern. Or is it modernity that looks very classical? Aquinas' statement that rational beings are those who *non solum aguntur sed per se agunt* already contains the full force of Rousseau's concept of freedom as autonomy (the very concept for which Kant calls him the Newton of his ethics).[41] This power is already present in the Socratic concepts of *autarkeia* and *eleutheria*, and in the virtues of Aristotle's *phronimos*. The real difference between classicism and modernity is not in the subject's autonomy but in its meaning and authenticity.

---

40 Think of the radical and inhuman theses advanced by Peter Singer.

41 For Rousseau, "moral liberty [...] alone makes man truly the master of himself. For to be driven by appetite alone is slavery, and obedience to the law one has prescribed for oneself is liberty." Jean-Jacques Rousseau, *On the Social Contract*, trans by D. A. Cress (Hackett: Indianapolis, IN, 1987), p. 27.

The most important consequence of the difference between person and nature—or of considering freedom the defining characteristic of the person—is that one's focus shifts immediately from the universality and necessity of nature to the particularity and contingency of *freedom*. To observe freedom means to observe something that could have occurred otherwise, but actually occurred this way due to a non-determinate choice—namely, it means to observe something that is *personal*. Freedom is creative and unique. It comes from a unique principle and constantly nourishes it. To know a person does not mean to know his universal nature but to know the way in which his freedom has shaped, and keeps shaping, that nature. It is only at a minimal, or basic, level that respect of the person means respect of his nature and the ontological principle of his uniqueness (I am thinking of the respect rightly due to persons who cannot exercise, or have not yet exercised, their freedom: unborn babies, newborn babies, sick people, etc.). At a higher level, respect for the person is respect for the uniqueness that results from freedom. The person is like a castle that could have been built in a thousand different ways, and whose unique and original style can be admired and appreciated. Whether in private or in public life, the person does not want to be known, respected, and appreciated only as a human being (which, of course, is very important), but above all as Jake Nistler, Andy Kioko, or Matthew Currie. This kind of knowledge, respect, and appreciation is the ultimate way to *do justice* to the *person*.

In returning to our main question, "Person or Digital Self?" AI theories approach this question by assuming that if a digital machine will act exactly as we do, we could not say that there is a substantial difference between us and them. Fair enough! Yet the real question is, "Could they?" Could machines act exactly as we do? Among other things, this would imply that they are able to observe us and say, "There is no substantial difference between human beings and us because they act exactly as we do," and that in saying this they mean to pronounce a truth-statement. As I hope to have shown, this would mean that they are not machines at all. We are facing here deep and substantial differences: the difference between reality and appearance, on the one hand, and the difference between the existence of freedom and the existence of necessity only, or determinism, on the other. These are not minor distinctions.

V.

ULTIMATE END, HUMAN FREEDOM, AND BEATITUDE: A CRITIQUE OF GERMAIN GRISEZ

In his interesting and provocative article, "Natural Law, God, Religion, and Human Fulfillment," Germain Grisez claims that by criticizing the idea that "a person's will must have a single ultimate end in willing whatever it wills," he will disprove Aquinas' view that "human happiness (*beatitudo*, ultimate and perfect fulfillment) is to be found in God's goodness alone," and that "the human person attains divine goodness and finds happiness only in the vision of the divine essence."[1] Grisez's argument depends on four examples of people simultaneously willing "two or more ultimate ends." He also claims that Aquinas' thesis, namely, that man's ultimate end consists in the beatific vision, is logically inconsistent because "created persons" cannot "be fulfilled by *divine goodness itself*."[2] In what follows, I will show that Grisez's criticisms are logically inconsistent. I will focus, first, on the concept of an ultimate end (and on his four examples) and, second, on the beatific vision.

1. Ultimate End: Formal Necessity and Free Content

In both Aristotle and Aquinas, analysis of the ultimate end involves two distinct steps: (1) understanding the formal character of the ultimate end, according to which it is necessarily desired, and (2) identifying the content that bears this formal character and thus can fulfill man's desire. Thus formally (*secundum communem rationem beatitudinis*), every choice is for the

---

1   G. Grisez, *Natural Law, God, Religion, and Human Fulfillment*, op. cit., p. 16 (I quote from the manuscript I received before the conference, hereafter cited simply as "Grisez").

2   Ibid., p. 15, n. 34; emphasis original unless otherwise noted.

sake of the ultimate end. "As regards this," says Aquinas, "every man necessarily desires happiness,"[3] but with regard to the content of the ultimate end (*secundum specialem rationem quantum ad id in quo beatitudo consistit*), "not all desire happiness."[4] At the level of content, it is not a problem to say that the ultimate end (a) can differ from person to person and even in the same person over time; (b) is not usually well integrated with the multiplicity of goods characterizing daily human life; and (c) can be habitually the same even when it is contradicted by particular choices. In other words, we cannot choose whether to desire the ultimate end, but we need not desire that in which it in fact consists. Every choice is open to mistakes, and that is why it is so important to focus on what the ultimate end is.[5]

Considered formally, the ultimate end is the first principle in "the order of intention." It is the "principle moving the appetite," the underlying reason why we choose whatever we choose. If our intention did not rest on an end desired for its own sake we could not begin to choose anything—"nothing would be desired" and we would remain *immobile*.[6] So far, Grisez would probably agree, but this is not enough to understand the necessary way in which the ultimate end works in the agent's intentionality. Aristotle clearly distinguishes three formal traits of the ultimate end.[7] First of all, as we have just said, the ultimate end must be *in itself worthy of pursuit*. It cannot be desired instrumentally as a means to another end. This formal trait is not

---

3   *ST*, I-II, q. 5, a. 8. All translations are by the Fathers of the English Dominican Province (New York: Benzinger, 1947), except, for I-II, qq. 1–21, by John A. Oesterle (Notre Dame: University of Notre Dame Press, 1983).

4   Ibid. See also esp. I-II, q. 1, a. 7.

5   When Aquinas, in *ST*, I-II, q. 1, answers the questions "Is there an ultimate end for human life?" (a. 4), "Can a man have several ultimate ends?" (a. 5), and "Does man will all that he wills for an ultimate end?" (a. 6), he is referring to the common (formal) notion of ultimate end. But when he asks: "Is there one ultimate end for all men?" (a. 7), he clearly specifies: "With respect to the notion of the ultimate end, all agree in desiring the ultimate end [*quantum igitur ad rationem ultimi finis, omnes conveniunt in appetitu finis ultimi*]. But with respect to that in which this kind of thing is realized, all men are not agreed as to their ultimate end [*sed quantum ad id in quo ista ratio invenitur, non omnes homines conveniunt in ultimo fine*]."

6   See, *ST*, I-II, q. 1, a. 4.

7   See, esp. *NE*, I, 1097a31–1097b21.

enough in and of itself because "honour, pleasure, reason [knowledge], and every excellence [virtue] we choose indeed for themselves (for if nothing resulted from them we should still choose each of them), but we choose them also for the sake of happiness, judging that through them we shall be happy."[8] It is very interesting that both Aristotle and Aquinas do not hesitate in taking the best example of Grisez's basic goods (i.e., knowledge) to explain that it cannot be considered an ultimate end. For *scientia* "is desired as a good of the knower and is included in the complete and perfect good which is the ultimate end."[9] *Scientia* is loved "*non ut ipsa sit bona, sed ut habeatur*"[10] (to be possessed). It is also interesting that they do not hesitate in considering pleasure and all the virtues as ends pursued in their own right.

J. L. Ackrill has correctly emphasized that in order to understand how activities that have their own ends in themselves can still be subordinated to the ultimate end we must think of them in terms of "a relation like that of part to whole, the relation an activity or end may have to an activity or end that includes or embraces it."[11] The whole is the good of the agent: his happiness or beatitude. The parts are all the goods which characterize his complex being in different ways. For example, when an agent chooses to play tennis instead of reading a book on the ultimate end or eating a sandwich,

---

8   Ibid. When the concept of ultimate end is at stake "it makes no difference whether the activities themselves are the ends of the actions, or something else apart from the activities" (*NE*, I, 1094a16–18).

9   *ST*, I-II, q. 1., a. 6 ad 2.

10   *ST*, I, q. 60, a. 3 c.

11   J. L. Ackrill, "Aristotle on *Eudaimonia*," in *Aristotle's Ethics*, N. Sherman (ed.) (Lanham: Rowman & Littlefield, 1999), p. 61: "One may think of the relation of putting to playing golf or of playing golf to having a good holiday. One does not putt *in order to* play golf as one buys a club in order to play golf; and this distinction matches that between activities that do not and those that do produce a product. It will be 'because' you wanted to play golf that you are putting, and 'for the sake' of a good holiday that you are playing golf; but this is because putting and golfing are *constituents of* or *ingredients in* golfing and having a good holiday respectively, not because they are necessary preliminaries. Putting *is* playing golf (though not all that playing golf is), and golfing (in a somewhat different way) *is* having a good holiday (though not all that having a good holiday is)."

his *logical* point of view is his own good as a whole (his happiness). I choose tennis because I think that, *right now*, I am better off playing tennis. With respect to the whole, all the different goods are of course commensurable, just as the wheel, the carburetor, and the gas are commensurable with respect to a car. They are *parts* of it, not through their intrinsic qualities, but through the specific role they play with respect to the (qualitatively different) end of the car as a whole. In other words, they are *goods* for the car under only one *ratio boni*.[12] With his typical concise and technical style, Aquinas says that "whatever man desires, he desires it under the aspect of good (*appetit sub ratione boni*),"[13] or that "all things desirable to the will, as desirable, are of one genus."[14] This is meant to explain both that the human will cannot tend simultaneously to more than one ultimate end, and that it necessarily wills everything for the sake of an ultimate end. If there were several incommensurable ultimate ends of the human being, there would be no logical reason even to call them by the same name (basic *human goods*) and it would be epistemologically impossible to choose between them.[15] If there are several

12 I think the term "commensurability" is appropriate and does not need to be changed. The term "measure" is analogical, and it need not be used quantitatively as in proportionalism. In fact, it is classically used every time we consider different things under only one point of view. We say, e.g., that the mind of God is (the common) *measure* of ontological truth; or that the *res* is (the common) *measure* of logical truth; or that nature is (the common) *measure* of morality; or that God, as the ultimate end, is (the common) *measure* of the bounty of the universe (creation). I can see, however, why in order to stress the point I am making P. Simpson distinguishes between "commensurability" and "comparability": see, P. Simpson, "Grisez on Aristotle and Human Goods," in *The American Journal of Jurisprudence* 46 (2001): pp. 75–89. It only seems to me more an *ad hominem* distinction than a distinction required in itself.

13 *ST*, I-II, q. 1., a. 6 c.

14 Ibid., a. 5 c.

15 Grisez's hostility to the concept of (only one) ultimate end has two main reasons: (1) he thinks that we would not be free if there were only one ultimate end; and (2) he thinks that to talk about a plurality of ultimate ends is the only way to criticize proportionalism. Here I would like to raise an objection of logical consistency. If (a) we are free ("there is room and need for choice," Grisez p. 2) because there are several incommensurable ultimate ends, (b) in what sense can we be free in choosing between two or more instantiations of

human goods, they of course are all *human goods* by virtue of the same *ratio boni*, which is the good of the human being as a whole.[16]

Since being *in itself worthy of pursuit* is not a sufficient formal condition of the ultimate end, we need to add a second trait; it must be *"complete without qualification,"* absolute, and "always desirable in itself and never for the sake of something else."[17] It is impossible to desire the good of the whole for the sake of the part. While it is necessary to desire knowledge, power, play, marriage, riches, etc. (i.e., all the parts), for the sake of what we call happiness, it is impossible to desire what we call happiness for the sake of something else. This is true precisely because happiness (whatever it is) is the complete good of the whole, including in itself all the other goods. The ultimate end at work in the agent's intentionality is always and necessarily the good of the whole, not of the part. That is why it is formally intended by the agent as *complete without qualification*.[18]

the same ultimate end (e.g., eating fish instead of meat, marrying this woman instead of that other one)? Grisez and Finnis would probably answer that the basic values are open-ended: i.e., there is no logical need to choose, here and now, one particular instantiation; and this is the basic character of the practical syllogism. Why then could we not apply the same logic to the ultimate end, saying that it is open-ended with respect to all the particular human goods? In any case: (a) if there are several choices reducible to one and the same basic value (and therefore not incommensurable), and (b) we are free to choose one of them instead of the others, then (c) the correct account of freedom does not depend on the "incommensurability thesis," and (d) does not require us to deny the existence of only one ultimate end.

But if the "incommensurability thesis" does not work, is there another logical way to criticize proportionalism? The answer is: "Yes, it is the concept of ultimate end." If there is *only* one ultimate end that cannot be subordinated to anything else, we ought never do those actions which go directly against it or against what necessarily belongs to it. So, it is better to die than to blaspheme or to commit an action that constitutes a violation of the order God imprinted on creation, because that action directly denies God as the ultimate end.

16 For a similar criticism of Grisez see R. McInerny, "Grisez and Thomism," in N. Biggar, R. Black (eds.), *The Revival of Natural Law* (Ashgate: Aldershot, 2000), pp. 53–72.

17 *NE*, I, 1097a33–4 (emphasis mine).

18 If I were a car, I could not choose the good of the wheel just for the sake of

The second formal trait already enables us to speak properly about the ultimate end. Yet Aristotle adds a third and logically distinguishable trait: "for the complete good is thought to be *self-sufficient*."[19] It is important to stress that self-sufficiency is another *formal* aspect of the concept of ultimate end in itself. As "the first principle in the order of intention," the ultimate end is what the appetite finally tends toward without any further intentional subordination. Formally, it is what an agent necessarily intends which is in itself *sufficient* to satisfy the appetite. Logically, if it were achieved nothing more would remain to be desired.[20]

A sound account of the formal traits of the ultimate end enables both Aristotle and Aquinas to reflect on what its consistent content should be. For example, it becomes relatively easy to say that pleasure is not self-sufficient because it depends on an activity or good,[21] or that happiness cannot consist in an activity of the practical intellect because "the act of the practical intellect is sought not for its own sake but for the sake of the action," and the action is for the sake of an end.[22] It is even easy to say that the ultimate end cannot consist *simpliciter* in a good of the soul (i.e., in any of Grisez's basic goods) because nothing "belonging to the soul [...] is a complete good fulfilling the appetite," and the soul in itself depends on external objects to pass from being in potency to being in act. It cannot be the ultimate end of itself.[23]

---

the wheel in itself, but always for the sake of the wheel *as a part* of my good: i.e., in light of what is good for the car as a whole.

19 *NE*, I, 1097b8 (emphasis mine).
20 *NE*, I, 1097b16–21: "Further we think it most desirable of all things, without being counted as one good thing among others—if it were so counted it would clearly be made more desirable by the addition of even the least of goods; for that which is added becomes an excess of goods, and of goods the greater is always more desirable. Happiness, then, is something complete and self-sufficient, and is the end of action."
21 See *NE*, X, 1174b14–1176a29; *ST*, I-II, q. 2, a. 6 ad 1.
22 *ST*, I-II, q. 3, a. 5.
23 *ST*, I-II, q. 2, a. 7: "[H]appiness is something belonging to the soul" but "the object of happiness is something outside the soul." Hittinger's criticism of the immanentistic character of Grisez's basic values runs along the same lines. See R. Hittinger, *A Critique of the New Natural Law Theory* (Notre Dame: University of Notre Dame Press, 1987).

In each case that Grisez sketches of people who simultaneously will two or more ultimate ends he confuses the formality of the ultimate end with what the agent thinks about its content. Yet he is also too quick to identify goods like "playing baseball" or "civil marriage" as ultimate ends of the agents. [The mention of "pleasure of lechery" and "power" is ambiguous because all the examples were introduced as related with "ultimate ends," and even in Grisez's theory lechery and power cannot be described as ultimate ends.]

In the case of Joe,[24] formally the ultimate end always remains his good as a whole. He does not choose to play "simply for the sake of the game,"[25] but simply because *he* likes it (*ut habeatur*). The relation to the agent as a whole is logically involved in the relevant choice because the ultimate end is Joe's good, not the good of the game. If the latter were *formally* the ultimate end, Joe could not do anything else in his life other than play baseball and what playing baseball requires. On the contrary, the good of the *whole* potentially includes all the goods toward which Joe feels an inclination, and it is subject to hierarchy and subordination between them. Without need of thinking explicitly about the ultimate end, Joe sees "playing baseball *sometimes*" as part of his happy life, and he chooses to do this and he is happy doing this when the circumstances appear favorable. Even while playing, Joe does not think of baseball as the ultimate end of his life. It would of course be possible to do that, but Joe "lives in God's love and hopes to go to heaven." Whatever heaven means for him, it must be more important than playing baseball, and Joe would certainly stop playing *if necessary*. In a non-perfectly integrated way, Joe includes both heaven and playing baseball in his happy life, but the only ultimate end he explicitly recognizes is

24 Grisez, p. 16: "Consider Joe, an eleven-year-old boy who lives in God's love and hopes to go to heaven. He also plays baseball with his friends simply for the sake of the game. If Joe were catechized about how to relate those two goods to each other, he probably would subordinate playing baseball to heaven. But never having thought at the same time about the two ends, he never has chosen to play baseball with the ultimate intention of going to heaven. And, never having done that, heaven, though Joe habitually intends it, is in no way that for whose sake he chooses to play. So, when Joe is at play, he has at least two ultimate ends: heaven habitually and play actually."

25 Being "in itself worthy of pursuit" is not sufficient to identify formally the ultimate end.

heaven. It is the formality of happiness, not its content, that is necessarily involved in the choice to play baseball, and that same formality eventually pushes the agent to go beyond baseball.

Joan[26] also has only one ultimate end, both formally and materially. She is tending toward her happiness, which is her complete good as a whole, and she knows that her ultimate good lies in the love of God. However, now she feels that a civil union, apparently in contrast with that love, is necessary for her happiness. She does not at all think that the union is her ultimate end. She simply cannot practically understand how her human love can be against the love of God. Precisely because she recognizes only one ultimate end, she experiences a moral tension that she does not fully understand. Even while choosing the civil union she maintains the same habitual, ultimate end of loving God, but with the secret practical hope of finally harmonizing with it what appears incompatible. Joan's case is different than Joe's because Joe (as far as we know) does not experience any conflict (any moral tension) between heaven and playing baseball. For Joan, not only is the ultimate end as happiness present to her choice, but also her conscious (albeit practically confused) idea of it as loving God.

The same happens with the "deliberate venial sinners,"[27] which are

26 Grisez, p. 17: "Christians plainly have two ultimate ends when they commit themselves by a single choice to obduracy in mortal sin and to holding fast to their faith with the hope of eventual repentance. Consider Joan, a devout young woman who falls in love with a man and agrees to marry him before she finds out he is not free to marry. She might give up the man or give up her faith. But Joan chooses to marry the man civilly and to cling to her faith, hoping for eventual repentance and salvation."

27 Ibid.: "Many faithful Christians sometimes commit deliberate venial sins. Aquinas holds that God can remain such a venial sinner's habitual end. He seems to suppose that such sinners simply do not think beyond the proximate end so as to direct it to some ultimate end other than God. But that will not do. An ultimate end causes only by providing a reason for choosing to act for a proximate end, and God cannot provide any reason for choosing to act sinfully for any end. So, in sinning, deliberate venial sinners either have some ultimate end other than God or no ultimate end at all. But nobody can will anything except on account of some ultimate end. Thus deliberate venial sinners have some ultimate end other than God. Therefore, those in grace who commit deliberate venial sins simultaneously have at least two ultimate ends."

"venial," says Aquinas, because they do not go "against the law."[28] I think all "faithful Christians" will agree with me that when we commit a venial sin we do not think even for a second that God is not our ultimate end. Rather, the search for our good (our happiness) becomes disordered. We refuse to think that we are really going against God. With this secret, un-expressed idea, we get confused and we upset the harmony between the formality of the ultimate end (happiness) and our habitual understanding of it (God). Repentance is not "changing the ultimate end" but "finding again full harmony with it."[29]

The case of the politician[30] is much easier. He is merely living out a very selfish and disordered love for himself. He has probably never thought explicitly about an ultimate end in his life, but he places his happiness

28 "[S]ince he who sins venially neither does what the law forbids, nor omits what the law prescribes to be done; but he acts 'beside' the law, through not observing the mode of reason, which the law intends" (*ST*, I-II, q. 88, a. 1 ad 1).

29 *ST*, I-II, q. 88, a. 1 c.: "Venial sin excludes only actual reference of the human act to God's glory, and not habitual reference: because it does not exclude charity, which refers man to God habitually." A venial sin may be spending an entire day without dedicating some time to prayer, even if the idea that we should take a break and pray pops up in our minds a few times. A full harmony with our habitual end of loving God requires some time for prayer, but there is no law that prescribes it in some particular moments (except for Sunday Mass). So, when we do not take some time off to pray we do not *intend* to break any divine law, but we *use* the goods of this earth without being fully in harmony with our habitual intention of loving God. The formality of happiness as the ultimate end is there. The habitual idea of loving God is there too. If someone asked us, we would confidently say that everything we do is ultimately for the love of God. However, in the concrete choices we make God should be present more intensely. Our intentions and pursuit of happiness should be better integrated with our awareness of God as the ultimate end.

30 Grisez, pp. 16–17: "Many wicked people have multiple ends that they have not integrated with one another. Consider a politician who desires both the pleasure of lechery and the power of high office. Realizing that he is risking power when he pursues pleasure, he tries to conceal his adulterous affairs. Still, when his secret is exposed, he reluctantly sacrifices illicit pleasure to remain in power."

(formal ultimate end) above all in "the power of high office" and, second-arily, on "the pleasure of lechery." If we had to identify his habitual ultimate end *quantum ad id in quo beatitudo consistit*, we would probably say—on the basis of the little information we have about his life—that it is a vague mixture of these two elements, neither of which must be intentionally pres-ent in all his deliberations.

2. Beatific Vision: Why Human Beings?

Grisez criticizes Aquinas' view that man's ultimate *beatitudo* consists in the vision of God for two main reasons. On the one hand, he thinks that seeing God is not enough for human beatitude. In his mind it should also include what he calls integral human fulfillment. On the other hand, he claims that the beatific vision "will fulfill human persons, not insofar as they are human, but insofar as [...] they are truly divine," or "that the beatific vision fulfills the blessed insofar as they share in divine nature and that it cannot fulfill their human nature, which has no capacity for it."[31] Grisez's criticism is grounded on the idea that there are two ultimate ends: one for human be-ings as divine (the beatific vision) and one for human beings as human (in-tegral human fulfillment).[32]

The main (logical) problem with Grisez's approach to beatific vision is that: (a) if beatific vision does not fulfill human persons insofar as they are human ("they have no capacity for it"), then (b) there is no way to say that the beatific vision fulfills human persons at all, because the term "fulfills" necessarily implies a certain actualization of something that was already there to be fulfilled. In other words, to say that "beatific vision fulfills human persons as divine" is a contradiction: it is like saying that the beatific vision will fulfill dogs as divine. The question immediately follows: "Why should the gift of beatific vision be given to human beings instead, e.g., of dogs, trees or stones?" After all, they too have no capacity for it. However,

---

31   Ibid., p. 14.

32   A related problem that I cannot deal with here is that "*integral* human fulfil-ment" does not exist because it is not supposed to be anything beyond the plurality of incommensurable ultimate ends. See *God and the Natural Law*, op. cit., and *John Finnis* (Palermo: Phronesis, 2008).

if there is any relevant difference between human beings and the other material beings, we should wonder whether having a personal/spiritual nature implies a kind of capacity for the beatific vision.

As a starting point, we must assume that human beings certainly have a natural desire, tendency, or inclination toward a good (ultimate end) that goes far beyond the scope of every possible natural good, and that must be properly called "supernatural." Our natural ethical-religious experience consists in aspiring to a realization, a fulfillment—let us call it eternal life, final justice, final merit and demerit, etc.—that goes beyond the limits of this present life, beyond human nature as we can see it now, a nature destined for death and for ephemeral happiness.[33] Nothing natural can satisfy the ultimate and absolute aspiration of the human heart. Man is in exile on this earth; he is a pilgrim, and his nature exceeds the limits of the life he lives, and at least under this respect must be said to be somehow *capax* of a supernatural good.[34]

Of course, there is no way to achieve such a good by human effort alone. Nevertheless, that is what we naturally desire. This desire implies the knowledge of "what we call God."[35] Despite the fact that our knowledge is mediate and confused, we can rationally aspire to know God in himself. That means we can aspire to have a direct knowledge of the Creator: we can pray for it,[36] and we can act morally on the assumption that this will deserve the gift of eternal life.[37]

33 "What is good in this life is transitory" (*ST*, I-II, q. 5, a. 3).

34 See *Catechism of the Catholic Church*, Chapter I: "Man's Capacity for God (Homo capax Dei)."

35 See *ST*, I, q. 2, aa. 1, 3. "God is man's happiness" and what man "naturally desires, he also naturally knows" (a. 1).

36 To pray and to ask for the gift of the beatific vision, to thank God for that gift, to act morally in view of it, etc., are all human choices having the beatific vision as their reason. That is why Grisez is misleading and logically inconsistent when he writes that "if we have made [the commitment of cooperating with God] and God tells us he is prepared to give us a share in his very nature and intimacy, we have reason to ask for that gift, to thank God for it, and to cherish it. In that way, we can perform human acts bearing upon the beatific vision. Even so, since no human act can attain divine goodness in itself, it cannot be a *reason* for making any choice" (Grisez, p. 15). The *reason* to choose to pray is always that there is something we cannot achieve (or at least not

In the treatise on happiness[38] Aquinas explains that man's happiness consists in the beatific vision, and he focuses on the way in which we attain our ultimate end. Yet, he deals directly with the metaphysical possibility of the beatific vision in the *Summa Theologiae*, I, q. 12 ("how God is known by us"), a question that, surprisingly, Grisez does not quote in his article. Aquinas' first concern is to state that it is possible for a created intellect to see the essence of God (*Deum videre per essentiam*). To him the difference between the possibility of seeing God's essence,[39] on the one hand, and the possibility of doing so without grace,[40] on the other, is perfectly clear. Without the first possibility we could not have the beatific vision at all, with or without grace, because grace cannot change a created intellect into an uncreated intellect (grace does not create another God). This first possibility is what makes the beatific vision relevant to human beings and not, e.g., to dogs or stones. On the other hand, Aquinas is very clear that nobody can see the essence of God without grace. Yet, if grace did not act upon our nature—i.e., upon an act of *our own intellect*—then it would not be a human being that sees God's essence, but something else (in the last analysis, only God himself as he is the only uncreated intellect).[41]

easily) by our efforts alone (e.g., that we not enter into temptation). But I would say: no human act can attain the whole end in itself, even for somebody to be loved by somebody else, and still that love is a good *reason* to try to date a girl or to make your children happy, etc. In the same way, the beatific vision is a good reason for acting in a particular way in this present life.

37 The following words from *Veritatis Splendor* do not have merely a theological meaning: "The question which the rich young man puts to Jesus of Nazareth is one which rises from the depths of his heart. It is *an essential and unavoidable question for the life of every man*, for it is about the moral good which must be done, and about eternal life. The young men senses that there is a connection between moral good and the fulfillment of his own destiny" (John Paul II, Encyclical Letter *Veritatis Splendor*, n. 8). This idea of deserving eternal life through our morally good actions is already clearly stated in ancient Greek philosophy, especially in Plato.

38 *ST*, I-II, qq. 1–21.

39 *ST*, I, q. 12, a. 1.

40 *ST*, I, q. 12, aa. 4–5.

41 As a dog could not be *fulfilled* by the gift of an intellect, because if it received an intellect it would not be a dog anymore. So, if we were not able to see the essence of God by *our own intellect*, we would never be able to see it.

Aquinas is much more daring than Grisez. He does not wonder whether human nature can be fulfilled by the beatific vision "as human" or "as divine." He first wonders if a created intellect—angelic or human, with or without grace—can see the essence of God. "Can somebody other than God see the essence of God?" This is the relevant question. Grisez's answer, "human beings as divine," is contained in Aquinas's question. If Aquinas's answer, "Yes, created intellect can," does not work Grisez's answer will not work either because a "human being as divine" (whatever this phrase means) would still remain a "created being"—unless Grisez is proposing a sort of pantheism in which "human being as divine" means God himself, but even in this case we would not have any human being *to be fulfilled*. While criticizing Aquinas, Grisez actually renders his own discussion of the beatific vision meaningless.[42]

To fully understand Aquinas' explanation we must clearly distinguish: (1) the argument from natural desire; (2) the proof that the intellect can see the essence of God; and (3) the proof that grace is necessary.

First, the *naturale desiderium cognoscendi primam causam rerum* is, properly speaking, the proof of beatific vision as the content of human happiness.[43] Natural desire does not show in itself how a created intellect can see the essence of God. Nevertheless, it is in a sense the most important proof for this possibility because nature always manifests itself in a tendency (or movement) toward a certain act. Precisely because natural desire is an undeniable fact, we know that we are not indifferent to what God is in Himself, and we can focus on the structure that makes our intellectual nature open to the beatific vision. Of course, there is no room to talk properly about a potentiality because humans cannot reach the essence of God by

---

42 Grisez does not realize, in other words, that he is trying to criticize not Aquinas' understanding of the fulfillment of "human nature as human" by the beatific vision, but Aquinas' understanding of the possibility that some created being receives the gift of the beatific vision. Grisez's terminology is also misleading because it is perfectly clear in Aquinas, as we shall soon see, that *human nature* can receive the gift of beatific vision only because there is something *divine* in it (see, *ST*, I, q. 12, a. 2). The contrast between "human nature as human" and "human nature as divine" is not applicable to Aquinas. For him the distinction is simply between the natural and the supernatural.

43 *ST*, I-II, q. 3, a. 8.

their own acts alone. Certainly there is evidence for an opening (or capacity) that is both the mystery of our spiritual nature and the sign of a higher destiny. "*Si igitur intellectus rationalis creaturae pertingere non possit ad primam causam rerum, remanebit inane desiderium naturale.*"[44]

Second, to be able to see God we need a certain likeness of our intellect to Him—"*aliqua Dei similitudo ex parte visivae potentiae*"[45]—for knowing is a sort of identification with what is known; "*intellectus in actu est intelligibile in actu; sicut sensus in actu est sensibile in actu.*"[46] Normally, the similarity is *ex parte objecti*—"*ex parte rei visae*"—because the knower does not have the real thing (the stone) in himself, but only a certain likeness of it. Let us call it "form." In a sense, when the intellect knows something it makes the thing known similar to itself. Yet for God himself to be directly present to our intellect, the similarity must be *ex parte intellectus*. In this case, it is God who has to both make himself present to our intellect and make our intellect similar to his own. That is why Aquinas says that our intellect has a participated similarity to God ("*qui est primus intellectus*") both at the level of nature and at the level of grace and glory.[47] ["God said, 'Let us make mankind in our image and likeness [...] God created man in his image. In the image of God he created him. Male and female he created them" (*Gen* 1:26–7).]

Therefore, we can see God because there is *something divine* in us. Aquinas explains that the created intellect can "*in abstractione considerare quod in concretione cognoscit.*"[48] Even if it knows things only under the perspective of the *ens*—i.e., of an *esse* limited by a certain *essentia* [essence]—it "*potest ipsum esse secernere per intellectum, dum cognoscit quod aliud est ipse et aliud est ejus esse.*"[49] In other words, the created intellect is able to recognize the participated/created being as such, i.e., as a limited composition of *esse* and *essentia*, and can rationally consider the being whose essence it is to be: the *ipsum esse subsistens*. With respect

44 *ST*, I, q. 12, a. 1.
45 Ibid., a. 2 c.
46 Ibid., obj. 3.
47 Ibid., "*Sive hoc intelligatur de virtute naturali sive de aliqua perfectione superaddita gratiae vel gloriae.*"
48 Ibid., a. 4 ad 3.
49 Ibid.

to the participated being, this capacity of abstraction is a sign of an open-ing, a possibility, and a "capacity"[50] to be raised by grace to the direct knowledge of the *Ipsum Esse Subsistens*: "*Et ideo, cum intellectus creatus per suam naturam natus sit apprehendere formam concretam et esse concre-tum in abstractione per modum resolutionis cujusdam, potest per gratiam elevari ut cognoscat substantiam separatam subsistentem et esse separatum subsistens.*"[51]

Finally, grace is necessary because it is impossible to see the essence of God by means of a created image (*per similitudinem creatam*). "The essence of God is *ipsum esse ejus*" which cannot belong to any created form (*quod nulli formae creatae competere potest*) because "every created form is deter-mined according to some" essence [*omnis forma creata est determinata se-cundum aliquam rationem*]. "Hence to say that God is seen by some similitude, is to say that the divine essence is not seen at all; which is false."[52]

---

50 *ST*, I-II, q. 5, a. 1 c.: "That man has a capacity for the perfect good [*perfecti boni sit capax*] is evident from the fact that his intellect apprehends the uni-versal and perfect good, and his will seeks it. Hence man can attain happiness. It is also evident from the fact that man has a capacity for seeing the divine essence [*est capax visionis divinae essentiae*], as we have explained" (I, q. 12).

51 *ST*, I, q. 12, a. 4 ad 3: "Since therefore the created intellect is naturally capable of apprehending the concrete form, and the concrete being abstractedly, by way of a kind of resolution of parts; it can by grace be raised up to know sep-arate subsisting substance, and separate subsisting existence."

52 Ibid., a. 2 c. Aquinas distinguishes three reasons: "But on the part of the object seen [*ex parte rei visae*], which must necessarily be united to the seer [*quam necesse est aliquo modo uniri videnti*], the essence of God cannot be seen by any created similitude [*per nullam similitudinem creatam*]. First, because, as Dionysius says, *by the similitudes of the inferior order of things, the superior can in no way be known*; as by the likeness of a body the essence of an incorporeal thing cannot be known [*per speciem corporis non potest cognosci essentia rei in-corporeae*]. Much less therefore can the essence of God be seen by any created likeness whatever [*per speciem creatam quamcumque*]. Secondly, because the essence of God is His own very existence [*essentia Dei est ipsum esse ejus*], as was shown above, which cannot be said of any created form [*quod nulli formae creatae competere potest*]; and so no created form can be the similitude [*simil-itudo*] representing the essence of God to the seer [*repraesentans videnti Dei essentiam*]. Thirdly, because the divine essence is uncircumscribed [*divina es-sentia est aliquid incircumscriptum*], and contains in itself supereminently what-

Thus, for a created intellect to see God, he himself has to be directly present to its act of knowledge. However, the way in which God is exceeds the way in which the created intellect possesses the object of its own act of knowledge. "For knowledge is regulated according as the thing known is in the knower. But the thing known is in the knower according to the mode of the knower. Hence the knowledge of every knower is ruled according to its own nature. If therefore the mode of anything's being exceeds the mode of the knower, it must result that the knowledge of that object is above the nature of the knower."[53] Therefore, it is necessary in order for a created

ever can be signified or understood by the created intellect [*continens in se supereminenter quidquid potest significari vel intelligi ab intellectu creato*]. Now this cannot in any way be represented by any created likeness [*per aliquam speciem creatam*]; for every created form [*omnis forma creata*] is determined according to some aspect of wisdom, or of power, or of being itself, or of some like thing [*est determinata secundum aliquam rationem vel sapientiae, vel virtutis, vel ipsius esse, vel alicujus hujusmodi*]. Hence to say that God is seen by some similitude [*per similitudinem videri*], is to say that the divine essence is not seen at all; which is false. Therefore it must be said that to see the essence of God there is required some similitude in the visual faculty [*aliqua similitudo ex parte visivae potentiae*], namely, the light of glory strengthening the intellect to see God [*lumen divinae gloriae confortans intellectum ad videndum Deum*], which is spoken of in the Psalm, *In Thy light we shall see light*. The essence of God, however, cannot be seen by any created similitude representing the divine essence itself as it really is [*non autem per aliquam similitudinem creatam Dei essentia videri potest, quae ipsam divinam essentiam repraesentet ut in se est*]."

53 "*Cognitio enim contingit secundum quod cognitum est in cognoscente; cognitum autem est in cognoscente secundum modum cognoscentis. Unde cujuslibet cognoscentis cognitio est secundum modum suae naturae. Si igitur modus essendi alicujus rei cognitae excedat modum naturae cognoscentis oportet quod cognitio illius rei sit supra naturam illius cognoscentis*" (ibid., a. 4 c.). In the same article Aquinas explains that our "intellect naturally knows natures [*per intellectum connaturale est nobis cognoscere naturas*] which exist [*habent esse*] only in individual matter; not as they are in such individual matter, but according as they are abstracted therefrom by the considering act of the intellect [*secundum quod abstrahuntur ab ea per considerationem intellectus*]; hence it follows that through the intellect we can understand these objects as universal [*possumus cognoscere hujusmodi res in universali*]; and this is beyond the power of sense. Now the angelic intellect naturally knows natures that are not in matter [*connaturale est cognoscere naturas non in materia existentes*]; but this is beyond

intellect to have God himself as the object of its act of knowledge that it receive an "increase of the intellectual powers [*augmentum virtutis intellectivae*]," which is a "supernatural disposition" that "is called illumination of the intellect."[54] Grace does not create another intellect. Rather, it adds something to an act of our own intellect. That is why *we*, and not other beings (like the *divine* beings hypothesized by Grisez), will see the essence of God.

Personally, I find Aquinas' account of the created intellect's capacity for the beatific vision brilliant (especially considering the intrinsic difficulty of the subject). I do not think Grisez offers any consistent ground to talk about the beatific vision or any good reason to criticize Aquinas on this point.

Finally, to Grisez's theory of "integral human fulfillment" ("rich participation in all the human goods") as a necessary component of our beatitude (the fulfillment of human beings as human) I would like to raise here a very simple objection. It is clear that integral human fulfillment cannot be exactly the same for the blessed and for *pilgrims*. For example, think of marriage: "They will neither marry nor be given in marriage, but will be as angels of God in heaven" (Matthew 22:30–31). Think also of the need for eating, or for rationally seeking the truth, etc. We need a criterion to distinguish between what is essential and what is not essential to this ultimate fulfillment. Now, this criterion must be very strong because it must be able to make something as important as even conjugal love itself non-essential to human fulfilment.[55] Could it be that using a sound sequence of reasoning

the power of the intellect of our soul [*supra naturalem facultatem intellectus animae humanae*] in the state of its present life, united as it is to the body. It follows therefore that to know self-subsistent being [*ipsum esse subsistens*] is natural to the divine intellect alone; and this is beyond the natural power of any created intellect; for no creature is its own existence [*nulla creatura est suum esse*], for as much as its existence is participated [*sed habet esse participatum*]. Therefore the created intellect cannot see the essence of God, unless God by His grace unites Himself to the created intellect, as an object made intelligible to it [*nisi inquantum Deus per suam gratiam se intellectui creato conjungit ut intelligibile ab ipso*]."

54 Ibid., a. 5.

55 Marriage is for Grisez a basic human good; as such, it is a necessary component of integral human fulfillment and part of our ultimate beatitude. When he

at this level of human reflection, the only essential thing is exactly what Aquinas calls direct (loving) contemplation of God? After all, the created goods are nothing more than an imperfect image of what God is in himself, and in the order of charity everything is loved for God, in God and through God. Everything in heaven will be done and experienced as part of our loving contemplation of God. "The vision of the divine essence supplies the soul with every good, since the soul is united with the source of all goodness. Hence Scripture says, 'I shall be satisfied when Thy glory shall appear.'"[56]

raises the question, "How, then, can the one-flesh communion of marriage endure forever?" he says: "The answer is that it cannot endure insofar as it is based on sexual differentiation, it is limited to couples, and is fulfilled by having and raising children" (G. Grisez, *The Way of the Lord Jesus: Living a Christian Life*, Vol. II, Franciscan Press, Quincy, 1993), p. 608. That means that what we call marriage will not endure forever: i.e., it will not be in itself part of our heavenly beatitude. That is why when Grisez immediately adds, "Rather, it will endure in the resurrection without these limits and will be perfected within the greater one-flesh communion of the blessed in and with the Lord Jesus," we should reply without hesitation that this is even truer of the choice to renounce marriage (virginity or celibacy). If human love will endure in the resurrection without limits of sexual differentiation, couples, and having and raising children, it will be above all the kind of love lived by those who renounced marriage for the sake of the Kingdom of God. Not marriage or human sexuality in themselves, therefore, will endure forever, but rather that of which they are a sign: the love of God, and creatures being in God, for God, and through God.

56   *ST*, I-II, q. 5, a. 4 c., quoting Psalm 16:15. See also II-II, q. 180, aa. 1, 2–4, 7. "In both respects [by reason of the operation itself [*ratione ipsius operationis*] and on the part of its object [*ex parte objecti*] the delight thereof surpasses all human delight, both because spiritual delight is greater than carnal pleasure [...] and because the love whereby God is loved out of charity surpasses all love" (a. 7 c.).

VI

WHAT NATURE? WHOSE NATURE?: REFLECTING ON SOME RECENT ARGUMENTS IN NATURAL LAW ETHICS

What kind of nature is the foundation of morality? What does the adjective "natural" mean when it is followed by "law"? Everyone who makes a serious study of Aristotle and Aquinas usually agrees that nature is the measure of what is good, and that evil is somehow against nature. Yet the meaning and the ethical relevance of nature among contemporary Thomistic authors seem sometimes so far from their classical roots that one might easily wonder whether the alleged link between nature and morality is today no more than a slogan.

I think the concept of nature, as used in ethics by John Finnis, Germain Grisez, Joseph Boyle, William May, Robert George, and their followers, on the one hand, and by Martin Rhonheimer, on the other, is closer to modern philosophy than to Aquinas' realism at least under two main respects: (1) the tendency of making ideas themselves the first object of philosophical reflection rather than material reality; and (2) the tendency of focusing on the agent's subjectivity rather than on an objective (ethical) order. These tendencies are respectively the objects of my provocative "What Nature?" and "Whose Nature?" questions.

In this chapter, I want to focus on the way in which these authors tend to approach specific ethical issues because there is a consistency between metaphysical views and ethical methodology. I would like to show that some relevant mistakes they make in applied ethics depend on their peculiar and non-classical way of looking at nature. For my present purpose, it is very important to show how those tendencies can create a real methodological background. Consequently, my general strategy will be the following: first, through my "What Nature?" and "Whose Nature?" questions I will sketch the two tendencies and the way in which they affect ethical methodology;

second, I will analyze in more detail, in light of those tendencies, some arguments that the above-mentioned scholars proposed with respect to contraception and sodomitical acts; finally, I will sketch Aquinas' approach to nature as the basis of morality.

Another premise is *de rigueur*. The authors I am going to criticize are effectively trying to rediscover and to recover the foundations of classical philosophy, and are engaged in a fruitful and interesting dialogue with modern thought and contemporary analytic philosophy. From my viewpoint, their contributions should be favorably welcomed. What I will try to say is only that, as I see it, they become a little entangled in the same philosophical background of the arguments they criticize, and that this background prevents a more refined understanding of the Thomistic tradition of thought to which they refer.

Moreover, these scholars' theories are refined and nuanced, but also different from one another in many respects. Often, the generalizations involved in this chapter risk being unfair. Therefore, I must stress forcefully that the point of this chapter is not to give full justice to anyone's specific viewpoint but to underline common philosophical tendencies. I apologize for grouping very different and rich authors together, but if I am wrong in doing so it must be at the level of general interpretation of current philosophical tendencies, and not at the secondary level of the peculiar traits of someone's thought or of one or more specific points or arguments.

1. What Nature?

My "What-Question" is concerned with the tendency of focusing on a sort of world of values in itself as if it were something different from (and morally prior to) the real, *material* world. Nature as the ground for ethics becomes the nature of practical reason. Understanding (or studying) nature becomes equal to understanding the values which exist and act in our practical reason. This is a sort of immanentistic point of view which creates the problem of connecting the realm of values (ideas) with the realm of facts. A similar problem was created by Descartes' dualism of *res extensa* and *res cogitans* (or of body and spirit).[1] The values are grasped by practical reason,

---

1   Of course, this is not to say that there is not an explicit concern in the authors

not due to an understanding of the intrinsic meaning of material reality, but independently of it. They (the values) are then supposed to, so to speak, colonize material reality by giving it ethical *order* and meaning. The logical problem here is no longer the "is-ought" but the "ought-is."

This tendency is pretty clear, for example, in the opposition that Rhonheimer outlines between nature (natural order) and reason (moral order), as well as in his doctrine of "the measuring function of the reason," which tends to present human reason as a *non-measured measure* of morality.[2] With respect to the concept of nature, it is easy to detect an ambiguous terminology at this level of Rhonheimer's discourse. For example, he speaks (a) of a "nature" that does not contain the final moral orientation, and (b) of a "practical reason" that, consequently, "creates" (the moral order),[3] is the "measure of morality,"[4] "establishes the hierarchy,"[5] and "constitutes the difference between good and evil."[6] Elsewhere he speaks (a) of "natural inclinations" which do not contain in themselves the "ordering to the right end,"[7] and (b) of a "moral goodness," or "order of operative perfection (morality)," that goes "beyond the nature," "beyond the principles of the

I have in mind (especially in Rhonheimer) to avoid dualism. I only think that dualism remains as an unintended outcome of their philosophies.

2   M. Rhonheimer, *Natural Law and Practical Reason. A Thomist View of Moral Autonomy* [1987] (Fordham: New York, 2000), pp. 15–16, 307 ff; *La Prospettiva della Morale. Fondamenti dell'Etica Filosofica* (Armando Editore: Roma, 1994), pp. 127–128; "Sulla Fondazione di Norme Morali a Partire dalla Natura," in *Rivista di Filosofia Neo-Scolastica* 4 (1997): pp. 521–523. To avoid misunderstandings: I am not neglecting that Rhonheimer says explicitly that eternal law measures human reason. Even so, his view seems epistemologically much closer to a kind of Augustinian direct illumination by God than to a Thomistic (realistic) account of the way in which our intellect knows (and is measured by) the world God created. I think it is essential in order to understand Aquinas' view to focus on the existence of the eternal law in creatures as in the measured subjects. This existence gives our intellect a way to grasp, analogically and intentionally, the content of eternal law. On this point, see Chapters III and VII.

3   M. Rhonheimer, *Natural Law and Practical Reason*, op. cit., p. 69.

4   Ibid. p. 37; see also, pp. 40–42.

5   Ibid. p. 312.

6   Ibid. p. 311.

7   Ibid. p. 249.

essentia," and "beyond the order of nature."[8] For Rhonheimer, natural law is nothing more than the law of the practical reason. Consequently, "natural" refers to the nature of practical reason.

With regard to Finnis, Grisez, *et al.*, the tendency to which I am referring was already strongly criticized in terms of excessive separation between theoretical and practical reason, or—in the empiricist vocabulary—between facts (of nature) and values.[9] This way of thinking is typical of the world of analytic philosophy and, insofar as it underlines a complete autonomy of practical reason at the level of human value-knowledge, it can be properly called Kantian. Henry Veatch explained very well both the flaws of the "transcendental turn" in analytical philosophy and the reasonableness of a value-teleological reading of (the facts of) nature.[10] Yves Simon had already warned that the tendency of talking about values instead of natural laws is a dangerous outcome of immanentistic philosophy.[11]

1.1. Aquinas' Realism

In this regard, I would like to note that, on the basis of Aquinas' own gnosiology, we have to distinguish between three kinds of objects of human intellectual knowledge: (1) the ideas in themselves (*species intelligibiles*: object of second intention); (2) the bodily reality itself (*quidditas rei materialis*: proper object of first intention); and (3) the *ens in universali* (common object).[12]

---

8   Ibid. pp. 20–21.

9   See R. McInerny, "The Principles of Natural Law," in *The American Journal of Jurisprudence* 25 (1980); and the reply by J. Finnis and G. Grisez, "The Basic Principles of Natural Law: A Reply to Ralph McInerny," in *The American Journal of Jurisprudence* 26 (1981). See also, R.A. Gahl, Jr., *Practical Reasoning in the Foundation of Natural Law according to Grisez, Finnis, and Boyle* (Athenaeum Romanum Sanctae Crucis: Rome, 1994).

10   H.B. Veatch, *Human Rights: Fact or Fancy?* (Louisiana State University Press: Baton Rouge, 1985). See also, A.J. Lisska, *Aquinas's Theory of Natural Law: An Analytic Reconstruction* (Clarendon Press: Oxford, 1996).

11   Y. Simon, *The Tradition of Natural Law. A Philosopher's Reflections* (Fordham University Press: New York, 1965), pp. 50–51.

12   See, especially, Thomas Aquinas, *ST*, I, q. 85, a. 2; *De Veritate*, q. 1, a. 1 c. I will not explain here the meaning of the common object but let me refer, for

The first, says Aquinas, is not "the object itself" because the *species intelligibilis* is only "the form by which our intellect understands;" it is "the likeness [in us] of the thing understood [*similitudo rei intellectae*]."[13] Ideas are what actually exist in the intellect as they are abstracted from the particular, material things. But they are not what we actually think of, *id quod actu intelligitur*. The first and proper object of our thinking is, rather, the material thing itself—the *res*—insofar as it is intrinsically intelligible. It is the *quidditas, sive natura in materia corporali existens, de ratione autem hujus naturae est, quod in aliquo individuo existat*, through which our intellect "rises to a certain knowledge of things invisible."[14] Ideas (*species intelligibiles*) are instead the means by which our intellect knows and thinks of reality.

It is only in a second phase that we can think of our own thinking (reflect), i.e., think of the ideas we use to know reality: "*Sed quia intellectus supra seipsum reflectitur, secundum eandem reflexionem intelligit et suum intelligere, et speciem qua intelligit. Et sic species intellectiva secundario est id quod intelligitur. Sed id quod intelligitur primo, est res cuius species intelligibilis est similitudo.*"[15]

The ideas are therefore objects of second intention. They are the natures of the things *as known by us* (with all the limitations that this intentional relationship involves). However, the proper and first intention object is bodily reality itself: what we primarily think of, and know, in our constant, bodily, and existential contact with reality.

Now, even in light of this brief sketch, it should be evident that the values, at the level of our re-flective intellectual (practical) experience, are *species intelligibiles*: a second intention object. As such they are not what we actually know and think of. For example, our first intention is not for the value of friendship but for our best friend, Francesco. The value of friendship only exists in that relationship. Gnosiologically, our idea of friendship is an abstraction from the real, material friends we have: it is a *logical* entity. In turn, this means that in order to understand ethics we should not first focus on

all the topics of this section, to my *God and the Natural Law: A Rereading of Thomas Aquinas* (St. Augustine Press: South Bend, 2003).

13 *ST*, I. q. 85, a. 2 c.
14 *ST*, I, q. 84, a. 7 c.
15 *ST*, I, q. 85, a. 2.

our own thinking of values, rather on the teleological (ordered) material reality in which the values are *inscribed* or embodied (e.g., on the real friendship-relation between Francesco and I), and from which they are then *abstracted* by original insights of our reason. This also corresponds to the transcendental concept of good as a relation between *ens* and will. The will does not create anything, rather it goes toward the being known by the intellect. The consequences of this gnosiology for ethical discourse are significant. For example, we might think of the difference between trying to understand marriage either (a) by abstractly focusing on a kind of value of marriage in itself, or (b) by focusing on real happy marriages, that is on the value of marriage as the intrinsic teleological meaning inscribed in the two (bodily) sexes as they exist, interact, etc., in what we call "marriage."

2. Whose Nature?

The "Whose-Question" relates to a kind of reduction of morality to the intentionality of the agent, which loses sight of the objective ground to be found in a reality existing *outside* and *independently* from the agent's experience of values.[16] The Finnis-Grisez ethical methodology comes down to an analysis of the agent's intentionality toward the abstract (basic) values in themselves. What is immoral, according to this view, is simply going intentionally against one (or more) basic values. The evil of immoral actions seems equal to contradicting our own practical reason (our intentionality toward the values), as if every sin were *just* a sin against practical reason itself. This tendency looks very much like Abelard's ethics according to which what is morally important is only the consent of the will, and the external action does not add anything to the moral good or evil.[17]

An example of this is Rhonheimer's suggestion (which is actually timid and ambiguous in that he arguably contradicts it in other parts of his book) that "when someone kills an innocent person, the *moral* evil is not in the

---

16   It goes without saying that I continue to speak about *tendencies*, not about explicit and systematic elements, and tendencies that I see as connected with (and due to) a general philosophical background.

17   P. Abelard, *Ethics* [*Scito te Ipsum*], 25, 30, 35, 48. In P. Abelard, *Ethical Writings*, trans. P.V. Spade (Hackett: Indianapolis, IN, 1995).

death of the innocent but in the injustice of the murderer's will, in the deformation of his will."[18] To get an idea of the ethical paradox involved in this view, let us imagine an ideal moral world in which every punishment was objectively measured not according to the damage caused to the victims, but according to the degree of the aggressor's bad intention toward the values grasped by his practical reason.[19] Another clear example (to which

18   M. Rhonheimer, *Natural Law and Practical Reason*, pp. 328, 334, 396–397, 402. Grisez, Finnis, May and Boyle make a similar mistake: see below section 3, point f. I do not want of course to say that "the injustice of the murderer's will" is not a moral evil but, rather, that it is so because of the objective injustice/immorality of the death of the innocent. In the order of justice (which is neither *a-moral* nor *pre-moral*) the right (the *ius*) "besides its relation to the agent, is set up by its relation to others." Consequently, "a thing is said to be just, as having the rectitude of justice, when it is the term of an act of justice, without taking into account the way in which it is done by the agent" (*ST*, II-II, q. 57, a. 1 c). This means that, morally speaking, what matters is that the innocent does not die and, only secondarily that nobody wants to kill him.
  But what is the *objective* difference between an innocent dying in murder and an innocent dying of a natural cause (earthquake, etc.)? It is not just "the murderer's will?" The answer is no. The difference is that, according to justice, no innocent is to be killed by other human beings. Every innocent can claim a right to live from other human beings, but not from either God or every kind of natural event. This is the moral precept, and this is the moral order established by God. The term "right" makes (proper) sense only in the context of the relationships human beings have toward each other. And this means, in turn, that also the term "innocent," in the context of formulating the intrinsically evil action "killing the innocent," makes sense only in that same context. So, nobody is innocent with respect either to God or to natural events, and everyone is going to die. The death of the *innocent* (i.e., the death of he who has been unjustly killed by his fellow human beings) is an objective damage to the order established by God because, according to that order, the innocent had a *right* to live.

19   Usually, in criminal law once the guilt is ascertained, the better or worse quality of the agent's intentionality can lower or increase the punishment. But the relevant punishment to be lowered or increased is the one provided for by the law according to the objective damage caused by the crime to the common good. It goes without saying that the objective damage suffered by the victim is what the legislator should primarily look at in order to prudently evaluate the damage to the common good.

I will come back later) is Finnis', Grisez's and Boyle's suggestion that contraception and deliberate homicide belong to the same kind of evil action (contra-life): as if the death of an existing person were only a marginal circumstance with respect to the *genus* of the action, which must be determined *only by the agent's intentionality.*

These examples should be enough to show the point of my question: "Whose nature is the basis of ethics? *My* nature (the nature of my intentionality toward the values grasped by my practical reason) or a nature transcending me and that my intentionality should respect in order to be good?"

2.1. Why is the Good "Good"?

From the reductivist value-centered approach, several difficulties flow into ethical theory.[20] For example, think of the distinction between objective and subjective responsibility, or of the concept of non-guilty ignorance (both of which make secondary the importance of the agent's intentionality in itself). However, the main problem is perhaps that without connecting the values to the material structure of reality (the *bonum* to the *ens*), the very way of outlining values and of analyzing the agent's intentionality will be necessarily vague, not well determined, and *intuitive*. Intuitionism is actually a useful criticism of this immanentistic approach.[21]

---

20 For detailed criticisms see F. Di Blasi, *John Finnis* (Palermo: Phronesis, 2008); F. Di Blasi, "I Valori Fondamentali nella Teoria Neoclassica della Legge Naturale," *Rivista Internazionale di Filosofia del Diritto* 2 (1999); "Legge Naturale e Volontà di Dio: Finnis, Grisez, Suárez e la Teoria Convenzionale," *Iustitia*, 3 (2000).

21 In my book *John Finnis*, and in my article "I Valori Fondamentali nella Teoria Neoclassica della Legge Naturale" I show, e.g., that the descriptions of the basic values offered by Finnis, Grisez, and Boyle along the years, not only tend to change a lot and to become the more and more vague, but are also too shortly and simply sketched (no more than two or three pages each time); sometimes with clear contradictions, as in J. Finnis, *Natural Law and Natural Rights* (Clarendon Press: Oxford 1980), where "play" is, at the same time, a basic, incommensurable, value in chapter IV, and a kind of friendship (another incommensurable value) in chapter VI. Another, and more recent, example is the identification of marriage as another basic (irreducible, incommensurable) human good: G. Grisez, *The Way of the Lord Jesus: Living a Christian Life* (Vol.

Moreover, an existential doubt would otherwise dominate our lives: "Why are the values good?" If the values are good only because they are originally grasped as such by our practical reason, no other proof can be given for the real bounty of ethics than the existence in us of those original insights. The only possible salvation would be a sort of post-modern (Cartesian) external recourse to faith along the lines of "it is impossible that God is misleading me in my insights as to what is good." I think that there is something like this in Grisez, in his *hypotheses* of (and not analogical path to) the existence of God and God's freedom and *benevolence*, in his way of describing the value of religion,[22] in his *belief* that there is ultimately a connection between integral human fulfillment and human nature, etc. Moral bounty, in Grisez's view, is not written as such in the objective material world we see, which for similar reasons does not speak properly and directly even of God. This is another way of creating a separation between ethics and metaphysics. That is to say, a separation between natural finality and values, and between Creation (its intelligibility: the law as it exists in the measured subject) and God (the rational legislator).[23] Why should the basic human goods be *intelligible*—as Grisez likes to repeat—if not because they correspond to human nature? Here G.E. Moore's "open-question argument" would be appropriate: human values are always open to the question, "why?" The only possible answer to this question is nature. The only thing needed is a sound and viable (not factualistic) concept of nature.

It should go without saying that I am not questioning that the notion of good is *first* in the order of practical reason, that it is grounded on a kind

---

II, Franciscan Press: Quincy 1993); J. Finnis, *Aquinas: Moral, Political, and Legal Theory* (Oxford University Press: New York 1998). Now, the reader familiar with these writings cannot avoid raising the question: "How can marriage be incommensurable with, and irreducible to, at least the values of friendship and life?" If the act, e.g., of 'taking care of my children' can be described at the same time as an act of friendship, an act of love for my family, and an act of love for (human) life, the incommensurable values as described by Finnis and Grisez cannot account for the intentionality of that action.

22 See, G. Grisez, "Natural Law, God, Religion, and Human Fulfillment," in *The American Journal of Jurisprudence*.

23 See my, "The Role of God in the New Natural Law Theory," in *The National Catholic Bioethics Quarterly*, Spring 2013.

of original insight, or that, properly speaking, there is no deduction of ethics from metaphysics. Rather, I am questioning whether the original insight is grounded on our metaphysical knowledge of nature, and whether this metaphysical understanding is morally relevant.

An example of what I mean comes from *Contra Gentiles*, Book III, Chapter 141, "On the diversity and order of punishments." In this chapter we read that "external goods are subordinated to internal goods, and body to soul," and that "external and bodily goods are goods for man to the extent that they contribute to the good of reason, but to the extent that they hinder the rational good they turn into evils for man." From this we get a clear *moral* idea that we should have a greater fear of spiritual punishments than of bodily ones, and that "it will not be a punishment for a virtuous man if he be deprived of external goods as an aid to virtue." This moral insight as such cannot be deduced but still it is grounded on a theoretical understanding of what is higher and lower (subordinated) in human nature. This kind of *theoretical* "why" is precisely the final *moral* answer for which people always look.

3. Contraception and the Contra-Life Argument

It is well known that Finnis, Grisez, Boyle, and May propose an argument against contraception centered on an alleged *necessary* contra-life intention involved in every choice to use a contraceptive. Whatever further purpose one might have, they say, this choice's "relevant immediate intention [...] is that the prospective new life not begin."[24] Now, despite the great attention that these authors' views deserve, I have to say that in this particular case I find their argument interesting above all because of the great number of inconsistencies, and theses which are against common sense, that it entails. I think that scholars as brilliant as they are cannot lose sight of so many

---

24   G. Grisez, J. Boyle, J. Finnis, and W.E. May, "Every Marital Act Ought to be Open to New Life: Toward a Clearer Understanding," *The Thomist* 52 (1988): p. 370. The best criticism I know of their argument is J. Smith, *Humanae Vitae: A Generation Later* (The Catholic University of America Press: Washington, D.C. 1991), pp. 105–106, 340–370. There is also a short critique in M. Rhonheimer, *Etica della Procreazione* (Mursia: Roma 2000), pp. 37–40.

obvious points unless it is due to a deep misunderstanding at a very general philosophical level. If this is true, the need for clarifying this baseline misunderstanding is more important than any specific argument that it might engender.

Let me very briefly summarize the main points of their thesis on contraception:

a) They think that contraception is essentially immoral because it necessarily involves a contra-life intention that they describe in the following way: people who contracept "find the prospect [of a possible baby] repugnant," and their will is properly characterized, with respect to the baby, in terms of "practical hatred."[25]

b) They think that the definition of contraception does not involve any intention to enjoy sexual pleasure or engaging in sex.[26]

c) Consequently, they state that "the morality of contraception" does not belong to "sexual ethics."[27]

d) And since people who contracept only *"usually* [...] are interested in sexual intercourse,"[28] they say that "a dictator [...] who would engage in no sexual behavior whatsoever, and might not will any such behavior," but "who wanted to control population [...] might contracept by having a fertility-reducing additive put in the public water supply."[29]

e) Since "contraception must be defined by its [contra-life] intention,"[30] they think it is "similar to deliberate homicide."[31]

f) And, to make the way they are focusing on *intentionality* clear, they say that "although the goodness of the life which is destroyed provides the reason why deliberate killing is wrong, the moral evil of killing primarily is

---

25 "Every Marital Act Ought to be Open to New Life," op. cit., p. 373.
26 Ibid. p. 370. "Contraception," they write, "is only contingently related to marital intercourse. For the definition of contraception neither includes nor entails that one who does it engages in sexual intercourse, much less marital intercourse."
27 Ibid. p. 371.
28 Ibid. p. 373 (Emphasis mine)..
29 Ibid. pp. 369–70. It goes without saying that the dictator's action would better be described as violence against his citizens' freedom and bodily integrity.
30 Ibid. p. 371.
31 Ibid. p. 372.

in the killer's heart." They add, as an example of the same point, that "a man can commit adultery without ever touching a woman"[32] (as if the sixth commandment were exactly the same as the ninth).

g) Since contraception is always wrong because using contraceptives necessarily involves a contra-life intention, and since they agree that "women who are victims of rape" are "morally justified" in using contraceptives (of course, not abortive), they try to show that these women somehow choose to use contraceptives without a real intent to avoid conception. These women, they say, do it out of "a defense of the woman's ovum [...] against the rapist's sperm" but "*without ever projecting and rejecting the baby.*"[33] [It goes without saying that if this break between contraceptives and the agent's intentionality is possible their whole (contra-life-intention) argument fails because it would be possible to choose to use a contraceptive without having a contra-life intention.]

h) Even if it is possible for people who contracept to have the same good reasons as people who practice natural family planning (NFP), they also say that (a) contraception is wrong because of the contra-life choice "to impede the baby's coming to be," while (b) NFP is good because "it is a choice *not to do something* [...] with the *acceptance as side effects* of both the baby's not-coming-to-be and the bad consequences of his or her not-coming-to-be."[34] [Here, the mere difference between action and omission seems to enable change in the nature of the relevant human action. Moreover, the difference between end, means, and side effects becomes vague and confusing. The end of NFP's abstention is basically the same as contraception's positive act: to avoid—right now—having a baby. They are both, under this respect, a means to this end. How can it (the end) become an unintended side effect? And why only in the case of NFP?]

---

32   Ibid. pp. 372–373. Matthew 5:28 clearly indicates the distinction between sins of thought and sins of action (and between the sixth and the ninth commandment) when it adds the key words "in his heart." "But I say to you, everyone who looks at a woman with lust has already committed adultery with her in his heart." Committing adultery "in one's heart" is not the same as committing adultery for real, so to speak, by having sex with someone else.

33   "Every Marital Act Ought to be Open to New Life," op. cit., p. 390 (emphasis mine).

34   Ibid. pp. 401–2.

3.1. The Tendency against Philosophical Realism

My purpose now is not to dwell at length on all of Grisez, Finnis, May and Boyle's arguments on contraception. I am concerned here only with the philosophical tendency underlying their discussion. I think the above sketch is enough to state my point. What are the fathers of the "contra-life argument" looking at? It is not difficult to see that they are looking only at a value in itself and at our intentionality toward it. In doing so they attempt the impossible: connecting a *value* (which does not come from facts) with a factual state of affairs, i.e., connecting the contra-value intentionality with the mere *fact* of using contraceptives. It was probably while moving into a sort of ideal (Platonic) value-world that they lost sight of (material) reality and common sense: blurring the difference between contraception and NFP, between the fifth and the sixth commandments, and between justice and chastity, etc.

To a more *realist* eye, what is obvious about contraception is exactly the conjugal act and its nature (with the meanings inscribed in it). When we talk about contraception as a moral issue, we do not talk about factual instruments as such or about violence (as in the dictator's case). We talk, rather, about people who:

(a) Want to engage in a complete sexual act (this is the relevant *end*);

(b) For whatever reason (good or bad) do not now want to have a(nother) baby;

(c) Do not want to wait to have sex; and

(d) Decide to engage in sex while doing something to impede possible procreation (this is the contraceptive *means*).[35]

Beyond this description there is no moral question about contraception. That is why the (moral) definition of contraception includes the intention to have sex, and why contraception is not a sexual act in itself, of course,[36] but an obvious sin against the sixth commandment (for those who believe that it exists). Thus, it belongs to sexual ethics and to the virtue of chastity.

---

35 This is how Paul VI defines contraception: "Every action which, either in anticipation of the conjugal act, or in its accomplishment, or in the development of its natural consequences, proposes, whether as an end or as a means, to render procreation impossible" (*Humanae Vitae*, n. 14).

36 This is another confusing point of "Every Marital Act Ought to be Open to New Life" (see, especially pp. 369 and 371).

"Women who are victims of rape" do not have any intention to perform the conjugal act: that is why they do not commit the contraceptive intrinsically evil act. People who use NFP do not choose to perform the conjugal act at the cost of positively modifying its nature (which includes its cycles). The *bonum delectabile* (pleasure) does not prevail on the *bonum honestum*. That is why abstention is a different moral act than contraception: it involves a different end/means structure, and a different moral intentionality—not toward the end of not having a baby, of course, but toward the objective meaning of the conjugal act (i.e., respect *vs.* denial). It is, more or less, like abstaining from food when continuing to eat would require one to vomit—as apparently ancient Romans did, "eating till they vomited" and "vomiting in order to eat more."[37] These two choices (abstaining *vs.* vomiting) do have different moral intentions toward the objective meaning of eating (again, respect *vs.* denial).

Despite what it may seem, I do believe I am not sketching a sort of perverted faculty argument here. The conjugal act is something very special for human beings, and long before any theory comes to the picture: this is an undeniable *moral fact* and a starting point for the ethicist. The moral importance of the conjugal act must not be deduced, but explained. It is so important we do not have any sense of perfect marriage without it. Both traditional doctrine and common sense see the performance of the conjugal act as an essential element for making the marital bond perfect. The "first night" is the moment of full possession and of total self-giving. And it is a potentially procreative moment in which the other person with whom I become *one flesh*, precisely due to this total bodily union, becomes a potential father or a potential mother. The conjugal act is the only place in which the two ends of marriage (union and procreation) coexist *bodily*. In this act union is procreation and procreation is union. For a *philosophical realism*, this fact has tremendous importance.

Philosophical realism means that all our knowledge comes from our five (external) senses—from the material reality we experience. From this viewpoint, there is no dualism between body and spirit. If material reality does not speak to us of spiritual things, then we simply do not know

---

37   See G. Woolf, *Ancient Civilizations: The Illustrated Guide to Belief, Mythology and Art* (Thunder Bay Press: San Diego, CA 2005), p. 389.

spiritual things (soul, values, or God). If our knowledge of marriage, chastity, family, responsible parenthood, etc., does not come from material reality, then it is simply false. Yet it is true insofar as those concepts (marriage, family, etc.) are means by which our (theoretical and practical) intellect knows the *material* reality of the human being's existence as male and female. The existing (factual) reality of sex is what comes first, and our certainty in sexual ethics depends on how much it speaks clearly to us.

This is why the conjugal act is so important. It is simultaneously the summit of sexual reality and the clearest element of it. It is the aim of all our sexual attraction (the analogy with other animals is very helpful here). It makes the final meaning of the person's sexual identity undoubtedly clear, but it also clarifies that sexual union is not an end in itself. The summit of human bodily union is a pro*creative* moment that looks beyond the couple. That is why everybody spontaneously connects the reality of sex with marriage and the family. The point is that we know what marriage is—and we are certain about its two ends, about the evil of contraception, etc.—because the conjugal act is what it is, and not the other way around. There is no other sexual act—from holding hands to embracing, kissing or caressing each other—that has an intrinsic procreative meaning, although such acts do form part of the overall sexual picture of which the conjugal act is the highest point. This is why the conjugal act is the only specifically sexual act for which we have the moral problem of not separating the two meanings of marriage. This is also why if the conjugal act did not exist we could not be sure that marriage had two intrinsic and inseparable ends. Conjugal union (marriage) is the *theoretical* meaning of the existence of the twofold human being, and the conjugal act is the seat of that meaning.

I do not want now to develop a detailed argument against contraception. My only concern is to say that sexual ethics, far from committing itself to show that the immorality of contraception does not depend on the conjugal act's *nature*, should rather deepen the understanding of its nature and explain why it is so *important*.

4. Abstinence and Contraception

I think Rhonheimer's explanation of the immorality of contraception is more reasonable and refined than that of Grisez, Finnis, Boyle, and May.

He explicitly criticizes the contra-life argument and rightly underlines, for example, the ambiguity of talking about natural and artificial methods, the deep unity which exists between unitive and procreative meanings of conjugal love, the need for a deep understanding of the agents' intentionality towards that love, etc. However, Rhonheimer's basic methodology is harmed by the dualism he sees between nature and reason, or between bodily facts and rational values. In this respect, his approach to ethical issues is similar to Finnis', Grisez's, etc. For this reason his own argument against contraception cannot in the end reach the desired conclusion. Let me state very clearly once again that I am not saying that Rhonheimer's specific ethical arguments regarding contraception are similar to Finnis's, Grisez's etc., but that his general approach to ethics is.

The basic point governing Rhonheimer's ethical methodology is that the measure and rule of morality cannot be found in the order of nature—that is, in the natural inclination, "sexual drive,"[38] biological laws, or "biological-procreative openness"[39]—rather, in reason itself.[40] Consequently, in dealing with specific moral issues he tends to shift the focus from what he sees as the *mere biological facts* of human nature to the *general rational values* of practical reason, as if these values were somehow coming *from the outside* to inform human (factual) biological nature. This methodological step is dominated by the distinction/opposition between nature and reason as I already mentioned. It requires exactly the same further (but logically impossible) step we have already seen in the contra-life argument. It consists in an attempt to create a *necessary connection* between rational *values* and the mere *factual states of affairs*.

4.1. The Principle of Inseparability

In his most accurate and detailed study on the immorality of contraception,[41] Rhonheimer's argument explicitly takes three main steps:

38 M. Rhonheimer, *Natural Law and Practical Reason*, op. cit., p. 122.
39 Ibid. p. 114.
40 Ibid. p. 111.
41 M. Rhonheimer, *Etica della Procreazione*, op. cit. See also, "Contraception, Sexual Behavior, and Natural Law: Philosophical Foundation of the Norm of 'Humanae Vitae,'" in *The Linacre Quarterly* 56/2 (1989).

(1) explaining the anthropological meaning of the principle of inseparability and defining the object of the conjugal act (he says this is the corner-stone of the argument); (2) explaining the meaning of procreative responsibility in the context of a virtue-ethics; and (3) explaining the difference between contraceptive sex and periodic continence (he says this is the heart of the argument).[42]

The first step contains remarkable passages on the substantial bodily-spiritual unity of the human person[43] and on the marital union as the truth of human sexuality.[44] The principle of inseparability means that it is impossible to *intentionally* separate the two meanings of the conjugal act (unitive and procreative) without destroying both of them. This is because the procreative meaning essentially belongs to the same marital loving union (the inseparability of the two meanings is willed by God).[45]

Rhonheimer distinguishes very carefully between *mere biological* functions and *intentional* meanings. The meanings belong to the essence of the conjugal act as a human action. So, even biologically infertile acts can still be intentionally ordered by the couple to procreation. Without this intentionality even the unitive meaning would be destroyed.[46]

This distinction surprises me. If the meanings belong to the action as intentionally chosen, what Rhonheimer himself recognizes would become impossible. The possibility of reciprocal self-giving by the spouses in the conjugal act independent of the intention to procreate could not occur.[47] Another thing that surprises me is the distinction between "the traditional doctrine of the two ends of marriage" and the doctrine of "two meanings of the conjugal act." Rhonheimer thinks that the former is not concerned with intentionality but only with the description of marriage as "a special type *of social reality*." If it were not so, the (primary) procreative end would make the (secondary) loving union instrumental.[48] Now, my difficulty with this approach is not only that, following the same trend

42 See M. Rhonheimer, *Etica della Procreazione*, op. cit., p. 45.
43 Ibid. pp. 46–49.
44 Ibid. p. 60.
45 Ibid. pp. 52–58.
46 Ibid. p. 55.
47 Ibid. p. 58
48 Ibid. pp. 60–62.

of reasoning, the very love of God would make the other people (loved ultimately for God's sake) mere instruments; but above all that, in the history of canon law, the traditional doctrine of the ends of marriage is associated precisely to the understanding of the necessary intentionality the agents should have in order to contract a valid marriage. The traditional doctrine has always belonged to an ethical context and to the study of intentionality.

Finally, Rhonheimer defines the (intentional) object of the conjugal act as a "bodily loving union" which essentially includes the procreative meaning.[49] Yet, he hastens to add that up to this point there is nothing in his argument that can support the thesis of the immorality of contraception. We still do not know, he says, why the bond between the two meanings should be respected even at the level of every single conjugal act. To answer this question we need another argument showing that contraception is intrinsically opposed to "procreative responsibility."[50]

4.2. The Argument from Abstinence

The obvious question at this point is: "Why this need for another argument?" If the procreative meaning belongs essentially to the conjugal act and if, according to the principle of inseparability, it is impossible to intentionally separate the two meanings without destroying both of them, it should necessarily follow that not even *one* contraceptive conjugal act can be performed without simultaneously destroying the unitive meaning of it. This is why here I can interpret Rhonheimer only as shifting his focus from the material nature of the conjugal act to an abstract, general meaning of human love in itself.[51] Only if the procreative meaning belongs primarily to *conjugal love* do we still need the link with every single (conjugal) act. Moreover, from my point of view, Rhonheimer's new focus is another sign of his tendency to not pursue moral answers by means of an interpretation of nature.

Rhonheimer's proper argument against contraception begins with

49   Ibid. p. 59.
50   Ibid. pp. 64–5.
51   Ibid. pp. 70–71: here this shift appears clearly.

"procreative responsibility" (or "responsible parenthood")[52] as an integral part of the virtue of chastity. I like to call it the *argument from abstinence* because its methodological hinge seems to be *the positive need for abstinence* in order to live chastity and responsible parenthood.[53] I apologize for the oversimplification of a nuanced and rich analysis, but I will summarize his argument in the following three points:

(1) Procreative responsibility (or responsible parenthood)—defined as "the making use of, and compliance with, a natural striving, in the framework of an *ordinatio rationis*"[54]—requires the exercise of the virtue of chastity; or better, it is part of this virtue.

(2) Chastity—"the virtue that establishes and preserves the order and measure of human sexuality"[55]—requires marital abstinence.

(3) Marital abstinence—"the governing of the natural inclination through reason and will;"[56] the "*mastery over the sexual drive itself*;"[57] the "bodily act of procreative responsibility"[58]—cannot be exercised in contraceptive acts.

4.3. Abstinence from What?

In *Natural Law and Practical Reason* the positive need for abstinence was much clearer. However, Rhonheimer's view does not seem substantially different in *Etica della Procreazione*, where the focus is always on the recurrent statement that in contraceptive acts spouses do not need to modify their sexual behavior according to procreative responsibility (or the governance

---

52 The difference between these two concepts is not very clear in Rhonheimer: see, ibid. pp. 66–8.

53 Ibid. p. 107: "Contraception is a measure that make *superfluous* procreative responsibility in the performance of sexual acts and the corresponding virtue of *temperantia*."

54 *Natural Law and Practical Reason*, op. cit., p. 112; *Etica della Procreazione*, op. cit., p. 68.

55 *Natural Law and Practical Reason*, op. cit., p. 112; *Etica della Procreazione*, op. cit., pp. 67, 69.

56 *Natural Law and Practical Reason*, op. cit., p. 114.

57 Ibid., p. 122.

58 *Etica della Procreazione*, op. cit., pp. 72–3.

of reason).[59] In any case, it is evident that Rhonheimer's argument works (even if tautologically) insofar as abstinence is defined either as required by procreative responsibility or as required by the virtue of chastity. Now, the obvious question is, "Why should governance, mastery, or procreative responsibility necessarily require the *negative act* of abstinence?"

I agree, of course, that chastity requires abstinence, but only accidentally: when the values inscribed in human sexuality cannot be realized by engaging in a sexual activity here, now, and in this particular way. The reason for abstinence is the *factual*, material way in which human sexuality exists. This factual existence is the only starting point for answering the question, "Abstinence from what?" We must abstain from homosexual actions, for example, because they deny the male and female sexual identity and its unitive and procreative meaning. We must abstain from sodomy because it denies the objective unitive and procreative meaning of genital organs. We must abstain from contraception because it denies the objective unitive and procreative meaning of the conjugal act. If we do not *abstain* in all these cases, we go against the love of God (who made the natural order in this way) and we lose a contemplative (self-giving) moral disposition toward reality. We turn reality into an instrument of our pleasures and desires.

It seems to me that Rhonheimer's argument cannot answer the question "Abstinence from what?" precisely because it loses sight of the *nature* of the conjugal act.[60] It cannot clarify why contraception should be an intrinsically evil act—why it cannot be done even as an exception. In other words, it cannot cover the distance between the general need for abstinence and every single action. As a matter of fact, we can easily imagine a couple that lives in a better way with chastity and abstinence than many others, and use contraception only every once in a while. We can compare it with another imaginary couple that has never been abstinent at all and has fifteen

---

59 See, ibid. pp. 75–77, 107.

60 Actually, in his second-step attempt to connect value and fact he sometimes timidly suggests that the relevant facts are not *just facts* (see. e.g., *Natural Law and Practical Reason*, p. 120; *Etica della Procreazione*, p. 77). But this little welcomed inconsistency is not enough to cancel the break between values and nature due to his "without-*ordinatio-ad-debitum*-order-of-nature" premise.

kids after fifteen years of marriage. If abstinence is the key to sexual morality, why do we not talk about intrinsically evil actions in this last case? Actually, it seems that Rhonheimer tends to refer to people who use contraceptives as those who cannot control their sexual impulses and are not able to modify their sexual behavior according to a reasonable plan.[61] It goes without saying that in plenty of cases this is not true at all.

Rhonheimer's argument tends to reverse the terms of the question about abstinence in a way that goes against common sense. Abstinence is not a positive requirement at least in this sense. We do not have to live our lives looking for ways to abstain. Rather, it is always a negative requirement. That is to say, we have to abstain every time looking for pleasure would deny (or endanger) the meaning of our *bonum honestum*, which in the case at hand is our sexual identity.

4.4. The Starting Point

It is obvious, in a sense, that the starting point of an argument against contraception cannot be responsible parenthood—or procreative responsibility—in itself, because the point of responsible parenthood is to understand if it is good or not to have a child right now, which is a very prudential question. On the other hand, the point of contraception is that, whatever the objective good with regard to having children might be, one cannot voluntarily engage in complete sexual intercourse using contraception. Refusing contraception does not essentially involve actualizing a responsible-parenthood intentionality. To put it another way, if a married couple has a *non-contraceptive* conjugal act in the context of a *totally irresponsible* attitude towards children, we still do not talk about intrinsically evil actions, but if the couple uses contraceptives in the context of a perfectly good reason to delay the pregnancy, we do. In both cases the intrinsically-good/evil question does not depend on responsible parenthood.

The starting point cannot even be the twofold meaning of the conjugal *love* in itself. The obvious reason for this is that there are thousands of morally good ways to instantiate conjugal love (hugging, kissing, planning a vacation together, etc.), and *all but one* are allowed even when the couple

61 M. Rhonheimer, *Etica della Procreazione*, op. cit. pp. 75–7.

does not want to have a child. The *required abstinence* is only for the conjugal act. Of course, then, there should be something in the *nature* of the conjugal act that explains the precise reason of the immorality of contraception.

5. Value of Marriage and Acts of the Reproductive Type

In their "Marriage and the Liberal Imagination,"[62] Robert George and Gerard Bradley criticize Stephen Macedo's thesis that "whatever values can possibly be realized in the acts of genital union of sterile spouses can equally be realized by those spouses—or similarly committed couples, whether of the same sex or opposite sexes—in oral or anal sex acts."[63] Macedo claims that the point of sex in an infertile marriage, since it is not reproduction, should necessarily be the same as it is in the case of loving gay couples. In response, George and Bradley think that a sound criticism of Macedo's view implies, first of all, rejecting the traditional doctrine of reproduction as the primary end of marriage,[64] and, second, focusing on the value of marriage in itself.

Their argument involves two basic steps. (1) On the one hand, they maintain that sex is morally right only when it aims at the "intrinsic good of marriage itself"; otherwise, it "damages personal (and interpersonal) integrity by reducing persons' bodies to the status of means to extrinsic ends"[65] (including the reproductive end). (2) On the other hand, they explain that "sodomy is intrinsically not-marital" because marriage, "considered as a two-in-one-flesh communion of persons," "is consummated and actualized by acts of the reproductive type."[66]

---

62 I quote from the reprinted version in R.P. George, *In Defense of Natural Law* (Oxford University Press: Oxford, 1999), pp. 139–160.

63 Ibid. pp. 139–40. Macedo's article to which they are referring to is: "Homosexuality and the Conservative Mind" in *Georgetown Law Journal* 84 (1995).

64 R. George, G. Bradley, "Marriage and the Liberal Imagination," op. cit., p. 141: "St Augustine, among others, seems to have treated marriage as a purely instrumental good whose primary value has to do with procreation and the nurturing of new human beings."

65 Ibid. p. 147.

66 To my current purpose (i.e., underlining their general philosophical tendency) it is not relevant if either George or Bradley changed their respective explanations after the article that is partially reproduced here.

Now, what surprises me most in this strategy is that it would have been much easier to say (a) that primary end does not mean singular end, and (b) that what is immoral is to pervert the primary end, not to enjoy the secondary. For example, there is nothing wrong in eating ice-cream just because we like it, even if it does not contain any nutritive value. Yet, it would be immoral to eat thirty-five ice-cream cones using special drugs to impede the digestion process in order to eat more. Pleasure is not wrong as long as it does not deny the natural order. In the same way, enjoying sex is good insofar as nothing is done which denies either its reproductive or its unitive meaning. From my point of view, the only way to understand why sodomitical acts deny the meaning of marriage is to focus on the perversion they imply with respect to the way sexual identity and the genital organs are made and how they are perceived. This perversion is evident to all people who are willing to look sincerely at the *facts* of the natural order. To them St. Paul's simple warning is enough: "For this cause God has given them up to shameful lusts; for their women have exchanged the natural use for that which is against nature, and in like manner the men also, having abandoned the natural use of the woman, have burned in their lusts one towards another, men with men doing shameless things and receiving in themselves the fitting recompense of their perversity" (*Rm* 1: 26–7).

However, George and Bradley seem unwilling: (a) to focus on evident facts of nature, and (b) to explain their meaning with respect to the human being as a whole (union between body and spirit; sexual identity as part of personal identity; relationship between pleasure and good; love of God and self-giving; etc.). Rather, they choose to go the other way around by (a) focusing on a value of marriage that in itself does not depend on reproduction, and then (b) trying to connect it to a supposedly extrinsic—factual—state of affairs, which is the reproductive character of the conjugal act. Their attempt cannot work.

5.1. Reproduction and the Definition of Marriage

First of all, George and Bradley claim that reproduction is secondary or extrinsic to marriage, but the definition of marriage they offer makes sense only if procreation *is* the primary intrinsic end of marriage. They define marriage as a "two-in-one-flesh communion of persons that is consummated and actualized by sexual acts of the reproductive type."[67] How could the objective character of marriage's *proper acts* be either secondary or extrinsic to the good of marriage? This is a logical point. If (a) reproduction is what intrinsically defines the acts of the reproductive type as the *specific* kind of acts they are, i.e. those acts objectively ordered to reproduction, and (b) these *specific* acts as such are what consummate and actualize the good of marriage (defining it as the *specific* communion of persons it is), it follows that (c) procreation, far from being extrinsic or secondary, is exactly the *defining trait* of marriage as a *specific* communion of persons.

5.2. Intentionality and Technical Necessity

They could protest that I am missing their point, i.e., that to commit a "sexual act of the reproductive type" does not mean necessarily to tend intentionally to the end of reproduction. Actually, they assert quite clearly that "spouses have a reason to mate quite irrespective of whether their marriage will, or even can, be productive."[68]

Yet given their definition of marriage this sounds really strange. We have acts of the reproductive type, which (a) actualize marriage but (b) are committed without any relevance, according to the agents' intentionality, for procreation (i.e., for their objective meaning as acts of the reproductive type). In this case, the term "act," as used in the phrase "acts of the reproductive type," should logically refer not to *human acts*—which, according to their theory must always be defined by the agent's intentionality, as *what is chosen*—but to some factual body-joining mechanism. If so, that is, if the defining character of the relevant acts does not have any intrinsic value in the very process of committing them, the link between these acts and the good of marriage does not have anything to do with values but is rather a kind of *technical necessity*. It is like saying: "As a matter of *fact*, you cannot actualize the good of marriage other than by engaging yourself in that material situation." Such technical necessity should be explained accurately. If it were true, for example, we could no longer exclude as immoral the sexual

---

67   R. P. George, G. Bradley, "Marriage and the Liberal Imagination," op. cit., p. 139.
68   Ibid. p. 147.

acts committed by someone who, after a successful sex-change operation, was able to mate according to the acts of the reproductive type.

Alas, this technical necessity is inexplicable and the *non sequitur* remains. If reproduction does not have anything to do with the intentionality that spouses should have toward the good or value of marriage, then spouses should be excused if they do not intentionally pursue "acts of the reproductive type" when they want to actualize their marriage.

5.3. Naturalistic Fallacy

But we must go further. Making the acts of the reproductive type the core of the definition of marriage would imply—according to the interpretation of the is-ought question that George and Bradley share with Grisez and Finnis—committing a naturalistic fallacy, that is, trying to confer an absolute value to a *factual* state of affairs. It would be like trying to create a *necessary* link between the value of marriage, on the one hand, and the biological function (reproduction) of some *material* act, on the other. George and Bradley would commit the very logical mistake that all the new-classical theorists accuse the so-called conventional natural law theory of having committed.

Of course, the problem here does not lie in considering whether or not *reproduction* is a part of the value of marriage.[69] Even in this case we could pursue reproduction (and marriage as well) outside of the acts of the reproductive type (e.g., through the in-vitro-fertilization). The problem lies in the attempt to create a *necessary* connection between a general rational value (that does not come from nature), on the one hand, and a particular factual situation (performing acts of the reproductive type), on the other.

5.4. Narrow Starting-Point and Wrong Conclusion

Even if we agree on the existence of a kind of necessary link between marriage and sexual acts of the reproductive type, it would appear to mean that

---

69   As George does, together with Patrick Lee, in "What Sex Can Be: Self-Alienation, Illusion or One-Flesh Union," in R.P. George, *In Defense of Natural Law* (Oxford University Press: Oxford, 1999), pp. 161–83.

no other act could actualize the good of marriage, and that every other kind of act would be immoral. What is even more stunning is how narrow the proposed definition of marriage is, so narrow in fact that it cannot work as it is meant to work.

Let us recall George and Bradley's strategy. In short, they want to discover a criterion to judge the morality and immorality of sexual acts. The criterion they find is that only *marital* acts are morally good. Of course, that begs the question of what is marital, and they answer, "sexual acts of the reproductive type." So, when sexual acts are not of the reproductive type we are able to argue that they are *non-marital* and, therefore, *immoral*. However, this argument proves too much because it tries to use (in a mere material way) the most unitive sexual act as the only criterion of morality in marriage.

As I say above in the section on contraception, there are plenty of ways (more or less sexual) to actualize the good of marriage, from giving a kiss and living together, to choosing the house, the appropriate school for the kids, etc. This is why, for example, spouses can live a wonderful marriage even when, because of an accident, they become unable to have complete sexual intercourse. Yet, if we agree that sexual acts of the reproductive type are (maybe the most important but) not the only possible *marital acts*, and that there are a number of other sexual acts (kissing, embracing, caressing, etc.) which are not intrinsically evil, then the original strategy to condemn sodomy appears definitively frustrated, and the proposed definition of marriage inadequate.

In fact, this is where the entire problems lies. George and Bradley's starting point is inadequate, not only because the conjugal act is not the only marital act, but also because it is not just a sexual act of the reproductive type. The conjugal act is rather an act with a twofold meaning: unitive and procreative. It is an act in which the unitive meaning exists in, and is qualified by, the natural reproductive structure of human sexuality. Without knowing this natural structure we would not even know what marital unity really means.

Paradoxically, while trying to criticize the primacy of procreation, George and Bradley make it the only defining trait of the conjugal act. This is why an unintended but necessary consequence of their description is that spouses cannot engage in sexual intercourse without tending to the reproductive end.

Another unintended consequence is that sexual intercourse becomes the only way to actualize the good of marriage.

6. Sketching Aquinas' Approach to Nature as the Basis of Morality[70]

In Chapter 129 of the third book of the *Summa Contra Gentiles* Aquinas tries to show "that things prescribed by divine [revealed] law are right, not only because they are put forth by law, but also because they are in accord with nature [*secundum naturam*]."[71] Generally speaking, in the part of the *Contra Gentiles* in which he deals with the different kinds of moral precepts it is clear that: (1) *agere secundum rationem* (acting according to reason) is equal to *agere secundum ordinem naturalem* (acting according to the natural order); and (2) understanding the order of nature requires understanding: (a) its natural ends or goods; (b) the natural measures according to which those ends should be pursued; and (c) the natural hierarchy existing between the various ends. Accordingly, Aquinas' description of the natural order is much richer than the perverted faculty argument suggests.

To begin with, let us see how the term *ordo naturalis* appears in Chapter 129:

> Indeed, as a result of the precepts of divine law, man's mind is subordinated to God, and all other things that are in man's power are ordered under reason. Now, the natural order requires [*naturalis ordo requirit*] that lower things be subject to higher things. Therefore, the things prescribed by divine law are naturally right in themselves [*naturaliter recta*].

The meaning of this passage is quite clear. The divine revealed law contains a moral hierarchy. Therefore, what the divine law prescribes is *etiam secundum naturam* precisely because the natural order possesses the same moral hierarchy. But let us continue:

70 This section is an excerpt of a longer argument I develop in *God and the Natural Law*, op. cit. See Chapter III, section 4.

71 *CG*, III, Ch. 129.

Again, according to the natural order [*secundum naturalem or-dinem*], the body of man is for the sake of his soul and the lower powers of the soul are for the sake of reason, just as in other things matter is for the sake of form and instruments are for the sake of the principal agent. But, because of one thing being ordered to another, it ought to furnish help to that other, and not offer it any hindrance. So, it is naturally right [*naturaliter rectum*] for the body and the lower powers of the soul to be so managed by man that thereby his activity of reason, and his good, are least hindered and are, instead, helped. But, if it happens otherwise, the result will naturally be sinful. Therefore, drinking bouts and feastings, and inordinate sexual activities through which rational activity is hindered, and domination by the passions which do not permit free judgment of reason—these are naturally evil things [*sunt naturaliter mala*].

In this passage, both the existence of an intelligible hierarchy in the natural order and the grounding of the moral conclusion upon the understanding of the natural order are unquestionable. Yet the natural order also contains *the measure* according to which we should use the "lower things":

Furthermore, we showed above that man has this natural endowment, he may use lower things for the needs of his life. Now, there is a definite measure [*mensura determinata*] according to which the use of the aforesaid things is proper to human life, and if this measure is set aside the result is harmful to man, as is evident in the immoderate eating of food. Therefore, there are some human acts that are naturally fitting [*naturaliter convenientes*] and others that are naturally unfitting [*naturaliter inconvenientes*].

In Chapter 129, the natural inclinations of the order of nature also include the inclination to God. This is consistent with the meaning of the entire chapter because (a) the divine law requires the love of God as the ultimate end, and (b) it should also be, under this respect, *secundum naturam* (in conformity with nature).

Besides, those acts by which he inclines towards his natural end [*finem naturalem*] are naturally appropriate to an agent, but those that have the contrary effect are naturally inappropriate to the agent. Now, we showed above that man is naturally ordered to God as his end [*homo naturaliter ordinatur in Deum sicut in finem*]. Therefore, the things by which man is brought to the knowledge and love of God are naturally right, but whatever things have the contrary effect are naturally evil for man.

Finally, the chapter concludes:

Therefore, it is clear that good and evil in human activities [*bonum et malum in humanis actibus*] are based not only on the prescription of law, but also on the natural order [*non solum sunt secundum legis positionem, sed secundum naturalem ordinem*].

In light of this sketch of Aquinas' approach, the following statement that we find in Rhonheimer's book is surprising: "If we begin this way, and say that 'nature' is the norm of morality—as *mensura* (measure) or *regula* (rule) [...] we have disoriented ourselves in gaining access to the texts of St. Thomas, in which one searches in vain for a statement that nature is the measure of what is good."[72] Just as surprising is the claim that "the assumption that practical judgments are ultimately grounded in theoretical judgments about the 'order of nature'" was "not at all" Thomas's viewpoint.[73] As a matter of fact, there is no doubt that, in the passages I just cited from Aquinas, nature is *methodologically investigated* as the norm and measure of what is good, and that practical judgments are ultimately grounded in theoretical judgments about the order of nature.

There is a very interesting passage in the *Contra Gentiles* that relates the *ordo naturalis* to the *agere secundum rationem*. Let us read it.

Just as the exercise of sexual capacities is without sin, provided it be carried on with reason [*si secundum rationem fiat*], so also

72 M. Rhonheimer, *Natural Law and Practical Reason*, p. 8.
73 See ibid. p. 555.

in the case of the use of food. Now, any action is performed in accord with reason [*secundum rationem*] when it is ordered in keeping with what befits its proper end [*quando ordinatur secundum quod congruit debito fini*]. But the proper end of taking food is the preservation of the body by nutrition. So, whatever food can contribute to this end may be taken without sin. Therefore, the taking of food is not in itself a sin.[74]

It goes without saying that in this passage Aquinas leaves the natural hierarchy out of consideration. The actual question is only about the intrinsic goodness of eating (or having sexual relations). Nevertheless, the use of the term *secundum rationem* is clarifying. *Secundum rationem* is whatever "befits its proper end." Therefore, if an action is conformed to a natural inclination's proper end it is, in itself, *secundum rationem* and not evil—it could become evil (not *secundum rationem*) only under the hierarchical point of view: if, here and now, it goes against the proper end of a higher natural inclination. This natural-hierarchy-conformity character of the moral action is stressed in another passage of the *Contra Gentiles*:

> But sin does occur in our act of appetition, because, since our nature [*natura nostra*] is composed of the spiritual and the corporeal there are several goods for us. Our good in regard to understanding is indeed different from what it is according to sensation, or even according to the body. Now, there is a certain order [*ordo quidam est*] of these various things that are man's goods, based on the fact that what is less primary is subordinated to what is more primary. Hence, a sin occurs in our will when, failing to observe this order [*tali ordine non servato*], we desire what is only relatively good for us [*secundum quid*], in opposition to what is absolutely good [*simpliciter*].[75]

I think it should be clear enough that, for Aquinas, we act *secundum rationem* when we (try to) respect the order of nature in all its intelligible

---

74 *CG*, III, Ch. 127.
75 Ibid. Ch. 108.

aspects as we know them. Yet before ending this chapter I would like to quote a long passage in order to give a clear example of Aquinas' manner of doing ethics by way of reading the (*facts* of the) natural order. I think that many modern misinterpretations of his ethics come, not from mis-reading specific points, but from a general inability to adopt either his own point of view on nature or, that is to say, his ethical methodology. The passage I have in mind involves an argument against the particular case of fornication in which the agents do not take any precautions to avoid a possible pregnancy (Aquinas methodologically distinguishes this case from the other in which the fornicators use contraception).[76] Going slowly through Aquinas' words, the reader will appreciate his style and his way of looking at reality. I am sure that it will become evident *in what sense* there is no difference in Aquinas' ethics between the *facts* of nature and the values grasped by our practical reason.

> Likewise, it must also be contrary to the good for man if the semen be emitted under conditions such that generation could result but the proper upbringing would be prevented. We should take into consideration the fact that, among some animals where the female is able to take care of the upbringing of offspring, male and female do not remain together for any time after the act of generation. This is obviously the case with dogs. But in the case of animals of which the female is not able to provide for the upbringing of offspring, the male and female do stay together after the act of generation as long as is necessary for the upbringing and instruction of the offspring. Examples are found among certain species of birds whose young are not able to seek out food for themselves immediately after hatching. In fact, since a bird does not nourish its young with milk, made available by nature as it were, as occurs in the case of quadrupeds, but the bird must look elsewhere for food for its young, and since besides this it must protect them by sitting on them, the female is not able to do this by herself. So, as a result

76 I explain in detail Aquinas' twofold case against fornication in *God and the Natural Law*, op. cit. See Chapter III, section 4.

of divine providence, there is naturally implanted in the male
of these animals a tendency to remain with the female in order
to bring up the young. Now, it is abundantly evident that the
female in the human species is not at all able to take care of the
upbringing of offspring by herself, since the needs of human
life demand many things which cannot be provided by one person alone. Therefore, it is appropriate to human nature [*est igitur conveniens secundum naturam humanam*] that a man remain
together with a woman after the generative act, and not leave
her immediately to have such relations with another woman, as
is the practice with fornicators.

Nor, indeed, is the fact that a woman may be able by means
of her own wealth to care for the child by herself an obstacle to
this argument. For natural rectitude in human acts [*rectitudo
naturalis in humanis actibus*] is not dependent on things accidentally possible in the case of one individual, but, rather, on
those conditions which accompany the entire species [*secundum
ea quae totam speciem consequuntur*].

Again, we must consider that in the human species offspring
require not only nourishment for the body, as in the case of
other animals, but also education for the soul. For other animals
naturally possess their own kinds of prudence whereby they are
enabled to take care of themselves. But a man lives by reason,
which he must develop by lengthy, temporal experience so that
he may achieve prudence. Hence, children must be instructed
by parents who are already experienced people. Nor are they
able to receive such instruction as soon as they are born, but
after a long time, and especially after they have reached the age
of discretion. Moreover, a long time is needed for this instruction. Then, too, because of the impulsion of the passions,
through which prudent judgment is vitiated, they require not
merely instruction but correction. Now, a woman alone is not
adequate to this task; rather, this demands the work of husband,
in whom reason is more developed for giving instruction and
strength is more available for giving punishment. Therefore, in
the human species, it is not enough, as in the case of birds, to

devote a small amount of time to bringing up offspring, for a long period of life is required. Hence, since among all animals it is necessary for male and female to remain together as long as the work of the father is needed by the offspring, it is natural to the human being [*naturale est homini*] for the man to establish a lasting association with a designated woman, over no short period of time. Now, we call this society matrimony. Therefore, matrimony is natural for man [*matrimonium homini naturale*], and promiscuous performance of the sexual act, outside matrimony, is contrary to man's good [*contra hominis bonum*]. For this reason, it must be a sin.[77]

Of course, Aquinas is not undertaking here an explanation of the indissolubility of marriage, nor does he want to analyze all the possible reasons why matrimony is natural for man. Instead, he is merely focusing on those aspects of the natural order that seem to him sufficient to conclude that there is a need for a lasting association, and that promiscuous performance of the sexual act, outside matrimony, is contrary to man's good. If we do not pay too much attention to his *cultural* idea of men and women, and if we add to his picture our much deeper knowledge and sensitivity about the importance of both father and mother for the lives of the children in all their aspects, in other words if we focus on the rationale of the argument in itself, we will have a good idea of Aquinas' reasonable way of understanding ethics by reading the natural order.

---

77   *CG*, III, Ch. 122.

VII.
NATURAL LAW AS INCLINATION TO GOD

This chapter aims to contribute to the debates over faith and reason and the interpretation of Thomas Aquinas' ethics. More particularly, my goal is to clarify how according to Christian thought one can speak of *natural law as an inclination to God*. To do so I adopt an analytic methodology, explaining the relevant concepts involved in the title one by one, and trying to make its overall meaning understandable and reasonable. Of course, talking about inclination to God is not the only way to speak of natural law but, as I hope to show, it is a relevant and revealing one.

Although my approach here is philosophical, I will also reflect on some central notions of Catholic faith and doctrine. From this viewpoint, Aquinas' teaching on natural law deserves special attention not only because he is the most important figure in the history of natural law theory, but above all because he is the *Doctor Communis* of the Catholic Church.

Here are a few other methodological premises:

I will try to be as brief as I can. It is not my intention to deal here with either the current or the historical debate on natural law theory, nor is it my intention to delve deeply into the many topics traditionally related to it.[1] I only want to convey as clearly as possible some key interpretative principles about both Aquinas' thought and Catholic doctrine. Those who are well trained in natural law theory will easily recognize the many nuances and implications of my discussion.

I will also try to be an old-fashioned scholastic by using reason in order to understand the faith better and more consistently. I maintain (a) that

---

1   For a fuller discussion, see in addition to the other chapters of this book, F. Di Blasi, *God and the Natural Law*; and, Idem, "Natural Law and Natural Rights," in A. C. GRAYLING AND A. PYLE (eds.), *Encyclopedia of British Philosophy* (Thoemmes Continuum: Bristol, 2006).

there is a formal distinction between truths known in the light of faith and truths known by unaided reason, and at the same time (b) that there is a unity of knowledge. That is to say, there is one truth but two means by which man comes to know it: revelation (faith) and natural reason. The proper order between these two means of knowing is contained in St. Anselm's *credo ut intelligam*. In the words of the Pope St. John Paul II's *Fides et Ratio*:

> faith liberates reason in so far as it allows reason to attain cor-
> rectly what it seeks to know and to place it within the ultimate
> order of things, in which everything acquires true meaning. In
> brief, human beings attain truth by way of reason because, en-
> lightened by faith, they discover the deeper meaning of all
> things and most especially of their own existence.[2]

1. Faith and Natural Law

Before beginning an analytic explanation of the phrase *natural law as inclination to God*, I would like to recall, in this and the next section, some central points of Catholic doctrine regarding natural law, as well as the
traditional definition of ethics in terms of its material and formal objects.
As we engage in our main analysis, I hope that the reader will appreciate
the harmony and consistency between these points and Aquinas' view of
natural law theory.

1.1. Revelation and Natural Law

Natural law belongs to the *depositum fidei*. That is to say, it does not belong
only to the so-called *natural revelation*—i.e., to what God revealed to man
about himself and his will through the perfections of nature—but it belongs
also to *supernatural revelation*—i.e., to what God revealed to human reason
through the Tradition of the Church and the inspired authors of the Bible.
Therefore, both the existence and the content of natural law are at the same
time truths that belong to human reason and to the faith.

2   John Paul II, *Fides et Ratio*, n. 20.

1.2. Natural Law and the Covenant

Natural law indicates what Jews, Christians, and all human beings are called to do even before receiving the highest demands coming from the new law: the law of grace and the sacraments. In other words, natural law is the content of what can be called the basic covenant between God and the human beings. This covenant depends on the primary relationship that binds creatures to their Creator, and which invites human beings to a loving answer to the gifts of existence, of freedom, and of the responsibility of being *ministers* of this world. As ministers, we are the only beings able to understand it according to the truth and to knowingly direct it back to God the Creator. Natural law is the only path to the love of God: "He that hath my commandments, and keepeth them; he it is that loveth me" (John 14:21).

1.3. The Pedagogical Character of the Law and the Commandments

Many people today try to remove the concepts of law and authority from ethical theory to the advantage of some ideals of ethical spontaneity and autonomy. Thus, it is especially worthwhile to reflect on the fact that both biblical pedagogy and the tradition of the Church have always presented the demands of the moral life by using the semantics of *obedience to the law of God*, which is not only the natural law but also, and more generally, the eternal law and the divine positive law from the old and the new covenant. The Commandments given to Moses have always been understood as a perfect historical expression of the natural law and, therefore, as the basis and the ground of man's moral life. The recent *Catechism of the Catholic Church* follows this ancient tradition, and presents the moral life of the faithful by commenting on the Ten Commandments one by one. With regard to ethics and the moral life, the concept of law and more specifically of natural law is not merely a part (that can be neglected or disregarded) of revelation but is instead its core. It is the right dialectic of the biblical moral life as *obedience* (loving-God-more-than-ourselves) *versus disobedience* (loving-ourselves-more-than-God).

1.4. Natural Law, Free Obedience, and Moral Conscience

In this context, the main conceptual structure underneath John Paul II's encyclical letter *Veritatis Splendor*—on the fundamentals of the Catholic Church's moral teaching—can be correctly understood. This structure rests entirely on the relationship between the concepts of freedom, law, and moral conscience. Human beings' true freedom resides in listening to the law of God, which manifests itself in our moral conscience. This is where we produce judgments about the good and the evil of every action, thought, and omission. Therefore, listening to our moral conscience is an act of obedience to the law: "Moral conscience does not close man within an insurmountable and impenetrable solitude, but opens him to the call, to the voice of God. In this, and not in anything else, lies the entire mystery and the dignity of the moral conscience: in being the place, the sacred place where God speaks to man."[3]

Here, it clearly appears that *legal language*—i.e., the language of the law—does not have just a pedagogical meaning in the Bible or the Catechism. Rather, it is a language chosen by God, which expresses an intrinsic

---

3   John Paul II, *Veritatis Splendor*, n. 58. See also, Pastoral Constitution on the Church in the Modern World *Gaudium et Spes*: "In the depths of his conscience, man detects a law which he does not impose upon himself, but which holds him to obedience. Always summoning him to love good and avoid evil, the voice of conscience when necessary speaks to his heart: do this, shun that. For man has in his heart a law written by God; to obey it is the very dignity of man; according to it he will be judged. Conscience is the most secret core and sanctuary of a man. There he is alone with God, Whose voice echoes in his depths. In a wonderful manner conscience reveals that law which is fulfilled by love of God and neighbor. In fidelity to conscience, Christians are joined with the rest of men in the search for truth, and for the genuine solution to the numerous problems which arise in the life of individuals from social relationships. Hence the more right conscience holds sway, the more persons and groups turn aside from blind choice and strive to be guided by the objective norms of morality. Conscience frequently errs from invincible ignorance without losing its dignity. The same cannot be said for a man who cares but little for truth and goodness, or for a conscience which by degrees grows practically sightless as a result of habitual sin."

truth of our dealing with him which we cannot do without. The reason why Aquinas so much countenances natural law was not to pay some homage to thinkers from the past or to contingent political powers (as Straussian Thomists seem sometimes to suggest), but to pay due attention to the Word of God.

1.5. Natural Law, Reason, and Revelation

Natural law can be known by natural reason. That is, we can know the truth of natural law by believing in God, but we can also reach the knowledge of natural law using our reason only. This does not mean that we could also go on in our moral life without revelation. God revealed natural law because without his help we cannot follow our nature, nor can we even perfectly understand it. "Because," as Aquinas explains, "on account of the uncertainty of human judgment, especially on contingent and particular matters, different people form different judgments on human acts; whence also different and contrary laws result. In order, therefore, that man may know without any doubt what he ought to do and what he ought to avoid, it was necessary for man to be directed in his proper acts by a law given by God, for it is certain that such a law cannot err."[4]

One could ask: "Why all these difficulties? Why didn't God make us able to do better on our own?" An answer to this question can perhaps be found in the John Paul II interview, *Crossing the Threshold of Hope*. God is not "the God of the deists." "He is not the Absolute that remains outside of the world, indifferent to human suffering. He is Emmanuel, God-with-us, a God who shares man's lot and participates in his destiny." In God's original design neither the world nor man is supposed to be "self-sufficient."[5] Nature cannot be nature by itself alone, and God wants to walk together with the good man. Nature and grace belong, so to speak, to the same primordial *system* of creation.

When we say that natural law can be known by natural reason we do not imply that man does not need supernatural aid. Just as a baby cannot

4   *ST*, I-II, q. 91, a. 4 c.
5   See John Paul II, *Crossing the Threshold of Hope* (London: Jonathan Cape, 1994), 50–63.

develop his natural capacities without his parents, his family and, in general, the milieu provided by other human beings, so man cannot reach the full moral truth without listening to the Word of God. He cannot do good actions (i.e., he cannot act according to natural law) without "the hidden action of grace."[6] "*On the path of the moral life the way of salvation is open to all*," precisely because the "influence of grace" is always present in the actions of those who try to follow "the dictate of conscience" and "to lead an upright life," even if, without fault, they do not "know anything about Christ or his Church" or "have not yet attained to the express recognition of God."[7] Revelation, grace, natural reason and natural law are parts of a single design. Natural law is the only vehicle available to us, but it has always been supposed to function with a special fuel called grace.

1.6. Natural Law and Love of God

Natural law is summed up in the precept of love: "You shall love the Lord your God with all your heart, and with all your soul, and with all your mind. This is the greatest and first commandment. And a second is like it: You shall love your neighbor as yourself. On these two commandments hang all the Law and the prophets" (*Mt* 22:36).[8]

Loving God and other human beings is the *ratio* of natural law, and it is therefore the central truth that all people should understand by their reason. If they do not, they will never act righteously. It is not by chance that the main passages of Scripture in which it is clearly stated that we can come "to know God by the light of reason alone"[9] are truly *moral passages*, in which the pagans' *refusal* to know God is the cause of their bad behavior in every field. Moreover, both failures, the refusal and the bad behavior, are strongly condemned.[10] "And as they liked not to have God in their knowledge, God delivered them up to a reprobate sense, to do those things which

---

6   See John Paul II, *Evangelium Vitae*, n. 2.
7   See *Veritatis Splendor*, n. 3. See also, *Lumen Gentium*, n. 16.
8   See also, *Deut* 6:5; *Rom* 13:9–10; *Catechism of the Catholic Church* (*CCC*), n. 2055.
9   *CCC*, n. 37.
10   *Wis* 13:1–9; *Rom* 1.

are not convenient; Being filled with all iniquity, malice, fornication, avarice, wickedness, full of envy, murder, contention, deceit, malignity, whisperers; Detractors, hateful to God, contumelious, proud, haughty, inventors of evil things, disobedient to parents; Foolish, dissolute, without affection, without fidelity, without mercy" (*Rom* 1:28–31). Our attitude toward God and our knowledge of natural law appear in the Bible as two sides of the same coin.

1.7. Natural Law as a Preamble of the Faith

Natural law is surely a preamble of our faith in a broad sense, as it is the good work of moral reason preparing us for the gift of faith. Yet we might even say that it is *strictly speaking* a preamble of the faith, in the precise sense that we cannot receive (supernatural) faith without some previous knowledge of the natural law. Faith is not only something theoretical but also practical: it affects both the human mind and the human heart. Thus, in order to receive faith we should be *naturally* able, not only *to know* God, but also *to love* God with all our heart, soul, and mind, discovering in him our final end and the source of our personal dignity.

The structure of the first part of the *Catechism of the Catholic Church* (entitled "The Profession of Faith") emphasizes that with regard to faith the first move is God's, who decides to reveal himself to human beings (Chapter Two, "God Comes to Meet Man"). Only the second move is man's (Chapter Three, "Man's Response to God"). Yet, first of all, before the Catechism speaks of God's revelation, there is a first chapter entitled, "Man's Capacity for God." The theoretical reasoning behind this chapter is that if man were not *capax Dei* he would not be able to receive God's subsequent *message*.[11]

This first chapter of the *Catechism* underlines, as is obvious, that man's natural reason starting from "the physical world and the human person" is "capable of coming to a knowledge of the existence of a personal God" (Parts II and III). That is why it is possible to speak "about him to all men and with all men," and to "dialogue with other religions, with philosophy and science, as well as with unbelievers and atheists" (Part IV). Yet the

11   Of course, the original move, so to speak, was by God, who reveals himself through creation (natural revelation), thus making human nature *capax Dei*.

beginning of the chapter (Part I) is devoted to the natural *moral* capacity for God, "The Desire for God." Early in this section, the *Catechism* recalls the following passage from *Gaudium et Spes*:

> The dignity of man rests above all on the fact that he is called to communion with God. *This invitation* to converse with God is addressed to man *as soon as he comes into being*. For if man exists, it is because God has created him through love, and through love continues to hold him in existence. He cannot live fully according to truth *unless he freely acknowledges that love and entrusts himself to his creator*.[12]

We may wonder whether our moral capacity should not be the *second step*, insofar as we cannot desire what we do not know. This is the reason that ethics is always grounded in, even if not deduced from, metaphysics. Nevertheless, practical knowledge is first in its own order. In our lives it is more important in a sense because we cannot act without the original (unchosen) attraction for an end. We could not even speak of God's existence if we were not *interested in* the truth about God. From this viewpoint, the strategy of the Catechism appears perfectly justified: it opens with desire, with ethics, and in a sense, as we shall see, with natural law in its basic (natural) religious meaning.

1.8. The Question about Morality, Natural Law, and Ethics' Religious Aspect

Veritatis Splendor likewise stresses many times the religious character of ethics. The beginning of the encyclical is almost entirely devoted to qualifying the question about morality which the rich young man asks Jesus as a question about God: a question "about the full meaning of life." "This is in fact the aspiration at the heart of every human decision and action, the quiet searching and interior prompting which sets freedom in motion. This question is ultimately an appeal to the absolute Good which attracts us and beckons us; it is the echo of a call from God who is the origin and goal of man's

---

12   Emphasis mine.

life."[13] Moreover, the question about morality "is *an essential and unavoidable question for the life of every man*, for it is about the moral good which must be done, and about eternal life. The young man senses that there is a connection between moral good and the fulfillment of his own destiny."[14]

A few lines later, John Paul II clearly states the connection between the question about morality and the natural law. "*To ask about the good*, in fact, *ultimately means to turn towards God*, the fullness of goodness. Jesus shows that the young man's question is really a *religious question*, and that the goodness that attracts and at the same time obliges man has its source in God, and indeed is God himself. God alone is worthy of being loved 'with all one's heart, and with all one's soul, and with all one's mind' (Mt 22:37). He is the source of man's happiness. Jesus brings the question about morally good action back to its religious foundations, to the acknowledgment of God, who alone is goodness, fullness of life, the final end of human activity, and perfect happiness."[15] "The statement, 'There is only one who is good' thus brings us back to the 'first tablet' of the commandments. This calls us to acknowledge God as the Lord of all and to worship him alone for his infinite holiness (cf. *Ex* 20:2–11). *The good is belonging to God, obeying him*, walking humbly with him in doing justice and in loving kindness (cf. *Mic* 6:8). *Acknowledging the Lord as God is the very core, the heart of the Law*, from which the particular precepts flow and towards which they are ordered."[16]

This religious view of moral life constitutes the background and final answer to all the main subjects the encyclical discusses: from natural law to moral conscience, to intrinsically evil acts, etc. At the end of our philosophical analysis, I hope it will be easy and useful for the reader to compare at least these first passages of *Veritatis Splendor* with Aquinas' view on natural law and eternal law.

2. Ethics and Natural Law

Ethics can be defined as the discipline, or *scientia*, that studies human beings and their actions as good or evil in the absolute sense (*simpliciter*). This

13   *Veritatis Splendor*, n. 7.
14   Ibid., n. 8.
15   Ibid., n. 9.
16   Ibid., n. 11.

is distinguished from a relative or technical sense of good and evil as when we say, "You played a good match," "This is a good gun," "You trained good muscles," and the like.

2.1. Man as the Subject of Ethics

Materially speaking—i.e., from the viewpoint of its material object—ethics studies the human being as a subject whose being and action are characterized by rationality. Man is an ethical being because he knows according to the truth—namely, he understands the meaning of things—and he freely acts as the owner of himself and of the things that surround him. Other beings, on the other hand, do not ask themselves why things are and what they are. Instead of *acting* they are *acted upon* by the laws of nature, by their instincts, etc. It is plainly obvious that even the non-human animals that move in an astonishing rational way—like the ants or termites in the anthill or the beavers in building their dams—do not do it based on calculus, thoughts, or studies about why they do it and what the best ways to reach their goals are. Rather, they move, so to speak, automatically. On the contrary, as a specific way of existing, being human means to know according to the "why" (according to the truth) and to act based on this unique kind of knowledge. For this reason, for human beings to be *moral* (or *good simpliciter*) it involves a free life-plan or life-vision whose result cannot be taken for granted. This is unlike other beings that are automatically *good* with respect to their natures' ends—as the ant is *per se* a good member of the anthill—unless they have physical defects.

2.2. The Importance of Virtue

In the first place, ethics concerns the way in which man through his specific way of existing and acting can become good *simpliciter*, simply speaking. This is what makes the concept of (moral) virtue so important in ethical theory. Virtue primarily indicates not the moral goodness of the actions, but of the agent. In fact, from an ethical viewpoint the most important thing is not to have a good action, but to have a good man who is *the cause* of the good actions.

When we say that a man is (morally) good, we point to a stable quality of his being, namely something that he possesses, like being courageous, loyal, sincere, and the like. This quality is something that man supposedly acquired through his specific way of acting (free and rational), and this is why possessing a moral virtue is meritorious. Virtue is therefore a sort of piece of cloth—a *habit*—made of moral goodness. Once this piece of cloth is bought or acquired, man always wears it and keeps weaving it with richer and more precious fabric.

It is only secondarily that ethics deals with specific human actions (like homicide or giving alms) as good or evil. To be clear: the moral character of the actions is of course extremely important to evaluate. What I mean, rather, is that the main focus of ethical theory should be the good person as such: his moral character and fulfillment.

2.3. Human Action as Ethical Action

As far as actions are concerned, ethical theory deals with specifically *human* actions, namely the actions that make man either good or evil. In other words, in order to do ethics we need truly *human actions* in which both our intellect and our will are fully involved, and not merely *acts of man* like the growth of our hair or body or the digestive process. Yet, most importantly, we need to look at human actions in their absolute meaning rather than just according to the relative goals they happen to have. From the viewpoint of ethical theory there are two basic meanings of good involved in each action: a relative one and an absolute one. For example, to eat something when we are hungry is surely a good thing to do, but is it the good thing for us to do here and now?

Robert Spaemann explains the difference between the relative good and the absolute good:

> The doctor says, "It would be a good idea to spend another day in bed." To be precise the word "good" should be qualified in two ways. The doctor should say, "It is a good idea for you", and "It is a good idea for you if your first priority is to get well." These qualifications are important. If for example someone were planning a robbery involving murder for a particular day, then, all things considered, it would doubtless be "better" if that person picked up a lung infection which would put a stop to his

project. Conversely, on a particular day, one of us might have something so pressing and urgent to do that we will disregard the doctor's advice to stay in bed, and take the risk of getting a relapse of influenza. But with regard to the question of whether or not it is "good" to act in this way, the doctor, as a doctor, can make no pronouncement. From a doctor's point of view "good" means "good for you, if your first priority is your health". That is the doctor's area of responsibility. Whether or not our health should always be our first priority is something about which the doctor can make a pronouncement as a fellow human being, but not in his special capacity as a doctor.[17]

The work of our moral conscience occurs precisely at the level of absolute good. That work is nothing more than to judge—here and now, and taking into account all the relevant circumstances we can reasonably foresee—the relative ends of our actions in light of the absolute end of our life: the final end.

2.4. Natural Law as an Approach to Ethical Theory

In light of the above definition of ethics and speaking very generally, we can say that natural law theory is an approach to ethics under the aspect of its final foundation. For natural law is exactly the norm that decides or tells our conscience what is good and evil, here and now, in the absolute sense.

Of course, natural law is not just a label to express a specific branch of moral philosophy: i.e., the one involving the question about the ultimate grounds of moral duty. As we shall see, natural law is also a very specific answer to that question. Basically, the term "natural law" means a philosophical view according to which nature is transparent to the wisdom and will of God (i.e., it is known as *created*), appearing somehow as a gift. Man understands that "freely taking care of the good of nature" (in all the relevant senses of good) is exactly the way for him to love God; i.e., to respond to God's gift.

17 R. Spaemann, *Basic Moral Concepts*, trans. by T.J. Armstrong (London and New York: Routledge, 1989), 1–2.

3. The Term "Law": Some Implications

It is now time to begin making the conceptual and terminological clarifications at which this chapter aims. Of course, our first concern is for the term "law." In this regard, we have to deal with the following related concepts: (1) the two-subject relation and the common good; (2) the first meaning of law; (3) the rational character of law; (4) the extrinsic principle; (5) the law's effectiveness; and (6) the law's autonomy.

3.1. The Two-Subject Relation and the Common Good

The concept of law refers immediately to a relation between at least two subjects: a legislator, on the one hand, and one or more subjects (citizens) on the other, with the legislator having the power to impose his will on the citizens.

For Aquinas, this power is justified by the end of the law, which is what makes the law *rational* (or irrational, whenever it drifts away from it), and which coincides with the good that is *common* to the entire political community. It goes without saying that the ordering to the good of the whole pertains either to the whole as such or to someone who represents it. This is the reason why private persons cannot legislate, because "to order anything to the common good" and to make a law belong "either to the whole people or to a public personage who has care of the all people."[18]

Most likely, when Aquinas cited the case in which the law is passed by the whole people he was thinking of something similar to what we would call today a democratic process, with a voting assembly endowed with legislative power. Certainly, he was not thinking of a utopian society in which everybody always agrees about the common action to undertake (which would be a situation of perfect political unanimity). In fact, he adds that, when the ordering to the common good is done by the whole people it is the people themselves that will retain the *vis coactiva quam debet habere lex* in order to force the recalcitrant and the dissenters.[19]

At any rate, the "whole people" case is not an exception to the need for a two-subject relationship. This is because the official act of the people

18 *ST*, I-II, q. 90, a. 3 c.
19 *ST*, ad. 2.

acquires the nature of law precisely by assuming the public character of a directive authoritatively addressing all the citizens, and sanctioned by some sort of punishment. Even when it democratically represents the citizens, public authority conceptually remains a subject different from all the citizens addressed by the laws.

A key interpretative principle in Aquinas' treatise on law is offered precisely by his recurrent assertion that law may be in something—may exist—in two ways: "first, as in that which measures and rules" (the legislator), and "secondly, as in that which is measured and ruled" (the subject). In this sense, therefore, when we properly use the term law, we should always ask ourselves who the two relevant subjects are, in which law *exists* according to those two ways. This is the reason—as I recalled in chapter III, sec. 3— why Aquinas says that "properly speaking, none imposes a law on his own actions."[20] Yet, this is also the reason why he can write that "each one is a law to himself, in so far as he shares the direction that he receives from one who rules him."[21] For law, as "participated," always exists in the subject who is measured by it and who therefore, in this sense, possesses the law in his own being.

3.2. The First Meaning

It follows that the first meaning of law is that of command because what matters about law is first of all its possibility to be effective, or to oblige somebody to act in a certain way. To avoid misunderstandings about a possible voluntaristic approach behind this statement, we only need to specify that the first meaning of something is also the last in the series of the definition. That is to say, it is the meaning that *specifies* the nature of something. For example, in the definition of man as rational animal, the meaning of animal—as the generic element of the definition—comes before the meaning of rational, which is its specific element. However, the first meaning of man, the meaning that *specifies* what man means, is that of rational. Man is everything that animal means plus something else—the specifying element—which is indicated by the adjective "rational."

20   *ST*, I-II, q. 93, a. 5 c.
21   See, *ST*, I-II, q. 90, a. 1, 3; q. 91, a. 2.

Likewise, in the case of law, the first meaning that—inside the genus to which law belongs: i.e., the genus of the acts of reason—specifies it is that of command. Law is everything that act of reason means plus something else that comes from the concepts of command, common good, authority, and promulgation. Among these concepts, command—as we have seen in Chapter III—seems to be the primary one that specifies the nature of the law as a particular kind of rational act.[22]

In a sense, it is obvious that law belongs to reason because law is always an act of an intelligent being which aims at obtaining a particular effect. Law belongs to reason "since it belongs to the reason to direct to the end."[23] This is how we evaluate the rationality, or reasonableness, of a law and judge its goodness: by looking at its end and at its chosen means to achieve it.

Yet it is also obvious that this reference to reason would not be enough to define law. Again, rationality can define law only *generically*, as the act of an intelligent being, but not *specifically*, as a particular kind of rational act. Law directs to an end (generic nature) to be achieved by means of the authoritative imposition of particular conduct (specific nature). The function of law is that of government, namely to make use of a variety of things by directing them to only one end (common good) or by imposing an *order* on them.[24] From this viewpoint, a more precise definition of law, as offered by Aquinas, is, "a dictate of reason, commanding something [*rationis dictamen per modum praecipiendi*]."[25] In the well-known definition "*quaedam rationis ordinatio ad bonum commune, ab eo qui curam communitatis habet, promulgata*,"[26] the preceptive character is implicit in its mention of the authority as the proper source of the law.

The primary meaning of law is therefore heteronymous because it refers the law to a subject (the legislator) external to those who are *bound* by it.

22 See the third chapter, "Law as Act of Reason and Command."

23 *ST*, I-II, q. 90, a. 1 c.

24 See, e.g., *CG*, III, 64; *ST*, I-II, q. 93, a. 1.

25 *ST*, I-II, q. 92, a. 2 c.: "Just as an assertion is a dictate of reason asserting something, so is a law a dictate of reason, commanding something [*sicut enuntiatio est rationis dictamen per modum enuntiandi, ita etiam lex per modum praecipiendi*]."

26 *ST*, I-II, q. 90, a. 4 c.: "[A]n ordinance of reason for the common good, made by him who has care of the community, and promulgated."

This is a common sense observation. I think nobody can deny that the first idea of law we have in mind is related to the concepts of command and obligation. This is not an invention by either classical voluntarism or modern legal positivism, and there is no need to criticize it if we want to criticize these currents of thought.

This is why Aquinas begins his discussion on law by saying that "*lex* [law] is derived from *ligare* [to bind], because it binds one to act."[27] While this etymology is probably false, the supposed root of the word *lex* undoubtedly reveals the first meaning of the concept, at least in Aquinas' understanding. The imposition of the name relates to grasping the nature of something.

With this first meaning of law as (rational) command, we can now restate the two-subject relation by saying that we can always look at law from at least two perspectives: that of the legislator *who commands*, and that of the subject *who obeys*.

3.3. Extrinsic Principle

The reason why Aquinas begins the treatise on law by focusing on its belonging to reason is exactly because the first common-sense-meaning of law is that of command. That is why it is so important to avoid the risk of voluntarism, by stressing immediately that law is basically a *rational* act.

Yet, we should recall that the principle ordering the treatment of law in Aquinas' work is not reason, rather, it is the concept of extrinsic principles of human acts. The entire second part of the *Summa Theologiae* is devoted to human acts. In order to deal with them, Aquinas distinguishes intrinsic principles—comprising the "powers of the soul" and the "habits"[28]—from extrinsic principles.

> We have now to consider the extrinsic principles of acts. Now the extrinsic principle inclining to evil is the devil, of whose temptations we have spoken in the First Part. But the extrinsic principle moving to good is God, Who both instructs us by means of His Law, and assists us by His Grace.

27   *ST*, I-II, q. 90, a. 1 c.
28   See, ibid., I, q. 77 ff; I-II, q. 49 ff.

These are the opening words of the treatise on law,[29] in which man is looked at basically as the *measured* subject, or the obedient subject, of the law-relation. As principle of human acts law comes from the outside: from an authority. It is intrinsically heteronomous, and God is the source of all laws because human law also binds man insofar as it is grounded on eternal (or natural) law.[30]

3.5. Effectiveness

From the point of view of the legislator, law always requires a (rational) command, on the one hand, and a principle of effectiveness on the other.[31] That is to say, it would be senseless to command something without having the power to make the command effective. The legislator must therefore have "the coercive power, such as the law should have, in order to prove an efficacious inducement to virtue [...] or to inflict penalties."[32]

This principle of effectiveness indicates the way in which *the law exists in that which is measured and ruled*. At the same time, it determines the real existence of a legislator as such. As a matter of fact, the legislator is exactly he who has the *coercive power* to make his will effective in a particular place and at a particular time.[33]

Generally speaking, from the point of view of the (rational) subject who obeys the law effectiveness might depend on:

(1) The *reasonable confidence* in the legislator, grounded in the shared common end/good of the law. This implies: (a) the reasonableness of the very existence of the authority as a way to orderly direct the political

---

29   Ibid., I-II, q. 90.

30   See, ibid., I-II, q. 96, a. 4.

31   For the issues involved in this and the following sections, see especially the third chapter, section 3.

32   See, ibid., I-II, q. 90, a. 3 obj. 2.

33   John Finnis, having grounded authority on its reasonableness, rightly asserts: "It remains true that the sheer fact that virtually everyone *will* acquiesce in somebody's say-so is the presumptively necessary and defeasibly sufficient condition for the normative judgment that that person has (i.e. is justified in exercising) authority in that community," *Natural Law and Natural Rights* (Clarendon Press: Oxford 1980), p. 250.

community (the need for authority), and (b) the reasonableness of the action of the effectively existing authority both at the general level of the legal system's order, and at the specific level of each individual statute. This is the physiological way for a law to be effective: when citizens see the reasonableness of it and spontaneously conform their conduct to it.

(2) The *threat of punishment* in the case of refusal to obey. This is the pathological way for the law to be effective. If most people obeyed most of the legal rules for this reason only, the legal system would be on the path to destruction.

(3) A *mixture* of both (1) and (2): reasonableness and fear. I think this matches the most normal way good citizens abide by the laws of their legal systems in the case of arguable issues like speed limits, the use of helmets, specific taxes, and the like. Even the good citizen sometimes breaks these laws, and other times abides by them *only* to avoid punishments.

3.6. The Autonomy of the Law

Both the reasonable confidence and the threat of punishment (as different ways in which law can be effective in the lives of the measured subjects) require a much deeper principle of effectiveness. That is to say, for the legislative command to have any force there must be something that is (already) good for the subjects, which they are willing either to achieve by obeying or not to be deprived of by disobeying. For example, before the carrot and the stick can be effective there must be pleasure and pain.

From the internal viewpoint of the obeying subject, the efficacy of reasonable confidence rests on the common good to be achieved through obedience, just as the efficacy of the threat of punishment rests on the private good not to be deprived of through disobedience (freedom, money, etc.).

In other words, the effectiveness of law presupposes what can be called a *principle of autonomy*, namely, something belonging to the nature of the agent and determining what is good or bad for him.[34] The human legislator cannot create this principle—i.e., he cannot command impossible things (hating children, walking always on one's hands) because *ad impossibilia*

---

34 I use the terms autonomy and heteronomy with the same meaning they have in *Veritatis Splendor*, no. 41.

nemo tenetur. If he did citizens would eventually react against him. This is basically why every human law is derived from natural law, because human law—like the arts—must operate (in order to achieve its end by binding human beings) *as nature itself would have acted.*

Now, if a legislator could impose even the principle of autonomy by his will, he would be the perfect legislator. He would make nature act according to his plans. To this legislator, the term "law" would apply in its fullest sense. This is why the use of "law" for the *ordo creationis* (eternal law)—as I explained in Chapter III—is not metaphorical but analogical: "For the natural law above all has the character of law [*lex enim naturalis maxime habet rationem legis*]."[35] Paraphrasing Aquinas on the names of God, we could say that, as regards to the imposition of the names, the term "law" is primarily applied by us to human law, which we know first. But as regards the *res significata*, it is "applied primarily to God," because what we call law exists in God's action "in a more excellent way."[36]

4. "Natural"

By now we have enough elements to understand correctly the impact of the adjective "natural" when applied by Aquinas to the term "law."

(a) First of all, it means that the natural order (*ordo creationis*) is the passive subject of a legal two-subject relation in which God is the Legislator.

(b) Second, it means that the natural order as such (as *ordo*) is rational, and its rationality depends intrinsically on its being the product of the creative action of God.

(c) What matters most in order to understand the specific nature of the concept is the first meaning. The natural order obeys a command. It behaves necessarily in a certain way because it is subordinate to a legislator who created it. "God imprints on the whole of nature the principles of its proper actions. And so, in this way, God is said to command the whole of

---

35 *ST*, I-II, q. 90, a. 4, obj. 1.

36 See, ibid., I, q. 13, a. 6 c. For a sound understanding of the logical meaning of analogy, see R. McInerny, *Aquinas and Analogy* (Washington, D.C.: The Catholic University of America Press, 1996).

nature [*Deus imprimit toti naturae principia propriorum actuum. Et ideo per hunc modum dicitur Deus praecipere toti naturae*]."[37]

5. (Natural) Inclination

We should also have enough elements to correctly approach the concept of (natural) inclination. Inclination is the way in which law exists in the subjects measured by it. If a law works, if it is *effective*, it means that (one way or another) it is able to generate an inclination to act according to its directives in the subjects it addresses. At the same time, the inclination is what grounds the effectiveness and the autonomy of the law. The natural inclinations are the principle of perfect effectiveness of God's law on creation—i.e., on the natural order. They make God's law perfectly autonomous insofar as they exist as internal principles of movement in the nature of every created being.

If we are to correctly frame the issue, external principle and inclination are the two key concepts to be understood, insofar as the former indicates the heteronomous character of law and the latter indicates the autonomous character of law.[38]

In the following passage, Aquinas makes it absolutely clear what the term "inclination" means when it is used in defining the concept of law:

> Since law is a kind of rule and measure, it may be in something in two ways. First, as in that which measures and rules: and since this is proper to reason, it follows that, in this way, law is in the reason alone. *Secondly, as in that which is measured and ruled. In this way, law is in all those things that are inclined to something*

---

37   See, ibid., I-II, q. 93, a. 5 c.

38   Of course, the reasonable confidence and the threat of punishment, insofar as they make the law effective with respect to its subjects, also come analogically under the notion of inclination. They cause a sort of inclination toward the end of the law, but as we said, their efficacy depends on the *natural* inclinations already operating in the subjects. From this viewpoint, the New Law also properly falls under the *ratio legis* because of its effectiveness: grace acts effectively, in a sense creating in man a further and more perfect *inclination* to the supernatural end.

by reason of some law: so that any inclination arising from a law, may be called a law, not essentially but by participation as it were.[39]

Every created thing necessarily obeys the will of God because it can only behave according to its natural inclinations. It does not choose to move according to its nature. It simply is already in movement: the dog toward the meat, the boy toward the girl and the girl toward the boy, etc. The existence of natural inclinations is the basic reason why the is-ought question is a false problem: *the world is already in motion*. No one can choose to stop it or to create a new movement. We can only work on the movements already existing, as an artist uses the natural properties of the colors, the stones, the clay, etc. Moral life too is *already in motion*; it causes happiness or unhappiness, regrets, praises and blames. The ethicist cannot create values from the outside. For instance, he cannot *decide* that children are important (this would definitively be a *fallacy*). Yet if they are—and it seems obvious that they are—then this *movement* has particular rules to work well, to be fulfilling for the agent, etc. What ethics does, if done well, is not to create "oughts," but to try to understand the moral movements already existing in us and their rules. Sometimes this tells us that whether we like it or not this "ought" is working in us in such a manner because this thing is or is not important or good for us in this precise sense and way.

5.1. Inclination and Freedom

Natural inclination is a very general concept applicable both to irrational creatures and to human beings (and to the angels as well), although in different ways. The rational creature receives a very special inclination intended to *effectively submit* his *free* acts to the order willed by God.

I know I am using a somewhat provocative and imperfect terminology, but I want to draw attention to a very important point that is often misunderstood. Up to this point in Aquinas' discussion, it is common to explain the difference between irrational and rational creatures more or less as follows: irrational creatures obey the natural law necessarily, while

39   *ST*, I-II, q. 90, a. 1, reply to obj. 1 (emphasis mine).

rational ones have to use reason to recognize their natural inclinations and to act freely according to them. This is right, of course, but it does not sufficiently describe the difference between them. This simplified view risks creating a wall of separation between the realm of necessity (proper to inclinations) and the realm of freedom (proper to reason), which leaves freedom out of any intrinsic guide provided by the law—i.e., out of the effectiveness of law and the realm of inclinations.

Actually, Aquinas says something different. He says:

> [I]t is evident that all things partake somewhat of the eternal law, in so far as, namely, from its being imprinted on them, they derive their respective inclinations to their proper acts and ends. Now among all others, the rational creature is subject to Divine providence in the most excellent way, in so far as it partakes of a share of providence, by being provident both for itself and for others. Wherefore it has a share of the Eternal Reason, whereby it has a natural inclination to its proper act and end [*naturalem inclinationem ad debitum actum et finem*]: and this participation of the eternal law in the rational creature is called the natural law.[40]

The most important thing to stress here is that Aquinas speaks in the singular. The idea is that there is *one* inclination for the rational creature guiding him toward his *debitum actum et finem*, where *debitum actum* is what reason recognizes here and now as the action to do or to avoid all things considered. Natural law is the moral guide for concrete (real) action. It is the "inclination to act according to reason,"[41] namely the inclination to do exactly the particular action that, after all the relevant train of reasoning involved, one's conscience judges as the right thing to do. In other words, the working of this basic inclination presuppose *the conclusion* of the moral reasoning based on all our knowledge of the natural order and, especially, of the several goods we have as human beings (i.e., our several natural inclinations), of the general moral principles grounded

40 See *ST*, I-II, q. 91, a. 2.
41 Ibid., I-II, q. 94, a. 3 c.

on them, and of the hierarchy existing between them with respect to our final end.[42]

In this sense, as Ralph McInerny has insistently clarified in his work, the first principle of practical reason, "good is to be done and pursued, and evil is to be avoided,"[43] is already a moral one. In this formulation, the term "good" "gives the formality under which the object is sought or pursued: as completive, as perfective" for the rational human (body and soul) agent. So, it expresses the *ratio boni perfecti*, also known as the *ratio ultimi finis*. "Natural law relates to inclinations other than reason, which have their own ends, by prescribing how we should humanly pursue those ends. For Thomas, natural law is a dictate of reason, not a physical law. It is by coming under the guidance of reason that goods that are not peculiar to man come to be constituents of the human good."[44]

In Aquinas's words:

> All the inclinations of any parts whatsoever of human nature, e.g., of the concupiscible and irascible parts, in so far as they are ruled by reason [*secundum quod regulantur ratione*], belong to the natural law, and are reduced to one first precept: so that the precepts of natural law are many in themselves, but are based on one common foundation [*communicant in una radice*].[45]

Now, of course, the set of inclinations we have are ruled by reason in the exact moment of choosing, every day, in each one of the thousand actions we do. This includes both mental actions and actions affecting the external reality (whether by a positive act or by omission does not matter). The regulation by reason does not happen in the abstract but is

---

42 See, for these concepts, the second chapter above.

43 See, *ST*, I-II, q. 94, a. 2 c.: "*bonum est faciendum et prosequendum, et malum vitandum.*"

44 R. McInerny, *Ethica Thomistica: The Moral Philosophy of Thomas Aquinas* (Washington, D.C.: The Catholic University of America Press, 1982 [1997 rev. ed.]), pp. 40–48. See also, R. McInerny, "Grisez and Thomism," in N. Biggar and R. Black (eds.), *The Revival of Natural Law* (Ashgate: Aldershot, 2000), 53–72.

45 *ST*, I-II, q. 94, a. 2, obj. 2.

always in the concrete moral experience, and so it cannot work without virtue.

This does not mean that we do not use general knowledge of the moral principles (or of the natural law simply speaking, *in universale*). This knowledge is of course necessary, and has a metaphysical and epistemological primacy with regard to the particular practical judgment by the moral conscience. However, it does mean that general knowledge in itself is not yet the proper work of practical reason, and it is not in itself the most basic meaning of natural law. That is also why the concrete (i.e., the *real*) moral action is properly qualified as an action according to or against virtue and not according to or against a general principle or rule. Virtue is exactly what determines the normative (the ought) character of the behavior in the particular circumstances of moral life. Here the deepest meaning of natural law and the concept of virtue go perfectly together, even though natural law as inclination maintains an ontological primacy (i.e., virtue is always the perfection of an inclination).

It is useful to recall that this is why Aristotle explicitly excludes practical knowledge from the realm of truth: "The object of theoretic knowledge is truth, while that of practical knowledge is action; for even when they are investigating how a thing is so, practical men study not the eternal principle but the relative and immediate application."[46] Furthermore, this is why he emphasizes that "men of experience are more successful than theorists", because "action deals with particular things," and prudence consequently requires "knowledge of particular facts even more than knowledge of general principles."[47]

Aquinas clearly has this doctrine in mind when, in the question "Whether the natural law is the same in all men", he writes that "as regards the general principles whether of speculative or of practical reason, truth

46 Aristotle, *Metaphysics*, trans. by H. Tredennick (Cambridge: Harvard University Press, 1989), II, 1, 993 b 20–5.

47 See, Aristotle, *Nicomachean Ethics.*, trans. by H. Rackham (London: Loeb Classical Library, 1934), VI, viii, 1141 b 14–23; *Metaphysics*, I, 1. This is also the main reason why Aristotle asserts that the young and immature "are not fit to be students of political science. For they have no experience of life and conduct, and it is these that supply the premises and subject matter of this branch of philosophy" (*NE*, I, i, 1195 a 1–4).

or rectitude is the same for all, and is equally known by all." Yet, "practical reason is busied with contingent matters, about which human actions are concerned [*sed ratio practica negotiatur circa contingentia, in quibus sunt operationes humanae*];" and, "although there is necessity in the general principles [*etsi in communibus sit aliqua necessitas*]," as to "the *proper conclusions* of the practical reason, neither is the truth or rectitude the same for all, nor, where it is the same, is it equally known by all [*quantum ad proprias conclusiones rationis practicae, nec est eadem veritas seu rectitudo apud omnes; nec etiam apud quos est eadem, est aequaliter nota*]."[48]

In the final assessment, there is an intrinsic law of our freedom—a special inclination imprinted in us—*commanding* us, through the judgments of our conscience, to perform a particular action here and now (the *debitum actum*). This inclination is the most basic meaning of natural law. The work of such inclination depends both (a) on general theoretical and practical knowledge (that is the most usual meaning of the term natural law) and (b) on a good experiential knowledge of the particular reality.

6. Inclination to God

We now have the vocabulary enabling us to approach the overall meaning of the term "natural law as inclination to God." This means that God wanted to make his will to be loved by us *effective*. Being the perfect legislator, he created the relevant *principle of autonomy* by imprinting in us an inclination to him, i.e., an inclination making him *important* to us.

We now have to check if this is a reasonable interpretation of what Aquinas had in mind. We are going to do this by clarifying: (1) the concept of natural law as participation in the eternal law; (2) our knowledge of the eternal law; (3) what might be called the "material object" and the "formal object" of natural law; (4) the *dilectio naturalis* of the human will; and (5) the relation between the inclination to God and our moral experience.

---

48   *ST*, I-II, q. 94, a. 4 c. See also I-II, q. 91, a. 3 ad 3: "The practical reason is concerned with practical matters [*operabilia*], which are singular and contingent: but not with necessary things, with which the speculative reason is concerned."

6.1. *Participatio Legis Eternae in Rationali Creatura*

Divine Wisdom, as moving all things to their due end [read: natural inclinations; intrinsic principles of effectiveness], bears the character of law. Accordingly the eternal law is nothing else than Divine Wisdom, as directing all actions and movements [*ratio divinae sapientiae moventis omnia ad debitum finem, obtinet rationem legis. Et secundum hoc, lex aeterna nihil aliud est quam ratio divinae sapientiae, secundum quod est directiva omnium actuum et motionum*].[49]

Once we understand that the eternal law directs all actions and movements, we can see that the natural law is not in itself different from the eternal law. So, it is obvious that when Aquinas asks "whether there is in us a natural law" the first objection he raises is: "It would seem that there is no natural law in us. Because man is governed sufficiently by the eternal law." The answer plainly follows: "This argument would hold if the natural law were something different from the eternal law."[50]

There is nothing belonging to the natural law that does not belong to the eternal law as well, because "all that is in things created by God, whether it be contingent or necessary, is subject to the eternal law."[51] Why then the special term 'natural law'? Of course, not merely because natural law is the piece of eternal law regulating human beings specifically. This would be odd because if this were the only reason for the special name we should or could give the eternal law a different name for every kind of creature.

Of course, we already know the answer from the *Summa theologiae*, I-II, q. 91, a. 2. In the case of man's rational nature there is a qualitative difference. It "is subject to Divine providence in the most excellent way, in so far as it partakes of a share of providence, by being provident both for itself and for others." More technically, man participates in the eternal law "by way of knowledge [*per modum cognitionis*]," somehow having a notion of the eternal law (*quia et notionem legis aeternae aliquo modo habet*).[52]

But what does it means for man to know the eternal law? Does it only mean that he has a rational nature? In other words, does it only mean that

---

49   Ibid., I-II, q. 93, a. 1 c.
50   Ibid., I-II, q. 91, a. 2 obj. 1.
51   Ibid., I-II, q. 93, a. 4.
52   Ibid., I-II, q. 93, a. 6.

he can recognize the meanings and the natural order of things, that he can act freely according to those meanings, and that in so doing he brings out the design of the eternal law? Of course, this would not be enough because the connection between eternal law and man's knowledge would be merely extrinsic. In fact, he would not know the eternal law as an eternal law, and the term "law" would be used only metaphorically.

I think we should take more seriously both the notion of eternal law and Aquinas' explanation of it. His point is that divine wisdom directs and moves man to act *consciously* according to the eternal law. God created man to be loved by him. Accordingly, by his natural reason man knows the eternal law as such, i.e., as God directing and moving the world. Man received a special natural inclination to act according to his knowledge of the eternal law, i.e., a natural inclination that (a) makes the design of God *important* for him, and (b) operates at the level of conscience and freedom. Thanks to this inclination man is created as a free steward (i.e., he can refuse the call) of God's providential action. He consciously helps God in "moving all things to their due end" (I-II, q. 93, a. 1) "by being provident both for himself and for others" (I-II, q. 91, a. 2).

Then again, let us see what Aquinas explicitly says about our knowledge of the eternal law.

6.2. Knowing the Eternal Law

When Aquinas explicitly explains how all people know the eternal law, he does not focus simply on the human capacity to know the intelligible aspects of nature (the natural inclinations and movements of all things toward their ends), nor does he refer to revealed truths or that part of eternal law regarding the divine law (old and new). Rather, anyone acquainted with Aquinas' metaphysics immediately recognizes in his statements the epistemological *a posteriori* structure of the (philosophical) ways to know God. In this respect, knowing the eternal law and knowing God are two sides of the same coin.

Aquinas literally says that eternal law is known "in its effects, wherein some likeness of that thing is found" because "no one can know the eternal law, as it is in itself, except the blessed who see God in his essence. But every rational creature knows it in its reflection, greater or less. For every knowledge of truth is a kind of reflection and participation of the eternal law." Furthermore, Aquinas does not deny the premise of the objection that we cannot know the eternal law because it is something divine. Rather, he says: "We cannot know the things that are of God [*ea quae sunt Dei*], as they are in themselves; but they are made known to us in their effects, according to *Rom* 1.20: 'The invisible things of God [...] are clearly seen, being understood by the things that are made.'" Moreover, "Although each one knows the eternal law according to his own capacity, in the way explained above, yet none can comprehend it: for it cannot be made perfectly known by its effects."[53]

Man's notion of the eternal law (that he somehow has, *notionem legis aeternae aliquo modo, rationalis natura, habet*)[54] is properly speaking a humanly limited—and possibly very confused—notion of God (i.e., of *ea quae sunt Dei*). It is not just the knowledge of an intelligible natural order, but rather the knowledge of the intelligible natural order *as related* (two-subject relation) to the creative will of God (the supreme legislator). This is the proper *natural knowledge* of the eternal law that we possess. In this regard, we should recall that Aquinas' philosophical proof for the existence of providence (that is another name for *lex aeterna*) is nothing but the fifth way to prove the existence of God.[55] That means that through the fifth way

---

53 Cf., ibid., I-II, q. 93, a. 2.
54 Cf., ibid., I-II, q. 93, a. 6.
55 Cf., e.g., *CG*, III, Ch. 64. "Moreover, that natural bodies are moved and made to operate for an end, even though they do not know their end, was proved by the fact that what happens to them is always, or often, for the best; and, if their workings resulted from art, they would not be done differently. But it is impossible for things that do not know their end to work for that end, and to reach that end in an orderly way, unless they are moved by someone possessing knowledge of the end, as in the case of the arrow directed to the target by the archer. So, the whole working of nature must be ordered by some sort of knowledge. And this, in fact, must lead back to God, either mediately or immediately, since every lower art and type of knowledge must get its principles from a higher one, as we also see in the speculative and operative sciences. Therefore, God governs the world by His providence. Furthermore, things that are different in their natures do not come together into one order unless they are gathered into a unit by one ordering agent. But in the whole of reality things are distinct and possessed of contrary natures; yet all come together in one order, and while some things make use of the actions of others, some are

we do not obtain simply the knowledge of God's existence. More precisely, we obtain the knowledge of the existence of God as the supreme lawgiver "directing all actions and movements."[56]

In other words, Aquinas' concept of eternal law should be read in light of the entire philosophical tradition that begins with the first pre-Socratic insights on natural teleology caused by an ordering love-intelligence. Aristotle interprets these insights as the discovery of the principle of movement and the final cause.[57] This tradition appeared already as a strong doctrine on divine providence in Socrates and Plato and became an explicit and developed universal-divine-law-view with the Stoics. Christian thought gave the further connotation of an efficient creative-cause to the Greek final-cause-ordering-intelligence. After the early reflections by authors like Theophilus of Antioch, Minucius Felix, Origen, and the Cappadocians, and the clear notion of eternal law in Augustine, the scholastic tradition delivers all the philosophical material Aquinas needed for his famous synthesis.

6.3. Material Object and Formal Object of Natural Law

Having clarified the sense in which the *participatio legis aeternae in rationali creatura* happens *per modum cognitionis*, we can now say, broadly speaking, that the *material object* of natural law is the knowledge of the *ordo creationis* (ourselves and the other human beings included) that we are able to achieve by our natural reason, while the *formal object* is the normative character under which that same natural order comes into our knowledge.

In other words, in the term "natural law," natural refers not only to human nature but also to everything we can know about the natural order. In this respect, the natural law and the eternal law (in its philosophical meaning, which does not include the divine laws, old and new) are the same thing.

helped or commanded by others. Therefore, there must be one orderer and governor of the whole of things."

56   For a deeper discussion of the structure of the five ways and the nature of our knowledge of God involved in them, see my *God and the Natural Law*, Chapter II, section 3.

57   See, *Metaphysics*, I, 1, 984 b 15 ff.

On the other hand, the term "law" means the normativity of nature, which for us cannot depend merely on the natural inclinations of things (man included). Rather, these inclinations bind intrinsically and necessarily everything except an *external* rational observer. The fact that the observer understands the need for iron to attract the magnet, the need for lions to go after their prey, or the need for mothers to nurture their children, does not imply any ethical urge for him. Nature's normativity needs something else. It depends on the understanding of what is behind the inclinations. To put it another way, it depends on the intelligible connection between the existing inclinations and the will of God (i.e., the *ratio legis*) who wants them.

When we mention the will of God, we do not slide into a sort of voluntaristic view of natural law theory. In this regard, it is certainly useful to recall that in Aquinas' (Aristotelian) metaphysics the notion of good does not add anything to the notion of being except that there is a relation with a will that wants it. Similarly, the notion of truth adds to that of being only a relation with an intellect that knows it. Absolutely speaking, something is not true or good in itself but only for someone, namely man or God (or the angels). When man realizes that there is a good (and beauty) in him and around him that is *independent of* and *more important than himself*, he likewise knows the will of God (with more or less awareness). That is why *everything* that belongs to nature appears important to the good man in an absolute (transcendental) sense, and not merely because of his desire.[58] Moreover, it should somehow be respected according to the meaning it intrinsically has.

In short: the term "natural law" indicates our knowledge of the natural order (material object) as created or willed by God (formal object), where the formal object is what makes the natural order absolutely important with respect to our conscience.

---

58 When I say "absolute sense" I mean "with respect to the will of God," and not, of course, "with respect to the other things." With respect to the will of God, every creature is important in an absolute sense, but it is also more or less important with regard to the place it occupies in the hierarchical order of all things, and with respect to the final end.

6.4. *Dilectio Naturalis* of the Human Will

Actually, it should be clear that what has been said so far is not yet sufficient. After all, we still do not have the principle of effectiveness—or of perfect autonomy—for the will of God as known by human beings. All things considered, we are still *external observers* of the will of God.

That is to say, let us grant that we are able to use our natural reason to know the intelligible order of nature, the existence of God (even if, for many people, in a very limited sense of a confused perception of a transcendental meaning of things), and the order of nature as created by God. Let us also grant that this is exactly why God wants the existence of man as a free being, so that he might be able to know and love Him. Yet, why should all this knowledge make the natural order absolutely *important* for us? Why should all this knowledge as such be *important* for us?

The only epistemologically sound answer is that God imprints in us, as the most basic inclination of our nature, the inclination to love him before and more than ourselves. The immanent and original work of this inclination would make the natural order morally important for us in the exact moment that we know it as created. This basic inclination would be the principle of perfect autonomy of natural law as such (i.e., as the natural order known by human beings as related, in a legal two-subject relation, with the effective/creative will of God), and it would also be the deepest ground of our moral conscience. Let us see what Aquinas says in this regard.

Speaking in I-II, q. 60, of the *amor seu dilectio naturalis* of the angels,[59] he first states that

> natural love is nothing else than the inclination implanted in nature by its Author, [so] it is common to every nature to have some inclination; and this is its natural appetite or love. This inclination is found to exist differently in different natures; but

---

59   It goes without saying that, since we cannot have a direct *experience* of the angelic nature, our philosophical understanding of it depends on the analogy between angelic nature, on the one hand, and human rational nature on the other. As such, it presupposes an in-depth study of both human intellect and human will.

in each according to its mode. Consequently, in the intellectual nature there is to be found a natural inclination coming from the will; in the sensitive nature, according to the sensitive appetite; but in a nature devoid of knowledge, only according to the tendency of the nature to something.[60]

Without *dilectio naturalis* nothing could move. With regards to man, without the inclination of his will toward his final end (happiness, *beatitudo*), he could not move because "all other desires are caused by this natural desire [*ex hac naturali voluntate causantur omnes aliae voluntates*]; since whatever a man wills he wills on account of the end." This is the origin of the difference between *dilectio naturalis* and *dilectio electiva*. In fact, "the love of that good, which a man naturally wills as an end, is his natural love; but the love which comes of this, which is of something loved for the end's sake, is the love of choice."[61]

Angels and man love themselves with both *dilectio naturalis* and *dilectio electiva*. This is coherent because a thing may be loved in two ways: as a subsisting good and as an accidental good. In other words, a subject may simply be inclined to procure what is good for itself (*dilectio naturalis*), and this inclination belongs both to irrational and rational creatures. "[H]ence angel and man naturally love self, in so far as by natural appetite each desires what is good for self." Yet angel and man may wish something *per electionem*, as a means for their good. In this case, they wish the means unto another (*alteri*), and they love themselves with *dilectio electiva*. Aquinas gives a clear example: when we wish for knowledge (*scientia*) we do not love it in itself (*ut ipsa sit bona*), "but that it may be possessed [*ut habeatur*]. This kind of love has been called by the name of *concupiscence*."[62]

At precisely this point, after having explained that angels (and man as well) love "another with natural love as he loves himself (*sicut seipsum*),"[63] Aquinas comes to the last and most important article of the *quaestio* 60, "Whether an angel by natural love loves God more than he loves himself

---

60 *ST*, I, q. 60, a. 1.
61 *ST*, I, q. 60, a. 2.
62 *ST*, I, q. 60, a. 3.
63 *ST*, I, q. 60, a. 4.

[*utrum angelus naturali dilectione diligat Deum plus quam seipsum*]."[64] Here his idea of human nature is extremely clear and sharp:

> From natural love angel and man alike love God before themselves and with a greater love. Otherwise, if either of them loved self more than God, it would follow that natural love would be perverse, and that it would not be perfected but destroyed by charity [*naturali dilectione etiam angelus et homo plus et principalius diligat Deum quam seipsum. Alioquin si naturaliter plus seipsum diligeret quam Deum, sequeretur quod naturalis dilectio esse perversa, et quod non perficeretur per charitatem, sed destruere-tur*].

The last words of this quotation unequivocally show how much Aquinas is aware of the implications of his philosophical view on *dilectio naturalis*. Man's inclination to "love God before themselves and with a greater love" is a necessary natural ground for the action of grace. Strictly speaking, it is a preamble of the faith [*preambulum fidei*]. If man did not already love God in such a way, human nature "would be perverse [...] and it would not be perfected but destroyed by charity." In other words, we cannot have, under this respect, a *natural final end* other than the *supernatural* one to love God.

The fifth article of the same question is full of important specifications.[65] For instance, (1) loving God more than oneself is not exclusive to the supernatural love of charity (see, *Obj. 4*), or (2) as a natural inclination, the *dilectio naturalis* operates necessarily, i.e., it remains even in the sinner, although in a perverse way (*Obj. 5*). However, what matters most to us now is how Aquinas stresses that his specific answer to the question is intended to deny that our love for God is related to our love of concupiscence. In particular, he wants to attack both: (a) the view that we naturally love God more than ourselves, but only as an aspect of our love of concupiscence (see

---

64 *ST*, I, q. 60, a. 5.
65 I briefly recall here only some main points, but I offer a more detailed comment of all of *quaestio* 60 in my *God and the Natural Law*, Chapter II, section 4.

the main *Reply*), and (b) the view that we do not love God more than ourselves exactly because of the love of concupiscence (see, *Obj. 2*). Again, his words are quite clear and unquestionable.

> *I answer that*, There have been some who maintained that an angel loves God more than himself with natural love, both as to the love of concupiscence, through his seeking the Divine good for himself rather than his own good; and, in a fashion, as to the love of friendship, in so far as he naturally desires a greater good to God than to himself; because he naturally wishes God to be God, while as for himself, he wills to have his own nature. But absolutely speaking [*simpliciter loquendo*], out of natural love he loves himself more than he does God, because he naturally loves himself before God, and with a greater intensity. The falsity of such an opinion stands in evidence [...].

It is important to note that what makes Aquinas certain of his own answer is exactly his knowledge of the precepts of the natural law as God reveals them. So, the only *sed contra* he states against the several objections that the angel "does not love God by natural love more than he loves himself" reads:

> On the contrary, All the moral precepts of the law come of the law of nature. But the precept of loving God more than self is a moral precept of the law. Therefore, it is of the law of nature. Consequently from natural love the angel loves God more than himself.

This *sed contra* vividly testifies how much Aquinas was thinking both of man and of his account of natural law when talking about angels. So, let us come back to the second objection regarding the love of concupiscence:

> *Obj. 2.* That on account of which a thing is such, is yet more so. But every one loves another with natural love for his own sake: because one thing loves another as good for itself. Therefore the angel does not love God more than self with natural love.

[…] *Reply Obj. 2.* When it is said that God is loved by an angel *in so far* as He is good to the angel, if the expression *in so far* [*inquantum*] denotes an end, then it is false; for he does not naturally love God for his own good [*propter bonum suum*], but for God's sake [*propter ipsum Deum*]. If it denotes the nature of love on the lover's part [*rationem amoris ex parte amantis*], then it is true; for it would not be in the nature of anyone to love God, except from this—that everything is dependent on that good which is God.

What does it mean that we do not love God with the love of concupiscence? It simply means that our human nature has a paradoxical structure. This is exactly the same structure that characterizes Christian ethics on the supernatural level of grace.[66] Namely, it means that since our deepest inclination is to love God before ourselves and with a greater love, we cannot fulfill our nature, we cannot reach our happiness (or *beatitudo*), if we intentionally pursue just our happiness (*Mt* 10, 39).

Here Aquinas' ethics goes hand in hand with Augustine's two loves grounding the two cities: "Two cities have been formed by two loves: the earthly by the love of self, even to the contempt of God; the heavenly by the love of God, even to the contempt of self."[67] Yet it is also perfectly in accord with the classical Aristotelian distinction between *good* (*simpliciter*) and *pleasure* as the two final formalities under which we tend toward the particular end of each action (the good as *useful* is only instrumental). Good and pleasure should go together. When we choose something mainly because it is good we also enjoy the pleasure coming from our action, but our intentionality takes us somehow beyond, or above, ourselves. However, due to our spiritual nature, we are able to separate good, *simpliciter dictum*, from pleasure and choose something only because of the pleasure we expect (whatever kind of pleasure, even intellectual). This intentionality (love of concupiscence in the broadest

---

66 "He who finds his life will lose it, and he who loses his life for my sake, will find it" (Mt 10:39).

67 Augustine, *The City of God*, W.J. Oates (ed.) (New York: Random House Publishers, 1948), Book XIV, ch. 28.

sense of the term) falls back on us. For both Aristotle and the Christian tradition, only by choosing the good in itself (*bonum honestum*: *quia honestum dicitur quod per se desideratur*) can man enjoy the greatest pleasure from his action (*bonum delectabile*: i.e., *quod terminat motum appetitus ut quies in re desiderata*),[68] because pleasure comes from the fulfillment of nature.

6.5. Inclination to God and Moral Experience

While it might seem odd to talk about such a natural inclination to God that works necessarily in the practical reasoning of all men and women, is it not rather the opposite view that should appear odd and queer, at least to common sense?

There are people who do not believe in God but who fight strongly—with *firm* belief and *absolute* certainty (even with unselfishness)—for certain ethical views. We should *rationally* wonder why they do so. If there is not anything higher, anything beyond the horizontal level of this existence, why do they have so much stress, worry and anxiety? From where does that firm certainty come? Most of the evidently unsound arguments of many moral philosophers cannot justify their ethical convictions. Of course, there is something more than *reason* in them, and in the current atheist ethical debate as well. (Too often, in the philosophical debate, the only difference between atheists and believers is that the former do not explicitly try to justify their faith.) Besides, we could get the same feeling of *rational exaggeration* when facing other people who give something approaching an *absolute* value to limited goods (job, sport, food, order, etc.), as if the importance of those kinds of goods somehow transcended their effective contingent and relative reality.

The natural inclination to love God before ourselves and with a greater love means that human moral life cannot work without an *absolute* point of view which transcends all the contingencies and limitations of this world. It means that man's authentic moral reasoning cannot work without *relativizing* himself in view of some higher value, that man needs some *absolute* moral truths, that he needs to *believe* in something, and that he is almost

68   See, *ST*, I, q. 5, a. 6.

always ready (knowingly or not) to sacrifice his *reason* for what he previously chose as his own *absolute* values. Again, it means that man cannot live without aspiring to *eternal life* and to an *infinite* good without hoping that his life be *absolutely* important for someone—beyond the transitoriness of human things—and without thinking that his good and bad actions will be a source of merit or condemnation after this brief life.

In other words, the natural inclination to God means that there is a notion of something absolute and transcendental behind moral life: a higher goodness, importance and truth. It is a notion—we should say according to the common ending of Aquinas' five ways to know God—of what everyone calls God. In this regard, it is worthwhile to recall that for Aquinas every man possesses (necessarily) a certain notion of God that grounds the (necessary) inclination to God. That is why, when he criticizes the so-called (after Kant) ontological argument, he does not deny that the idea of God is already working in every human mind. He only claims that such an idea is not enough to clearly (*simpliciter*) assert the existence of God. He says explicitly:

> To know that God exists in a general and confused way is implanted in us by nature [*est nobis naturaliter insertum*], inasmuch as God is man's beatitude. For man naturally desires happiness, and what is naturally desired by man must be naturally known to him. This, however, is not to know absolutely that God exists; just as to know that someone is approaching is not the same as to know that Peter is approaching, even though it is Peter who is approaching; for many there are who imagine that man's perfect good which is happiness, consists in riches, and others in pleasures, and others in something else.[69]

In the Christian tradition of ethical thought the alternative to God is not atheism but idolatry. That is, since man cannot do without his basic natural notion and inclination to God (his natural *capacity for God*), if he refuses God, the result will be to attribute the absolute and infinitive characteristics, which *rationally* belong only to the notion of God, to some relative end.

69   Ibid., I, q. 2, a. 1; also, *Contra Gentiles*, I, 10–11.

Under this respect (i.e., the working of the inclination to God in the concrete moral life of all mankind), a very important part of a sound natural law theory is precisely to deepen the inclination to God *in re* (i.e., phenomenologically). This shows the deepest feature of moral experience as (a) an experience of the transcendent (i.e., of the transcendental basis of the moral good), and (b) an experience of the paradox of finding oneself (fulfilling one's nature) through the total and absolute forgetfulness of oneself. Very often even the easiest arguments grounded on our knowledge of nature (e.g., that there is no difference between killing the unborn and born babies) are accepted by people in difficult situations only when they focus on the idea that God exists. This is coherent because this idea is finally what makes their moral choices absolutely important to human beings, and this is also why the reality of death is *naturally* so important for moral conversions.

As an example of this kind of understanding of the moral experience, one might recall what Spaemann says when speaking of moral duty: "Every 'ought' has to be linked to a want of some kind, otherwise we would have no reason to act on it."[70] Duty is not blind. The right question about moral duty concerns what we really want beyond all the relative goods we like. It concerns the final end of human life. Moral duty reveals the deepest inclination of our rational nature. Yet we must go further. The real voice of moral conscience requires self-sacrifice. It says that, whether you like it or not—no matter how much you might suffer—this action is good, and that action is bad. This aspect of moral conscience, in which man relativizes himself, epistemologically needs a transcendental ground. That is, it needs a final (moral) end which is more important than the rational agent himself. In this sense, we might say that the absolute imperative of conscience reveals the inclination to God. Even our own lives become absolutely important to us only when we look at God because, notwithstanding all the pains or sorrows we might suffer, God wants us to live. The last (and more beautiful and persuasive) natural law answer to suicide remains that God loves us eternally, and he is the final reason of our actions.

By loving God before and more than himself, man finds the *absolute* reason to love himself and others. God loves man in a special way. In this

---

70   See R. Spaemann, *Basic Moral Concepts*, op. cit., 14.

sense, from the viewpoint of the inclination to God there is no axiological difference between oneself and others. Maybe that is why the second commandment is like the first: "You shall love your neighbor as yourself" (*Mt* 22:36), where *as* seems to mean "no more and no less."[71]

7. Conclusion: Main Theoretical Presuppositions of Classical Natural Law Theory

As we mentioned in the beginning, natural law is a sort of synthetic term for an overall philosophical view according to which the deepest meaning of human life does not lie on this earth, and the experience of moral good (the moral experience) is somehow a transcendent experience. In other words, it is the experience of transcending self-love for the sake of what we human beings call God, the experience of a total and absolute self-giving. Again, it is an ethical view in which the work of moral conscience is already a religious experience requiring some notion of, and the inclination to, God.

According to natural law philosophy, the order, meaning, beauty, and bounty of the world reveal God to man. Man feels that his destiny and final good lie somehow beyond this world in God, and that this world is precisely the path to reach it. The world simultaneously appears to man as an image of God, a gift, a commitment, and something sacred that man has to administer.

Therefore, authentic moral experience implies the idea of belonging to a higher order rather than to oneself. It is the experience of profound inner peace of he who is not looking for his own will. A sound understanding of natural law theory sheds light on the strong and deep connection that is present in Christian ethics between the terms law, will, love, and obedience. Both in the supernatural and the natural order, *obedience* is the truth of human moral life. To the good man, one who opens his eyes to creation

---

71   It goes without saying that the inclination to God—besides giving the absolute moral character to all the moral precepts of natural law—implies *specific precepts* as well: exactly all those precepts implicitly involved in the first, and the hierarchically more important, three commandments of the law given by God (the commandments of the first tablet).

and his ears to his conscience, moral experience is exactly the *experience of the obedience of love to the will of God*. Even the most noble and rich human realities like family, children, and marriage reach their full natural and sacred meaning only in the religious man who looks at them as the main part of his *mission* in this world.

In conclusion, if we had to sketch the main theoretical presuppositions of classical natural law theory, we should say that they are that:

1) man's unaided reason is able to spontaneously grasp through the sensible reality offered by the senses a certain notion of God, even if sometimes it does so in a general and confused way;

2) man's will is naturally inclined more to God than to itself, or in other words that the love for God is the ultimate end of human actions and the *ratio* of natural law;

3) man is naturally able to use his reason to know an intelligible order present in nature (with himself being part of it), with an understanding of the several ends of things and of the hierarchical order that exists between them. [The specific knowledge of the objective natural order regulating the relationships between human beings traditionally goes under the label *ius naturale* and not under the label *lex naturalis*. In Aquinas' Aristotelian approach, it pertains to the treatise on justice];[72] and

4) man is able to recognize that order as willed by God (as created), therefore conferring on it an absolute (transcendental) value.

Of course, this last point (4) is just a corollary of the first one. The aspect of sensible reality which refers the human mind to God is nothing other than that fact that it is created and does not have the reason for its own existence in itself.

---

72 See, *ST*, II-II, q. 57 ff. Unfortunately, the English terms "natural law" and "natural rights" do not adequately translate the Latin distinction between *lex naturalis* and *ius naturale*. See my "Natural Law and Natural Right(s): Conceptual and Terminological Clarifications," in S. Brust and C. Wolfe (eds.), *Natural Law Today* (Lexington Books: New York, 2018).

VIII.

FRIENDSHIP OR EQUALITY?:
NOTES TOWARD AN IDEAL OF
POLITICAL PERSONALISM

What is the principle (or value) that grounds political society and determines its nature, identity, and justice? If we focus, on the one hand, on the current debate on political justice, and, on the other hand, on the birth of the modern state, its slow transformation into a constitutional State, and the development of contemporary international law as a universal human rights-based law, the answer should undoubtedly be "equality."

Of course, the concepts of equality and justice have entailed one another ever since the Greeks. From the eighteenth century, however, equality acquired a remarkable and revolutionary political power that gave birth to human rights and radically changed the classical (organic) political thought according to which the state comes before the individual.[1] Both the French and American revolutions happened in the name of an equality that first entails *equal* freedom of everybody before the law and second *equal* protection, respect, and promotion of the natural, or human, rights that everybody *equally* possesses simply due to one's being human. After these revolutions States have had to be grounded on the free and equal consent of each of their members, not just in theory but in practice as well.[2]

Equality grounds a morality of human rights, which today is widely

1   See N. Bobbio, *The Age of Rights* (Cambridge: Polity Press, 1996).
2   This does not entail that the idea of the social contract was not already present both in Greek philosophy (from Plato and Aristotle) and in Christian thought, including in Thomas Aquinas.

recognized as the only reliable and *just* foundation of political community.[3] We all more or less share the conviction that once democratic society (in which everybody is *equally* free) is historically established, and once national and international consent on human rights is secured, the proper foundations of a good and just political community have been laid.[4] Of course, we still have the problem of making equality *real* by removing obstacles and discrimination, and creating equal opportunities. Nevertheless, to agree upon and to foster these objectives is already clear evidence of a *just* society.

Despite all this, there are many political problems that cannot be answered—or, at least, answered easily—by simply focusing on equality and human rights. Think of solidarity. There are some ethical attitudes which are necessary to a sound social life and should be encouraged and fostered, but which cannot be *claimed* as if they were universal rights.[5] Solidarity is authentic only when it spontaneously arises from personal initiative toward somebody who is *passing by*: solidarity is neither *just* nor *egalitarian*.

There are problems apart from solidarity that apparently cannot be solved without having recourse to traditions and interpretative choices which are culturally determined. Think of the conflicts between human rights or the problem of multiculturalism.[6] Think of patriotism and

3   See Francesco Viola, *Dalla natura ai diritti. I luoghi dell'etica contemporanea* (Roma-Bari: Laterza, 1997).
4   An example of this strong conviction is in Bobbio. See *The Age of Rights*, Chapter 2.
5   E. Vidal Gil, on the other hand, advances the theory of a right to solidarity: see, Vidal Gil, *Los derechos de solidaridad en el ordenamiento jurídico español* (Valencia: Tirant Lo Blanch, 2001).
6   Some key texts to understand multiculturalism's criticisms of liberal theories are: A. MacIntyre, *After Virtue: A Study in Moral Theory* (Notre Dame, IN: University of Notre Dame Press, 1981); M. Walzer, *Spheres of Justice: A Defense of Pluralism and Equality* (New York: Basic Books, 1983); C. Taylor, *Sources of the Self: The Making of Modern Identity* (Cambridge, MA: Harvard University Press, 1989); M. J. Sandel, *Liberalism and the Limits of Justice* [1982], revised edition (New York: Cambridge University Press, 1989); W. Kymlicka, *Multicultural Citizenship: A Liberal Theory of Minority Rights* (Oxford: Clarendon Press, 1995). Also very useful is the recent volume by R. Bhargava, A. K. Bagchi and R. Sudarshan (eds.), *Multiculturalism, Liberalism, and Democracy* (Oxford: Oxford University Press, 1999).

national identities (or, these days, the European Union's identity). What is the real ground of political community, consent or tradition?[7] What values should be part of political discussion and action?[8]

Unlike modern political philosophy, the basic concept of classical Aristotelian political theory is friendship. The idea of political friendship has almost always been confused with the organic views which modern revolutions want to eliminate. It is not by chance that the natural rights of modern contractualism have been grounded on a denial of man's social nature by means of the state of nature pretense. Today, human rights supporters do not usually criticize Aristotle's statements on friendship. Yet if we carefully examine the nature of friendship, it is difficult to avoid the impression that friendship and equality are strongly incompatible.

Friendship always looks at the friend in a *special* way. It grows and becomes stronger as the difference between the friend and other people grows. It wants to be exclusive because intimacy excludes. Equality, on the other hand, seems to move irremediably in the opposite direction. It should avoid every partiality. It grows and becomes *substantial* as the difference between the friend and the others diminishes. It is inclusive rather than exclusive.

---

7   This is a different way to approach the debate between liberalism and multi-culturalism.

8   Rawls, for example, thinks that religion is something that political power should not deal with, as it is a controversial issue. For Rawls, the "citizen of faith" is a selfish person who does not comply with his civic duties because he does not put aside his personal beliefs for the sake of society. For Rawls' concept of public reason and what should be legitimately included in it, see J. Rawls, *Political Liberalism* (New York: Columbia University Press, 1993); "Reply to Habermas," in *Journal of Philosophy*, 92/3 (1995): 132–80; "The Idea of Public Reason Revisited", in *University of Chicago Law Review*, 64/3 (1997): 765–807. For a recent criticism to Rawls' exclusion of religion from public reason, see P. Neal, "Political Liberalism, Public Reason, and the Citizen of Faith," in R. P. George and C. Wolfe (eds.), *Natural Law and Public Reason* (Washington, D.C.: Georgetown University Press, 2000), pp. 171–201. Rawls is certainly one of our modern champions of equality, but it is very difficult to find equality and universality in this idea of what should be considered personal and controversial. At first glance, it seems that what is personal, controversial, and culturally determined is his strong stance against the importance of religion for political life and discussion.

How could somebody agree on which of the two should be put at the foundation of political community? Of course, friendship implies equality but equality with the friend, not with others. In this sense, if all people were equal there would be no friendship. This paradoxical conflict between equality and friendship can also be seen as a long-term feature of the political debate. Family is a good example. When the answer to the question on the vital principle of political society focuses on friendship, usually people tend to stress the importance of family for the political community. When it focuses on equality, it becomes easy to see family as a factor of inequality, or a substantial limit to the existence of equal opportunity (think of Rawls' radical assertion on the injustice of family).[9] Contemporary equality tends toward neutrality, but a neutral friendship is inconceivable.

This chapter focuses on the relationship between the principle of equality and the political value of friendship. It seems to me that Aristotle's approach reveals something about human beings *as persons* and about their political dimension to which the sole appeal to the equality of human rights cannot *do justice*. The point is not to deny either a human rights based morality or the principle of equality, but to try to integrate them into a broader perspective and to determine if the crisis of contemporary political systems shows an inadequacy of human rights talk. This chapter first addresses the political relevance of the classical concept of friendship and its connection with the concept of person. It then sketches an account of political justice which is slightly different than the most familiar ones based on human rights. This account draws remarkable consequences for approaching some of the most relevant issues at stake in the contemporary debate.

1. Friendship and Justice

In classical political philosophy since Aristotle, friendship is what[10] grounds the *polis*, or State. Friendship is "the greatest of goods for

9   See J. Rawls, *A Theory of Justice* (Cambridge, Mass.: Harvard University Press, 1971).

10   I deliberately do not define friendship here, and I try to avoid the term "value" with Aristotle because it is often abused today and it is too charged, so to speak, with a modern immanent meaning.

city-states."[11] It seems "to hold states together, and lawgivers to care more for it than for justice,"[12] because "when men are friends they have no need of justice, while when they are just they need friendship as well, and the truest form of justice is thought to be a friendly quality."[13]

In Book II of his *Politics*, Aristotle's critique of Plato's communism focuses on two leading ideas: [1] communism makes friendly bonds among citizens impossible, at every level of social life; and [2] communism deals with political community as if it were "a natural unity,"[14] something organic, similar to an individual's body. Aristotle considers Plato's project as an attempt to exceedingly increase the unity of the State, making the citizens share as many things as possible, and making them similar to a kind of big family, or all-encompassing individual.[15]

However Aristotle explains that two things "cause human beings to love and cherish something: their own and their favorite."[16] He continues that there is a certain pleasure in regarding a thing as one's own. This is not selfish pleasure coming from vice, but the morally good pleasure deriving from natural self-love. There is also a certain pleasure in helping one's friends, guests, or companions, and in doing them favors by using one's property. There are some virtues—like "temperance in regard to women (for it is a fine thing to stay away from another man's woman out of temperance), and generosity with one's property"—that in the Platonic system

11   *Pol.*, II, 1262b7. In this chapter, for the *Politics* I used C.D.C. Reeve's translation (Indianapolis, IN: Hackett, 1998).

12   *NE*, VIII, 1155a23–25.

13   *NE*, VIII, 1155a23–27.

14   *Pol.*, II, 1261b7.

15   There is something seductive in this desire of a strong political union built on the complete sacrifice of individual goods and interests to the advantage of common utility; a sacrifice that should go so far as to thrust one's children out without giving way to pity, and to give up one's family. See Plato, *Republic* (hereafter *Rep.*), IV, 415a–c; V, 457d. For the *Republic* I used Paul Shorey's translation (Cambridge, MA, Harvard University Press; London, William Heinemann Ltd., 1969), available on the internet at *Perseus Digital Library* (http://www.perseus.tufts.edu/). See also Giovanni Reale's evaluation of Plato's communism (too indulgent in my opinion) in his *A History of Ancient Philosophy, vol. 2 (Albany: State University of New York Press, 1987)*, pp. 197–200.

16   *Pol.*, II, 1262b21–23.

could never be practiced.[17] The State is not a natural unity, Aristotle concludes, as there are things that do not belong to it directly. To try to give these things to the state would mean to destroy them, and together with them to destroy the political unity that should instead come from the attempt. "It is as if one were to reduce a harmony to a unison, or a rhythm to a single bit."[18] The criticism is clear: in order for a melody to be successfully performed, every single note must remain itself and express its specific nature at its best. In Aristotle, the political bond is strong primarily if the bonds of friendship among individuals at the lower levels of social life are strong, starting with the family. In fact, inferior communities are by nature prior and more necessary than political community,[19] even if they are less self-sufficient.[20]

For the moment, I would like to draw attention not to the *political* importance of promoting the good of inferior communities by respecting their specific nature (also known as the problem of subsidiarity), and not even to the importance of not damaging the friendship lived by every citizen in his private life, but rather to the relationship that Aristotle draws between friendship and equality.[21] This relationship is not limited by the fact that, although different from each other, the two are intrinsically connected. It is true that friendship and justice are "concerned with the same objects and exhibited between the same persons,"[22] and that in every community "the demands of justice also naturally increase with friendship, which implies that friendship and justice exist between the same persons and have an equal extension."[23] Yet, this is not sufficient to describe the relationship between

---

17 *Pol.*, II, 1263a40–1263b22.

18 *Pol.*, II, 1263b34–35. This image of Aristotle's is very similar to Herder's image of the orchestra, which Charles Taylor praises in his "A Tension in Modern Democracy," in A. Botwinick and W.E. Connolly, *Democracy and Vision: Sheldon Wolin and the Vicissitudes of the Political* (Princeton: Princeton University Press, 2001), p. 90.

19 *NE*, VIII, 1162a17–20.

20 *Pol.*, II, 1261b10–15.

21 At least in this context, I consider justice and equality as equivalent political values.

22 *NE*, VIII, 1159b25–27.

23 *NE*, VIII, 1160a7–9.

justice and friendship. Rather, such a relationship also implies a real primacy of friendship over justice. In this sense, in order to realize a *just* political community, a good legislator and a good government should always have a special eye to friendship rather than to justice. This should exist both at the level of lower communities and at the level of the political good as such. Obviously, this does not mean that justice could be violated to favor friendship. It means, rather, that the meaning of friendship should provide the background to the concept of justice.

For the time being, we should limit our attention to the existence of an intrinsic link between friendship and justice without overstressing the primacy of the first over the second. In fact, what is most astonishing at first glance is precisely the idea that justice and friendship work together in grounding the political community. This is astonishing precisely because to focus on friendship is to focus on *one's own and one's favorite*. That is exactly what we would never expect from justice, because justice, as equality, is *impartial*.

1.1. Friendship and Equality

The most obvious reason why friendship and equality go together in Aristotle's ethics is that they both consist in relationships of equality. There is justice between two persons if a certain kind of equality exists between them, just as friendship exists between two persons if there is a certain kind of equality between them. Legal, or universal, justice is the equality of all citizens with respect to the common benefit or good, which can also be understood as their equal obedience to the laws that aim at that benefit. Particular justice is the equality of two or more persons with respect to either the distribution of a certain common good (distributive justice) or the propriety and possession of their own individual goods (commutative or corrective justice).[24] What then is the equality of friendship?

According to Aristotle, "equality does not seem to take the same form in acts of justice and in friendship; for in acts of justice what is equal in the

---

24　See *NE*, V, 1129a27–1132b20. For my present purpose I do not need to examine here in depth Aristotle's account of the different types of justice. Nor do I need to examine here the difference between the concept of corrective justice in Aristotle and the concept of commutative justice in Aquinas.

primary sense is that which is in proportion to merit, while quantitative equality is secondary, but in friendship quantitative equality is primary and proportion to merit secondary."[25] There is no need for us to focus here on the exact meaning of Aristotle's concept of merit. As far as friendship is concerned, what he wants to say is that it is more proper to its nature to have real equality (or parity) between what is given and what is received. If such parity is not established, due to some moral, economic, social, or cultural condition, there might still be respect for each other's rights, but not friendship. This is because friendship from both sides of the relationship lies "in loving rather than in being loved,"[26] and in giving more than in receiving. If the relationship is objectively unequal (father/son; aged person/youth; ruler/ruled) it is necessary for the one who receives more to make the effort to love and honor more. "It is in this way more than any other that even unequals can be friends; they can be equalized."[27]

For Aristotle, this real equality (according to quantity), which is required among friends, is above all *equality in virtues*. This is because benevolence, or goodwill, which is the first step on the path to friendship, does not arise from either benefit or pleasure, but "on account of some excellence [virtue] and worth, when one man seems to another beautiful or brave or something of the sort."[28] Thus, virtue is the first thing that friends give to each other. Aristotle says this is true of every kind of friendship, even of political friendship, or "concord," because concord "is found among good men,"[29] and "citizens want to be equal and virtuous."[30]

In my opinion, Aristotle's insight that friendship requires equality in virtues happily matches the contemporary ethos that considers human rights to be the foundation of political community. Yet it does not match the idea that human rights can be pursued in a neutral way. On the one hand, virtue essentially requires freedom for the moral agents. Under this respect, friendship can only flourish in an environment that fully allows friends to exercise

25 *NE*, VIII, 1158b29–33.
26 *NE*, VIII, 1159a26–27.
27 *NE*, VIII, 1159b1–2.
28 *NE*, IX, 1166b30–1167a21.
29 *NE*, IX, 1167b5.
30 *NE*, VIII, 1161a28–29.

freedom. On the other hand, to recognize and appreciate our friends' virtues implies a positive evaluation of the concrete exercise of their freedom. Thus, we have a first important consequence of considering friendship instead of mere equality as the basis of political community: the relationship between friends, even at the political level, cannot be neutral with respect to the *good life*. This does not necessarily mean that the political sharing of the good-life's values should be axiologically strong, to the point of establishing what today we would call an *ethical state*. I believe that there are already adequate theoretical resources in Aristotle to draw relevant differences among the spheres of friendship lived by individuals—including the political sphere—according to the degree of *intimacy* required by each of them. Political friend-ship is undoubtedly the relationship that requires the lowest level of intimacy and, consequently, the lowest level of sharing in the good life.

I think this is also a reasonable way to describe contemporary political communities in which a certain shared idea of the good life seems to be at the root of the very concept of human rights and of their interpretation. Sharing the human rights culture means to share a basic appreciation of the virtuous person as one who accepts and equally respects the human rights of everybody else. Under this respect, the language of friendship—which involves moral appreciation—seems more appropriate to express the fundamental value of political community than that of mere equality. Yet equality in the virtues is not something that *per se* distinguishes friends from other virtuous persons, or in the case of political community, from people who do not belong to the same community. Under this other respect, there-fore, friendship again seems coextensive with the universality of the value of equality. The only qualification is that it is equality itself that is incon-ceivable from a neutral viewpoint.

However, friendship also requires equality in *contribution*, namely, in what friends give to each other. As soon as the conceptual element of con-tribution comes into play, the equality that friends share in their reciprocal relationship sharply diverges from the equality they share with the other human beings. Every contribution, of any kind—moral, economic, cul-tural, etc.—is necessarily discriminatory, as are the concepts of nation, pa-triotic spirit, and the rights of citizenship. Here, friendship seems to come into more serious conflict with the concept of equality. It conflicts even with human rights, inasmuch as it implies the adoption of a selective criterion regarding both the protection of negative liberties and the continually imporoved realization of the positive. Every political community must look after its own citizens and those who reside in its territory or occasionally visit. It is only in a very indirect and secondary way that the political community can *indiscriminately* look after the human beings who live in the other parts of the world.

With regard to considering discrimination involved in the concepts of territorial membership and citizenship, the language of friendship seems much more appropriate to the political community than the language of equality. Yet it does not seem to offer a plausible justification for this discrimination. To find such a justification we need to delve more deeply into Aristotle's concept of friendship.

1.2. The Specific Character of Friendship

Friendship is the most extensively examined issue in the *Nicomachean Ethics* (two books out of ten), yet it is one of the few that does not receive a clear theoretical categorization. Aristotle appears somewhat uncertain about what friendship is. He begins by saying that "it is an excellence [virtue] or implies excellence."[31] In my opinion, the question of the exact relevance of friendship in Aristotle's ethics is far more difficult than the question raised by that hesitant exordium. There are good reasons to say that Aristotle would have conferred a higher theoretical value to friendship but he could not. On the one hand, he seems to perceive that the sense of ethics and of human life essentially depends on the sense and importance of personal otherness. On the other hand, he sees otherness—friendship—as something deriving from need and imperfection. Friendship as such cannot be divine. Strictly speaking, it cannot be part of the ultimate end.[32] Compared to this problem and to its theoretical interpretation, the link between friendship and virtue is definitely much simpler.

The entire Aristotelian ethics focuses on moral virtues because these are the virtues that fulfill, or perfect, the appetitive part of the soul, which

31 *NE*, VIII, 1155a2.
32 A less limiting concept of friendship enters the history of philosophy only with Christianity.

is the part responsible for our attraction to the good and the pleasurable. Since "it is on account of pleasure that we do bad things, and on account of pain that we abstain from noble ones,"[33] the fundamental ethical objective is to make the soul ready and willing "both to delight in and to be pained by the things that we ought."[34] Aristotle devotes very little room to the intellectual (dianoetic) virtues as if to say that if the appetite is (morally) correct then reason will not have much difficulty in finding the right action to perform. Excluding part of Book III and almost all of Book VI, from Book II until the books on friendship the attention is wholly for moral virtues whose main characteristic is to perfect the soul's inclination to the mean between two extremes: one in excess and one in defect. The soul's tendency toward these is due to an inordinate attraction to pleasure, that is, an attraction contrary to the right rule. Thus, moral virtue is an inclination (*exis*) to the courage that lies between rashness and cowardice, to the liberality that lies between prodigality and meanness, to the magnificence that lies between vulgarity and niggardliness, to the magnanimity that lies in between empty vanity and pusillanimity, to the truthfulness that lies between boastfulness and self-deprecation, and so on.

Friendship cannot be a virtue because virtue belongs to the agent's nature as an inclination in accordance with right reason, and friendship obviously cannot reside only in the agent. This is why Aristotle immediately retracts the statement that friendship is a virtue. He then includes among the conditions to be friend not only "reciprocated goodwill" or benevolence, but also the friends' "awareness" of that benevolence.[35] Friendship is a relationship that lies *between* the friends, not merely in the inclinations of one or both of them. Nevertheless, friendship is similar to virtue not just because it is essential to moral life, but also because it seems to answer to the same logic of perfecting inclinations with respect to two morally wrong extremes. In this case, the extremes are friendship grounded on (mere) utility and friendship grounded on (mere) pleasure. True friendship—the mean—is the one grounded on virtues, in which the friend is not loved instrumentally

33   *NE*, II, 1104b7–10.
34   *NE*, II, 1104b12–13.
35   *NE*, VIII, 1155b32–35, 1166b30–1167a21.

due to the benefit or pleasure that he or she supplies. "Men who are good
[...] wish well alike to each other *qua* good" and "are most truly friends, for
they do this by reason of their own nature and not incidentally."[36] "Bad
men," on the other hand, "will be friends for the sake of pleasure or of utility."[37]

Aristotle explains that apart from being the most useful and pleasurable, true friendship is lasting, requires living together in an intimate way,[38]
and leads to trust and like each other, and to "enjoy the same things."[39] It
"requires time and familiarity; as the proverb says, men cannot know each
other till they have 'eaten salt together.'"[40] For these reasons, "the friendship
of the good too alone is proof against slander, for it is not easy to trust any
one's talk about a man who has long been tested by oneself."[41]

It is clear that Aristotle does not think of friendship in terms of a sort
of *generic* relationship, in which time and living together are required simply
in order to get to know generic virtues that the other possesses. Such a
knowledge in and of itself would not be sufficient to bring about friendship.
Rather, friendship is an interpersonal relationship in at least two relevant
senses: (1) that it is built up on the knowledge and appreciation of the
friend's *unique* personality; and (2) that is itself a *unique* emanation of the
meeting of two unique personalities. In other words, what is *specific* to
friendship is rooted not in *nature* but in the *person*. Namely, it is not found
in the human being considered generically (or universally) equal to every
other human being, but in the human being considered as a unique and
original reality.[42]

36　*NE*, VIII, 1156b6–12.
37　*NE*, VIII, 1157b2–4: "[B]ad men will be friends for the sake of pleasure or of
　　utility, being in this respect like each other, but good men will be friends for
　　their own sake, i.e. in virtue of their goodness."
38　*NE*, IX, 1170b20–1171a20, 1171b29–1172a15.
39　*NE*, VIII, 1157b5–24.
40　*NE*, VIII, 1156b26–28.
41　*NE*, VIII, 1157a21–24.
42　Of course, when I write "specific" I do not mean to deny by any means the
　　importance of the "generic" sense of nature. I mean only to emphasize, from
　　a logical viewpoint, what it is that determines the specific, and therefore
　　proper, nature of what we call friendship.

1.3. Friendship and Person

The difference between person and nature was first worked out by medieval philosophy and theology, and it reaches its most detailed and nuanced definition with Thomas Aquinas. The famous definition of person that he inherits from Boethius—*rationalis naturae individua substantia*—is grounded on the concept of freedom. Individual substances of a rational nature are those which have dominion over their own actions, and which are not only made to act, like others, but which can also act of themselves ("*non solum aguntur, sicut alia, sed per se agunt*").[43] For Aquinas, *personal actions* are those actions which depend on a unique principle of spiritual nature and not only on universal, necessitating inclinations common to the species. That is to say, they do not depend *simply* on the common inclination to play, or to pair off and form a family (*universal nature*), but on my being Fulvio Di Blasi and not Joseph Kolf or Andrew Syski (*person as independent ontological principle*).[44]

In the definition defended by Aquinas, the person is free because he knows nature according to truth. When Aquinas approaches the question of whether man is free (whether he has free will, *liberum arbitrium*), he explains precisely that since the judgment of reason does not come from natural instinct it is a free judgment and, as such, it can originate different and opposed courses of action.[45] Rationality and freedom here are two sides of the same coin. From this viewpoint, Kant does not invent anything new when he tries to prove *a priori* the existence of freedom as a necessary condition of rationality. His argument perfectly follows the lines already drawn by medieval thought.[46]

The rationale of Boethius's definition was already present in Greek philosophy and it lies at the roots of the Aristotelian concept of friendship, among other things. Since its birth, moral philosophy has been linked to the idea of subjectivity, which transcends the realm of uniform necessity of nature. For this very reason, it is able to originate choices and actions that are really free. This is Socrates' original moral insight: man is the only being

---

43   Cfr., *ST*, I, q. 29 a. 1 c.
44   Cfr., *CG*, III, Ch. 113.
45   *ST*, I, q. 83, a. 1.
46   See, for example, Kant, *Ethical Philosophy* (Indianapolis, IN: Hackett, 1994), pp. 50–51).

whose action depends on knowledge of the truth and not on the necessitating work of nature (instincts and passions) or the values and universal inclinations that ground specifically human choices.

It is obvious that Socrates will say that *man is his soul* because what pertains to the physical realm—to the body—is necessity. Moreover, it is obvious that in the end he would center his ethics on knowledge, on the one hand, and on self-control, interior liberty, and autonomy, on the other. Man is that being who raises himself above the forces of nature, who is master and not slave, who has power over his own states of pleasure and pain, and whose moral realization cannot depend on any exterior force. Such a being experiences and interiorly enjoys his own freedom (*eleutheria*) by rationally controlling the impulses of his nature.[47] The goodness of this moral experience is radical and self-evident. When, after Socrates, Aristotle addresses the life of pleasure and enjoyment as a kind of life in which human happiness cannot reside, he simply writes that such a life is "slavish" and "suitable to beasts."[48] This criticism might appear weak and underdeveloped, but only to those who fail to notice the crucial value of freedom as a defining element of human being, which Aristotle inherits from Socrates and Plato. For Aristotle, a slavish life without freedom is not even worthy of special theoretical attention. Under this respect, the whole Aristotelian ethics should be seen as an ethics of freedom. It is an ethics in which the moral agent raises himself above the realm of necessity and develops his own personal subjectivity. He does this by living the virtues and, consequently, by acting not in the power of passions and pleasures but according to a truth-knowledge of nature (i.e., according to right reason).

2. Person, Friendship, and Political Community

The most important consequence of the difference between person and nature—or likewise, of considering freedom the defining characteristic of the person—is that one's focus immediately shifts from the universality and necessity of nature to the particularity and contingency of *freedom*. To observe freedom means to observe something that could have been otherwise

47 See G. Reale, *A History of Ancient Philosophy*, vol. 1, pp. 321–6.
48 *NE*, I, 1095b14–22.

but is actually this way due to a non-determinate choice. In short, it is to observe something that is *personal*. Freedom is creative and unique; it comes from a unique principle which it constantly nourishes. To know a person does not mean to know his universal nature but to know the way in which his freedom has shaped, and continues to shape, that nature. It is only at a minimal or basic level that respect of the person means respect of his nature and the ontological principle of his uniqueness (I am thinking of the respect for persons who cannot exercise, or have not yet exercised, their freedom: unborn babies, newborn babies, sick people, etc.). At a higher level, respect for the person is respect for the uniqueness that results from freedom. The person is like a castle that could have been built in a thousand different ways, and which can now be admired and appreciated for its unique and original style. Whether in private or public life, a person does not want to be known, respected, and appreciated just as a human being, but above all as Nicoletta Serio, Andy Kioko, or Matthew Currie. This kind of knowledge, respect, and appreciation is the only way *to do justice* to the person.

This point partially explains why the concept of narrative, which was developed by MacIntyre in the context of an original rereading of Aristotle's ethics, is today so attractive to many scholars.[49] Who the character of a novel is can be only known as the story unfolds, or as his actions come to existence due to somebody reading or writing them. These actions only have meaning if they are contextualized. The first way to introduce the reader to the identity of the novel's main character is precisely to describe the environment in which he lives his life: family, school, friends (and enemies), office, society, etc. All these things must be written not only because they accidentally reveal the character's personality, but also because they are somehow an *essential part* of it. It is extremely interesting to consider the link between individual and society as analogous to the link between the character and the setting of the story. It immediately emerges that the

---

49   See A. MacIntyre, *After Virtue*; and P. Ricoeur, *Oneself as Another* (Chicago: The University of Chicago Press, 1992). On the concept of narrative see also P. M. Hall, *Narrative and the Natural Law: An Interpretation of Thomistic Ethics* (Notre Dame and London: University of Notre Dame Press, 1994); and R. A. Gahl, Jr., "Comunità, ethos e verità," in L. Melina and J. Larrú (eds.), *Verità e libertà nella teologia morale* (Roma: Pontificia Università Lateranense, 2001), pp. 89–108.

personality (or identity) of the individual and the *personality* (or identity) of society are interrelated. Nobody is free to build up his own personality independent of his social context, which is in turn a contingent result of the coming together and interacting of many individual freedoms. From this perspective, it is certainly meaningful to talk about a right to take part in culturally shaping the political community and about a right to use, to that purpose, *any argument* that one might consider relevant to the development of his own personality and of the personalities of his loved ones. This is true whether this argument be freedom of religion, respect for some particular traditions, respect for one's own religion, etc. To deny this right is a violation of equality and discriminatory action.

2.1. Friendship's Act of Sharing

At this point let us go back to friendship. We said that friendship is grounded on equality in freedom and in the fundamental rights of the person. We also said that the proper character of friendship does not reside in generic elements of human nature but in the reciprocal sharing and appreciation of the novelty coming from the friends' free actions—that is, from their personalities. This is why every friendship is *unique* from the start and it deepens over time due to the creative nature of a primordial and original act of sharing. This act is a sort of agreement, or contract, which has both a constitutive and an evolutionary aspect (*in fieri*). It can also be more or less tacit or more or less explicit. "For friendship," says Aristotle, "is a partnership."[50]

If the act of sharing that grounds friendship ceases, friendship also ceases with it. Friendships break up with the vanishing of the motives of the primordial act of communion from which they had arisen. Sometimes this happens due to separation or a mere lack of frequentation. Lack of contact between persons progressively reduces a friendship's communion precisely because this communion does not come solely from a generic knowledge of values and virtues. The more a friendship is superficial, or not grounded on natural (family) bonds, the faster the relationship grows faint when friends do not see each other, until it eventually disappears. Other times, the breaking of a friendship depends on the change in values

---

50 *NE*, IX, 1171b32–33.

on the side of one or both of the friends. Even in this case, the breaking is faster or slower according to how deep or superficial those values are. However, this time the process is reversed: the stronger the values are, the faster a friendship breaks up. Think of a strong divergence between engaged people on the importance of children or the faith, or between two politicians on the interpretation of the basic values of their party. In these cases the crisis is rapid. "How could they be friends when they neither approved of the same things nor delighted in and were pained by the same things?"[51]

2.2. The Uniqueness of the Political Contract

All this is also true of the political community. It too originates above all from the recognition of human beings' basic freedoms, and is a unique encounter of personal beings with each other. It arises from a primordial and original agreement that has both a constitutive and an evolutionary aspect and depends on common values and authorities.[52] In contemporary states this primordial agreement is given especially by the several kinds of constitutional settlements, whether written or unwritten. As the outcome of the individual freedoms of those who approved them, these settlements are too unique and individual from the start and cannot be understood outside of the cultural context that determined them and keeps them alive. From this angle, the insights of contemporary legal hermeneutics concerning the constitutional settlements being more than the written documents certainly seem important.[53] Moreover, Rawls' fiction of an original position, in which nobody knows who he is and what he possesses, is inhuman (because it is impersonal). As a matter of fact, even two constitutions written exactly the same way could not be considered identical because their meanings would still remain inseparable from the culture and contingencies that produced them.

---

51   *NE*, IX, 1165b27–29.
52   I use "agreement" and "contract" here in a broad way that is applicable to both modern thinkers and classical authors like Aristotle, Augustine, and Aquinas. Read, for example, the following passage from Aristotle: "[Friendships] of fellow-citizens [...] are like friendships of association; for they seem to rest on a sort of compact" (*NE*, VIII, 1161b13–16).
53   See M. Jori (ed.), *Ermeneutica e filosofia analitica: Due concezioni del diritto a confronto* (Torino: Giappichelli, 1994).

After the constitutive agreement, the community grows and develops insofar as it remains dialectically connected to it. If it does not, we should speak of social revolution in the same way in which we spoke above about the breaking of individual friendships. The theme of returning to the origin that characterized humanistic and Renaissance political philosophy has much allure and much wisdom.[54] To understand who you are, you have to go back to your origins and revisit your past. This is true for any individual and any institution, especially in moments of crisis. Only in light of this historical self-consciousness is it possible to reasonably focus on what needs to be changed in the present and on how to build the future. Machiavelli's idea of reforming the Italy of the fifteenth century by looking at the pagan Rome of the republican period was probably wrong (Machiavelli, after all, was more of an ideologist than a historian). Yet his methodology of searching the past for the values upon which to ground the political unity of a nation contained a type of reasoning in political philosophy from which we should not stop learning.[55]

Will Kymlicka offers a useful distinction between two main kinds of multicultural society: one following the incorporation of cultures already existing in the territory, and one that depends on immigration processes.[56] In the first case, from the viewpoint of our analysis, the constitutive act of the political community should be taken as inclusive of the terms of the peaceful relationship established with the pre-existing cultures, and should develop consistently with those terms. If a peaceful life together is not established, the life of *one* (multicultural) political community in the relevant territory will never take shape. The original terms of the intercultural relationship can justify (i.e., make *just*) some discriminatory preferences in the life of the political community. This is the case with various special rights given to American Indians in the U.S. In the second case, the process of integration and the attention for minorities should happen in the context

---

54 See N. Abbagnano, *Storia della filosofia - Volume terzo: La filosofia del rinascimento* (Milano: TEA, 1993), pp. 3–11, 39–55.

55 See N. Machiavelli, *Discourses on Livy* (Chicago: University of Chicago Press, 1996), Book III, Ch. 1.

56 W. Kymlicka, *Multicultural Citizenship: A Liberal Theory of Minority Rights*, op. cit., p. 10.

of a constant respect and preference for the identity of the political community. In the case of conflict among rights, the traditional values of the receiving community must be preferred. This does not involve only the authorities of the receiving community. According to a *just* moral attitude, immigrants should make the effort of understanding, respecting, and reasonably integrating themselves in the traditions of those who are accepting them in their community. If they do this, it will be easier for their own traditions and values to be understood, respected, and often welcomed—this is the most mature step of the integration process.

Regardless of the kind of society, it is true that it will be stronger or weaker according to how relevant, pressing, and intense the original shared values are. Religion, freedom, moral values, defense, etc., are all factors of strong political union (or friendship). If statesmen neglect (or even attack) those values, the result is either a sharp breaking of political friendship or its dim and unperceived breaking due to the progressive dwindling of the factors of national unity among the citizens. This second breaking is similar to the break up of individual friendships due to lack of frequentation and common interests. To be Italian is *important* as long as it remains different than being American. In more or less the same way to be Joseph Kolf is *important* as long as it remains different than being Matthew Currie. Even if it were possible, a truly *neutral* democracy would end up destroying political unity, the feeling of belonging, and patriotism.

2.3. Primacy of Friendship and Criteria of Justice

The primacy of friendship over equality in the foundation of political community is analogous to the primacy of person over nature in the *suppositum* (the actually existing human being). When political philosophy is centered on the primacy of friendship it can be properly called *political personalism*. The person is more than the nature which he shares with his fellow human beings, just as the family and the political community are more than what makes their members and citizens equal to the members and citizens of any other family and political community. This something more comes from friendship. Due to the development of the discourse on human rights and equality, contemporary society came to understand that human relationships must be grounded at every level on the respect and protection of what makes all human beings formally equal: their nature.[57] However, human relationships are *personal relationships*, which come into existence and grow up in the unique encounter between individual freedoms. These relationships are more than the equal rights they have in common. Human rights are a necessary condition for the existence of the political community just as rational nature is a necessary condition for the existence of the person.[58] Yet no inclination common to the species can generate the person. Similarly, no *universal* element—such as human rights, democratic settlement, etc.— —that is not sufficient to distinguish the members of one political community from those of another, is sufficient to ground political communities and to nourish them.[59] It is important to reflect that patriotism cannot be reduced to criteria of universal equality. Human rights, as such, do not justify the particular attachment to one particular community (or to one particular family, football team, etc.). This is an important aspect of the human (*personal*) being that should not be underestimated.

Talking about political relationships as friendship relationships has many consequences. I will now briefly try to point out some of them that alter the concept of justice as it emerges from the sole consideration of equality.

2.3.1. Justice of Having Recourse to a Selective Criterion

The establishment of a human relationship necessarily involves embracing a selective criterion with respect to human nature generically considered. The relationship between two subjects A and B (say, husband and wife,

---

57 Let me consider, in this context, human rights talk as formally equivalent to the discourse on human nature.

58 From this viewpoint, respect for human rights can be compared to the concept of respect for the commandments as the "beginning of freedom"—or imperfect freedom—that from Augustine onward is common patrimony of Christian thought. See John Paul II, *Veritatis Splendor*, n. 17.

59 The point is not to interpret the political community as a kind of Platonic organic unity, as if it were an individual and personal autonomous being. The point, rather, is to highlight how much every political community depends on the *persons* who create it and nourish it with their *personal* choices. The fully existent political community because it depends on such free choices is contingent and not reducible to generic elements of human nature.

brother and sister, coach and player, boss and employer, citizen and citizen, etc.) means that all or part of the elements of the nature that A shares with the other human beings take on a privileged status in B's eyes, and vice versa. Whatever the intensity and the nature of the relationship, it will always be the case that B *ought* to take care of A's well-being more than of the well-being of anybody else, albeit to a certain extent. This is true both for (a) generic human goods (life, health, work, etc.) and (b) the novelty coming from A's choices (family traditions, language, religion, etc.). This preference looks like a discriminatory act if one gives priority to the concept of nature over the concept of person. However, if one considers the uniqueness of personal being it is clear that to neglect somebody whose existence *crosses our own* in some relevant way causes an injustice toward him. Yet a similar injustice does not exist (or exists to a lesser degree) toward those whom *we have never met*.

The person is a being who lives in unique and personal relations (this is a universal necessity of nature). We do him justice when we do not treat him generically, but according to the nature of those relationships. Respecting the selective criterion is *just* because it means *respecting the person*. This is true precisely because to do justice to the person means to respect not only his abstract freedom (or nature) but also its concrete exercise with reference to the unique relationships that it establishes with other people.

2.3.2. A Selective Criterion as Law's Internal Point of View

The establishment of a selective criterion seems to be an epistemological presupposition for the very existence of rights (whether human or not). In contemporary philosophy of law, it is clear that one cannot talk properly about rights in abstract terms but only in concrete terms. Even talking about a right to life or to freedom has no proper legal relevance if we do not *specify* (a) the subject who has a duty regarding it, (b) the subject who has the right, and (c) the concrete action or omission, object of the duty and the corresponding right. [In what sense would a person who is starving to death on a desert island, and of whose existence nobody knows, have *a right to life?*] From this viewpoint, the coming into being of a political community can be seen as the *first specification* (discriminatory, from a universal standpoint) of subjects and resources from which every concrete action in protection of rights can start. This likewise applies to an action which relates to subjects external to the political community.

This first specification takes place according to the internal and particular viewpoint of a certain political community. It depends on the basic cultural traits of that community, whether religious, ethical, economic, military, artistic, etc. There is no reason—or way—to place an a-priori limit on the list of elements which should be relevant to the initial definition of the identity of a community. That is to say, there are no *a priori* limits to the content of public reason. The internal point of view of the community leads to the discovery and rational interpretation of the very basic values of the law. The process of specification of rights originates and evolves diachronically in the context of a dialectical back and forth (or hermeneutic circle) between the particular culture of a community and its understanding of the rational universal elements of justice. Both extremes of this exchange should be taken into account for the purpose of defining what is just. If they want to be *just*, both the politician and the lawyer should know very well and respect the particular culture in which they operate.

2.3.3. A Selective Criterion and Balancing

The selective criterion accompanies the birth of the political community. It not only concerns the people toward whom the collective should first turn its attention, but also the way in which the hierarchies of values that exist in the community should be interpreted. At first glance, this seems to match both the Aristotelian concept of friendship and the predominant contemporary approach to the question of balancing. As we saw in section 1.2., "Friendship and Equality," equality in friendships cannot be neutral. In that sense, every community of friends originates from sharing—even at a minimal level—a certain conception of the good life that can depend on many factors: religious, moral, cultural, traditional, etc.

Now, if it is true (here a definitive answer is unnecessary) that cases of conflict between basic rights exist, which cannot be solved without the judge creating an *ad hoc* subjective hierarchy, it is also true that this procedure would be unjust if the reference *subject* of the *subjective* hierarchy (excuse me for playing with words) would be the same judge who creates it. The subjective hierarchy is just only if the *reference subject* is the *political community* that the judge serves. It should always be possible to describe the creation of the subjective hierarchy as an interpretive activity of the conception of the good life shared by the political community that the judge represents. Justice is always respect for freedom. In this case, it is respect for the freedom of the citizens, or to put it another way, respect for the constitutive act (*in fieri*) of the relationship of political friendship. The dialectical back and forth between the cultural viewpoint and universal rationality determines the development of legal civilization. Every culture tends to justify itself according to criteria of rationality.

2.3.4. The Justice of the Relevance of Tradition

At this point, it should logically follow that it is just to recognize, honor, and respect the history and the traditions of our nation from an internal viewpoint, and give more importance to whatever it is that people of the same nation hold as imperative. Both the internal stable cohesion of the community and the effectiveness of its continuous interpretative effort to reach universal values and human rights depend on this attitude. Even the capacity to welcome and assimilate new values and traditions (for example, those coming from immigration movements) depend on the same attitude.

The internal political debate of a community is only just toward the person if it occurs in such a context of valorization, understanding, and respect. In other words, it would only be just if it occurs in the context of a continuous interpretative reference to the personal identity of the political community given by its constitutive act (both as a historical act and as an act *in fieri*). Abrupt political changes are almost always to be avoided, because they are not only imprudent in a Machiavellian sense, but also *unjust*. Every change should always start and develop in the context of a respectful evaluation of the population's common feeling and understanding. The contrary would be ideological violence bearing divisions and social tensions.

The traditional values to be taken into account include culture, history, and every other element which characterizes the specific nation's civilization, including religion. From this viewpoint the recent debate on mentioning the Christian roots in the new European Constitution seems to be legitimate, insofar as it is reasonable to recognize the connection between the values of Christianity and the formation over the centuries of Europe's culture and civilization.

Let me give another example. If somebody tried fiercely, in today's Italy, to prohibit hanging crucifixes in the walls of public schools favoring a neutral attitude towards religion, the result would be not only a *non-neutral* stance against the relevance of religion in public life but also an injustice against Italian political community whose history, culture, and feeling are deeply tied to the Catholic religion. This is of course a prudential judgment that might be wrong.[60] My point, though, is that protecting freedom of religion in a political community is not in contrast with some preference given to a particular religion concretely chosen by the members of the community, and which has historically informed its very political and legal culture. Freedom of religion should also be respected in its concrete exercise. This does not mean that the religious attitude of a nation cannot change but that the change should not justifiably be politically superimposed by somebody who is indifferent to the culture and values of the people. By the same train of reasoning, if the right to freedom of religion were recognized today in Saudi Arabia it would still be unjust to eliminate every public privilege of Muslim religion.

2.3.5. Multiculturalism and Political Personalism

What is the relationship between this personalist approach and multiculturalism? This is not an easy question to answer because multiculturalism today looks more like a way to highlight the gaps of neutral (a-cultural) liberalism than an overall philosophical proposal. Some multicultural proposals actually seem naively compatible with the liberal principle of neutrality. They only shift the attention from respecting individual freedom, or identity, to respecting the identity of minority groups.[61] The main difference between these proposals and political personalism is that the latter focuses first on the identity

---

60 Some time ago when an Italian judge ordered the removal of a crucifix from the walls of a public school for reasons of fairness toward other religions (specifically Islam), even non-Catholic intellectuals reacted strongly against the judge's decision (which was eventually overturned) on account of the high relevance of the crucifix for Italian culture and history.

61 See, for example, Bhikhu Parekh, *Rethinking Multiculturalism: Cultural Diversity and Political Theory* (Cambridge, MA: Harvard University Press, 2000), whose conclusions seem to present, at the level of cultural groups, the same contradictions created by liberal neutrality.

of the political whole in which both the individual and the other intermediate social groups develop their own freedoms and personal identities.

Often, multiculturalism intertwines a cultural, or sociological, relativism in which the good, *relative* to a certain culture, comes before the right of the people living in that culture. In a model such as this there is no room for universal human rights. Political personalism is entirely different in that the person can practice his freedom (giving birth to culture) only by moving, so to speak, inside his own nature (i.e., inside the inclinations common to the species). Nature comes before culture and makes it possible. This model involves a constant dialectical exchange between the universal and abstract needs of reason and their particular cultural existence.

A clear example is the constant debate between the abstract declaration of the right to freedom of religion and the concrete evaluation of what actions should be regarded as legitimate expressions of it. For example, would it be legitimate for an Italian police officer who professes himself to be observant Jew not to try to save somebody on Saturday from a crime he happens to witness? Should we give special protection only to some public religions—even creating an official list—or to individual religions as well? In the latter case, should we protect a citizen who out of some individual religious reasons did not want to work on Tuesdays? In a political personalism of a classical fashion, nature (i.e., recognition of basic freedoms and rights) and culture go together because freedom and the creativity of culture are always (artistic) ways to express nature. What Michael Sandel says about "perfectionist multiculturalism" closely echoes this idea of political personalism.[62]

More generally, multiculturalism appears compatible with a classical political personalism when it stresses the insufficiency of the procedural republic[63] and the need for a political identity that stems from shared values and civic virtues and is grounded on some reciprocal commitment among the citizens.[64] This multiculturalism does not oppose the concept of liberal Western democracy, but only the neutral and abstract liberalism which dominates the debate between utilitarianism and Kantian deontologism.

---

62 See his preface to the second edition of *Liberalism and the Limits of Justice*.
63 See M. Sandel, *Democracy's Discontent* (Cambridge: Harvard University Press, 1996).
64 See C. Taylor, "A Tension in Modern Democracy."

A resolute attention to the equality of every human being and to human rights is perhaps the most important achievement of modern legal systems and contemporary political philosophy. The tendency of national States to look beyond their own territories, and the search for a universal cosmopolitan international order, are signs of great hope for the future of the human race. To a great extent, we owe this achievement and these signs to the way in which modern thought focuses on human nature and develops a strong rational discourse about its universal needs and rights.

On the other hand, classical Greek and medieval thought keep reminding us that the human being is not only nature, but above all a person. Human nature always lives and expresses itself in a culture, which is a nuanced and complex environment made of unique and unrepeatable individual choices. Social relationships are not only natural but also *interpersonal*. Friendship, which grounds them, is centered not on a generic human being, but on the person. Friendship depends on a special belonging to each other which is necessarily exclusionary and discriminatory. At the level of the political community, friendship especially manifests itself in patriotic values.

Just like the family and every other human association, political community is a work of art, of freedom built with the bricks and colors of nature. The current debates on globalization and multiculturalism reveal an insufficiency of the sole reference to human rights in politics. In the last two centuries, we focused most of all on the rationality of nature and on its universal needs. Now it is clear that we have to reach a further theoretical and practical synthesis that is able to harmonize, in a sense, the abstract and concrete of human existence. It is ever more evident that the refined and inexhaustible task of political theorists and statesmen is to try to complement the universal needs of human nature with the specific identity of each political community. They must recognize that such a community derives from the personalities of those who created it and continue to nourish its values. As I hope to have shown, this is a task of *justice* that has many direct and indirect consequences pertaining to our way of understanding and dealing with political and legal issues.

IX.

DEMOCRACY, CRISIS OF AUTHORITY, AND THE NATURAL LAW

It is fairly common today to talk about pluralism and relativism as if they were different and opposite ethical and theoretical responses, but to what question?

In his recent *Real Ethics*, John Rist emphasizes more than once that "in philosophy [...] ideas are not attractive merely because they are intellectually compelling," but also because they match values highly regarded in a certain time and place.[1] This statement recalls suggestive pages by Yves Simon on the relationship between ideology and philosophy. Ideology is "a system of propositions which, though undistinguishable so far as expression goes from statements about facts and essences, actually refer not so much to any real state of affairs as to the *aspirations* of a *society* at a certain *time* in its evolution."[2] Ideology carries "a heavy sociological weight"[3] and, for better of for worse, it always influences philosophy by determining the paths of its reflections. "A philosophy unaffected by any ideological feature would involve a degree of perfection that human affairs do not admit of."[4] "That society is blessed whose aspirations coincide with truth."[5] The philosopher's responsibility lies in keeping at bay, as well as he can, the influences of ideology on the objectivity of thought, without ever giving in to the temptation of accepting their advatnages. "A theorist is always in

---

1   J. Rist, *Real Ethics: Rethinking the Foundations of Morality* (Cambridge University Press: Cambridge 2002), p. 166.
2   Y. R. Simon, *The Tradition of Natural Law: A Philosopher's Reflections* (Fordham University Press: New York 1965), pp. 16–7.
3   Ibid. p. 20.
4   Ibid. p. 22.
5   Ibid. p. 24.

danger when he feels that there is in his public a 'will to believe' which, if needed, is ready to supplement the insufficient clarity of his analysis and overlook for a while possible gaps in his demonstrations."[6]

Why this debut? For the simple fact that the ethical and political debate on pluralism and relativism is contingent to our time, and it is charged with our ideological convictions about both the question of pluralism and relativism and possible answers. The question concerns the axiological foundation of liberal democracy, which is a political system grounded on its members' freedom. Hence, it must be preferred to any other political system. The possible answers are the good one—i.e., pluralism—and the bad one—i.e., relativism. I am not saying this because I want to impose my own answers on anybody else, but because I think it is undeniable that in our ethical and political culture (or our vastly shared ideology, if you like), democracy and pluralism have already won their battle. Our society wants to be democratic, and it does not want to be relativist but pluralist. For some reason, which certainly deserves to be explored in depth, the term "pluralism" expresses the values of freedom that we want our democratic systems to embody better than the term "relativism." From this viewpoint, the real question we should ask ourselves is not if pluralism is better than relativism, or vice versa, but, "Which pluralism, and how?"

If we look at the pluralism *versus* relativism alternative from the (common sense) viewpoint of the citizens of liberal democracies, this alternative appears factitious and ambiguous, especially because liberal democracy is already taken by everybody to be the *true* answer to the question about the best (and *just*) political system. Not even the most radical liberals would accept to *relativize* the liberal principle: i.e., they would refuse the idea that the majority could decide to overrule both the majority principle and the democratic government. If a majority tried to do such a thing, a civil war would follow, and it would be seen as a *just war*. Some Italian constitutional lawyers appeal to a legal fiction, which is as theoretically inconsistent as it is psychologically reassuring. They teach that the part of our Western constitutions relating to the democratic State's fundamental principles and freedoms could not be changed even by a hypothetical constituent or parliamentary unanimity. It is as if a transcendent reason existed according

6   Ibid. p. 39.

to which the historical majority that wrote a constitution must prevail on every other future majority until the end of time. As a matter of fact, this constitutional law approach presupposes the existence of trans-historical truths—or, more specifically, trans-majoritarian and trans-liberal truths. From this viewpoint, liberal democracy resembles a formal logic system, which, as scientists like Turing and Gödel teach, cannot be self-referential. When key truths of the system are at stake, the liberal majority principle is not applicable either synchronically or diachronically. Therefore, liberal democracies are not based merely on social agreements but on superior and objective ethical truths. They are not based on relativism.

But if the pluralism *versus* relativism alternative is factitious, why do people express it, or why do they express it in this way? There are probably many reasons. Partly, it is a rhetorical maneuver that gambles with the negative semantic connotation of the term "relativism" in order to make people focus on the risks, dangers, and defects of the democratic system. Another reason—a much more interesting one—is that the most successful philosophical and political ideologies that have tried to offer a foundation to the *truth* of democratic liberalism, both at its birth and still today, have strong relativistic presuppositions and implications. I realize this is a contradiction. Yet the success of philosophical theories almost never depends on their logical consistency. These relativistic presuppositions are as latent and contradictory as they are efficacious. They foster crises that do not have internal resources by which to be solved, namely crises related to *contents* for which liberal democracies experience need (think of things like solidarity, friendship, and the respect for the person), crises related to *superabundant* contents to select from (think of the current hyperbolic proliferation of human rights, or *alleged* human rights), and crises related to *fundamental* contents that often conflict with one another (the problem of the balancing of human rights).

A more subtle reason is that a sort of limited and moderate relativism seems to be convenient to many liberals. The main problem of contemporary political philosophy is the same as ever: to understand the limits of public power with respect to citizens' freedom(s). To use different words, it is to figure out how far the public force can and should go in order for individuals to live together, and for the society to grow and prosper in the best possible way. This problem manifests itself in the constant attempt to define a *sphere of justice* that is able to set precise limits on public action, or in the attempt to draw a sharp demarcation between public sphere and private sphere. There are many people who fear an *excessive coherence* (if there is such a thing) with respect to the fundamental truths of the democratic system—for example, the truths regarding human beings as holders of rights (who they are and what goods they have that must be protected and fostered under such and such circumstances). People fear that *too much coherence* about these truths might lead to totalitarianism, paternalism, and unjustified restrictions and censorships from which we have *freed ourselves*. Thus, it is better to adopt a *weak or thin thought* that will remain in constant tension with itself: a thought that states and does not state the fundamental truths of human freedom without getting too much into details of definitions and contents. In and through its weakness, this thought continues to protect an *acceptable quantity* of personal freedom.[7]

Personally, I do not believe that there are reasons to question our current favorable ideological attitude toward democracy and pluralism. Certainly, I do not intend to do it here. However, there are several crises today that cannot be constructively approached without disclosing some ideological exaggerations that have accompanied the history of liberal democratic systems. To do so, we must try to objectively justify—going beyond ideologies—the *transcendental* truths that ground them. Moderate relativism does not bring peace. On the contrary, it increases social tensions that cannot be solved without consistent truth statements. The current crises of the system are all linked to a deeper crisis. This crisis lies in another attempt to found liberal democracy in a total self-referential way—as if freedom could be the foundation of freedom, or autonomy could generate autonomy. A reasonable and consistent solution cannot avoid the search for a foundation of human freedom *external* to the system (*natural*, one might say), which is able to highlight and explain freedom's meaning and scope.

The background view of this chapter is that the only secure foundation of pluralism is an attitude of appreciation of, and respect for, nature. Such an attitude leads to an ever-increasing understanding and awareness of the foundation

---

7   Jeffrey Stout's rejection of metaphysical foundations of liberal democracy—in favor of pragmatic or expressivist explanations—works in the same way of what I call here "moderate relativism" (and with similar inconsistencies). See his *Democracy and Tradition* (Princeton: Princeton University Press, 2005).

of the dignity of the person and of the respect for his freedom. For reasons that are not necessary to it, theoretically speaking, the history of the modern liberal State walks hand in hand with the progressive crisis of the concepts of nature and authority. These two concepts go together because the respect for nature is an existential attitude before being an explicit theoretical option, and it grows and prospers in a context where even the Author of nature is recognized and respected. The current foundational crisis is highly related to the development of modernity's practical and theoretical atheism.

As is obvious, this view and its corollaries go far beyond the scope of one last chapter in a book. In what follows, I aim at a much more modest goal. On the one hand, I want to call attention to the roots of the relativistic attitude present in contemporary philosophical political thought—which, ironically, is meant to defend pluralism—and I want to explain how this attitude depends on the attempt to found society not on nature, but on the sole concept of freedom as autonomy. On the other hand, I will focus on Rawls and on the idea he made famous: the priority of the just over the good. I want to highlight the conceptual elements that entail the crisis of the concepts of nature and authority in the primordial doctrines of the modern State. This crisis is clearly visible when we specifically focus on some linguistic aspects of the modern turn in natural law theory.

1. Liberal Neutrality and the Priority of the Just over the Good

It is important to understand with reasonable accuracy what the sources of the relativistic attitude are in contemporary philosophical and political ideology. A good way to do that is to reflect—as briefly as the subject-matter allows—on the principle of neutrality and on the so-called priority of the right or just over the good.

> [The] priority of the right over the good in justice as fairness
> turns out to be a central feature of the conception.[8]

---

8   J. Rawls, *A Theory of Justice*, pp. 31–32. I don't need to dwell here on the evolution of Rawls' thought, but only on some key features of his original theory of justice, which can be considered as emblematic of contemporary political thought.

John Rawls is often considered the most important political philosopher of our time. His *A Theory of Justice* is emblematic of current trends of thought and it has made several ideas famous, one of which is the priority of the just over the good as a way to approach the contemporary debate. In this debate not only are so-called (contractualist) deontologism and (utilitarian) teleologism lined up on the different battlefronts, but also, and more generally, liberalism and communitarianism are placed in confrontation.[9] Rawls is a neocontractualist and a neokantian. Being just is for him what is required by social life, what grounds the agreement signed by the citizens, and what ought to be respected as a categorical imperative. Being good is what concerns the conceptions of moral life that everyone individually embraces: good is a private issue.

As Ronald Dworkin writes referring to a general objection that supposedly all critics address to liberalism—whether they are romanticists, Marxists, or conservatives—it is usually said that liberalism

> gives too much importance to the just, or to the principles of justice, and too little to the good, or to the quality and the value of the lives we live [...] In the last decades, it seems that liberal political philosophers have accepted the assumption common to these critiques. They assume that liberalism subordinates the questions about the good life to the questions of justice, or—to use a well-known expression by Rawls—that liberalism gives

9   "The debate between practical philosophy inspired by Aristotle and modern contractualism, especially in its liberal version, shifted today to the question if we should first safeguard the 'just'—as liberals argue (Rawls, Nozick, Dworkin)—or the 'good'—as communitarians argue. According to the former, a fundamental equality of opportunity (that is, justice) should be first guaranteed to each person, and then every individual should be left free to plan as he deems best his ideal life (which would be the good). According to the latter, on the other hand, justice itself presupposes intersubjective relationships, and therefore the belonging to a community, which establishes at the beginning what the shared values are, and which consequently is characterized by a precise conception of the good" (E. Berti, "Una critica all'individualismo moderno [A Critique of Modern Individualism]", in *Avvenire*, February 24, 1996).

the just *priority over* the good. This means that liberalism does not have by itself any opinion about the good life, but it only stipulates the principles of a just society, leaving to other theories or disciplines the task of imagining what the good life would be in this society. [...] Liberals do have an obvious reason to maintain this opinion about their political theory. A fundamental, almost defining, principle of liberalism is that the government of a political community should be tolerant as to the different, and often conflicting, convictions of its citizens about the good way of living [...] It is easier to understand, and maybe to defend, liberal tolerance if one accepts the view that liberalism does not derive or depend on any specific ethical ideal.[10]

The *principle of neutrality* is the most appropriate key to correctly reading classical liberalism, which could even be called *classical neutral liberalism* so as to clearly distinguish it from more recent *perfectionist* liberal approaches. From this viewpoint the question is not to be addressed in terms of which is prior to what with respect to the good and the just, but in terms of union or separation among them. That is to say, neutral liberalism aspires in general not to say anything about the good because everybody should be left free to take his own stance on the ethical questions and on the meaning of the good. However, since we are all surrounded by one another, neutral liberalism should solve the problem of creating the social conditions necessary to avoid everyone stepping on each other's feet. These are the conditions for the very possibility of social life, and somehow they are not supposed to match any ethical ideal: they are the conditions for the *just*, and the just ought to be neutral with respect to the *good*. The just and the good ought to be two different things.

Neutral liberalism presupposes a relativistic and individualistic conception of the good. It also presupposes that the dimension of the just be only instrumental. The idea of what is good needs to be multiplied by the number of subjects or citizens. The good should not be justified in a universal or objective way because this is precisely what the principle of

10 R. Dworkin, "La fonte di ogni libertà [The source of every freedom]", in *Il Sole-24 Ore*, March 10, 1996.

neutrality opposes. This is why the just cannot be justified by proclaiming its intrinsic value. That is to say, the just is not to be respected *because it is good*. The just *must* be universal and objective, or else it could not regulate intersubjective relationships. The priority of the just over the good is a relativistic claim because it means the impossibility of stating the existence, among all people, of a good that is objective: i.e., of a *common good*. Accordingly, the only reason individuals can find to respect the just is to see it as a useful tool for their own individual good. There would *always* be a reason to respect it only if it can be proven that it is always the best possible tool. The just is not an end but a means. Moreover, since the just relates to our social dimension—to our being or staying with the others—it follows that from a neutral liberal viewpoint it is the others who cannot be good for us: they can only be useful to our individual good. The other is not an end but a means. The most obvious alternative to neutral liberalism is not really about setting the good above the just, but about giving the just some intrinsic value: not "good before just" but "just as good."

The most common and spontaneous criticism to neutral liberalism is that it is impossible to maintain the neutrality of the good and insist at the same time on a theory of social justice. In other words, it is impossible to support the just without saying something about the good. It is interesting that this criticism has been raised—under the rubric of a discontinuity strategy—by a firm assertor of liberalism like Ronald Dworkin, who invited his fellow liberals to develop an *ethical foundation* of liberalism:

> Liberal philosophers who [...] adopt the restrictive interpretation according to which liberalism is a theory of the just but not of the good, face the problem of explaining what reasons people have to be liberals. They adopt what I will call the "strategy of discontinuity": namely, they want to find the moral or self-interest motives on the basis of which people might put aside, in their political action, their convictions about the good life. I think that liberals should reject this restrictive interpretation of their theory. Quite the opposite, they should try to connect ethics with politics, by building a thesis on the nature and the character of the good life able to make liberal political

morality continuous, rather than discontinuous, with attractive proposals on the good life.[11]

John Finnis is much stronger than Dworkin in stating this contradiction:

> It is sometimes argued that to prefer, and to seek to embody in legislation, some conception or range of conceptions of human flourishing is unjust because it is necessarily to treat with unequal concern and respect those members of the community whose conceptions of human good fall outside the preferred range and whose activities are or may therefore be restricted by the legislation. As an argument warranting opposition to such legislation this argument cannot be justified; it is self-stultifying [...] Those who put forward the argument prefer a conception of human good, according to which a person is entitled to equal concern and respect and a community is in bad shape in which that entitlement is denied; moreover, they act on this preference by seeking to repeal the restrictive legislation which those against whom they are arguing may have enacted. Do those who so argue and so act thereby necessarily treat with unequal concern and respect those whose preferences and legislation they oppose? If they do, then their own argument and action is itself equally unjustified, and provides no basis for political preferences or action. If they do not (and this must be the better view), then neither do those whom they oppose.[12]

In Rawls, the priority of the just over the good is functional to the principle of liberal neutrality, and it presupposes both a relativistic and individualistic conception of the good and that the dimension of the just is merely instrumental. To adequately understand this point we should dwell for a moment upon the basic conceptual elements of Rawls' peculiar contractualist theory (in its earliest version).

---

11 Ibid.
12 J. Finnis, *Natural Law and Natural Rights* (Clarendon Press: Oxford 1980), pp. 221–2.

As is well known, Rawls traces his theory back to the tradition of the grand modern contractualists: Locke, Rousseau, and Kant. He does not think the social agreement to be a real historical event. He agrees with Kant that the social contract is a fiction meant to rationally understand the basic requirements of common social life. Rawls' theory wants to show what we would choose for the social contract (its clauses and principles of justice) if we really were all reunited in the same room discussing the principles of living together that should be adopted in our community. Nonetheless, the social contract fiction, reflecting what we would all choose in that hypothetical situation, is also a mirror of the values that we really share and on which we implicitly ground our living together.

Rawls' theory revolves around three basic elements. The first is the *original position*, the social contract from which the political community originates. The original position is negotiated according to the hypothetical standards of perfect economic rationality. The hypothesis holds that the subjects coming to the original agreement do everything in their own *self-interest*, and also that they are perfectly able to calculate the best conditions to maximize this self-interest (perfect rationality). The second element is the *veil of ignorance*, which indicates the subjects' situation at the moment of bargaining and signing the contract. In order to obtain fair principles of justice, each subject is not supposed to know anything about himself and/or about his personal circumstances (family, patrimony, etc.) while discussing the social contract clauses. This way, allegedly, everybody will try to create the best possible conditions to maximize his self-interest independently from the position he actually holds (or will hold) in society. The point is that by aiming at one's self-interest each will indiscriminately pursue everybody's interest. Thirdly, there are the principles of justice. According to Rawls, the social contract leads to two fundamental principles of political justice. These are: a principle of equality (everybody has the right to the highest level of freedom compatible with the same level of freedom by everybody else), and a principle of inequality (social and economic inequalities can be accepted if they (a) are to the benefit of less advantaged people, and (b) relate to offices and jobs open to everybody in conditions of fair equality of opportunity).

It is important to stress that this ethical political theory implies that citizens are selfish at the moment of establishing the principles of justice.

They aim at their self-interest and pursue it with perfect economic rationality. A crucial flaw in this theory is that there are no reasons, whether selfish or not, for the citizens to accept the veil of ignorance. If indeed I am selfish, I will not be willing to forget my own advantages and privileges at the very moment of choosing the basic terms and conditions of my future life in society (terms and conditions which might make me lose them). If, on the other hand, I am not selfish, I will not want to forget, for example, that I am responsible for my five or seven children at the moment of choosing the basic terms and conditions of *our* future life in society since they might damage families with many children and other underprivileged people. An ethical person could not be willing to forget his own ethics and his own responsibilities at the moment of choosing the principles of justice.[13]

At any rate, I think it is apparent that beneath Rawls' theory there is a mixture of ethical relativism and individualism. In this theory, the sphere of justice is ultimately justified by its being instrumental to the *self-interest* of the contracting parties in the original position. Rawls, however, aims at affirming the existence of an absolute inviolability of the person which is grounded on the radical equality of all men as opposed to utilitarian instrumentalization. Such commodification would hold that social action can sacrifice the individual to the advantage of the greater good of the greater number. Rawls writes,

> Each person possesses an inviolability founded on justice that even the welfare of society as a whole cannot override. For this reason justice denies that the loss of freedom for some is made right by a greater good shared by others. It does not allow that the sacrifices imposed on a few are outweighed by the larger sum of advantages enjoyed by many. Therefore in a just society the liberties of equal citizenship are taken as settled: the rights

13　An interesting criticism to the veil of ignorance can be found in J. Rist, *Real Ethics*, pp. 183–186. Rist highlights that "to reason in a veiled world is not to reason in the world," nor it is rational to try to do so. Moreover, to be under the veil of ignorance would imply that one does not know his own experience (whether moral or otherwise), which, on the contrary, is essential to the rationality one uses at the moment of discussing the terms of an agreement.

secured by justice are not subject to political bargaining or to the calculus of social interests...These propositions seem to express our intuitive conviction of the primacy of justice.[14]

For Rawls, utilitarian instrumentalization depends on a particular conception of the good above considerations of justice, and by interpreting social action (justice) as the attempt to maximize the good according to that particular conception. Specifically, in the case of utilitarianism, it is the attempt to maximize the good in terms of *individual preferences* (which result from economic statistic calculations). The utilitarian instrumentalization, in other words, depends on having abandoned a neutral attitude toward the good at the moment of choosing the basic principles of social justice. This is why utilitarianism can be said to belong to teleological ethical theories, which are the theories in which "the good is defined independently from the right, and then the right is defined as that which maximizes the good."[15] In order to attain the desired inviolability, it is therefore necessary to set the conceptions of the good below considerations of justice. It is necessary to adopt a deontological theory—namely, "one that either does not specify the good independently from the right, or does not interpret the right as maximizing the good."[16] The just precedes the good because it sets the borders, so to speak, to the territory in which everybody can then pursue his own plan of life as he likes it. The just is an *initial bound* "upon what is good and what forms of character are morally worthy, and so upon what kind of persons men should be".[17] If, on the one hand, the good is and has to remain subjective—if the discourse about the good has to remain immanent to each individual person—the just, on the other hand, is the transcendent, the intersubjective, the common background for regulating mutual relationships.[18]

14   J. Rawls, *A Theory of Justice*, pp. 3–4.
15   Ibid. p. 24. Rawls says that he is using the definition offered by W. K. Frankena.
16   Ibid. p. 30.
17   Ibid. p. 32.
18   Ibid. See for example p. 9: "A conception of social justice, then, is to be regarded as providing in the first instance a standard whereby the distributive aspects of the basic structure of society are to be assessed".

Even at first glance, the elements of Rawls' thought that we briefly mentioned do not seem to be consistent with one another. The criticism of utilitarianism (and of teleological theories in general) comes from the obligation to never treat the individual as a means. Rawls explicitly refers to the Kantian imperative.[19] Now, utilitarianism is an example of ethical theory which is not relativist but individualist. It is precisely from its individualism that the possibility of instrumentalizing the person occurs ("the other" does not have inherent value). The definition of teleological theories is applicable only to this kind of theory because in a non-individualist conception (as, for example, the classical discussion of friendship)[20] the good neither precedes the just,[21] nor is distinguishable from it. From this viewpoint, Rawls' criticism becomes paradoxical: in order to make the other be an end in himself, he contrasts an individualist conception with a conception that is both individualist and relativist. An insoluble problem in Rawls's theory comes exactly from trying to infer the inviolability of the other from the veil of ignorance (ethical relativism) and from mutual indifference (individualism).

2. The Modern State and the Crisis of Authority

The debate on the priority of the just over the good and on Rawls' theory of justice very effectively reveals some basic problems of our liberal democracies. One is the problem of guaranteeing the inviolability of the person and of his rights against the instrumentalizations allowed by utilitarian thought. Another—as expressed by Dworkin—is the problem of finding an ethical foundation of liberalism able to preserve tolerance without falling

---

19   See, for example, ibid p. 253.

20   See the previous chapter, "Friendship or Equality? Notes towards an Ideal of Political Personalism".

21   Rawls himself seems to realize this when he states, "Whereas if the distribution of goods is also counted as a good, perhaps a higher order one…we no longer have a teleological view in the classical sense. The problem of distribution falls under the concept of right as one intuitively understands it, and so the theory lacks an independent definition of the good" (*A Theory of Justice*, p. 25). There is some ambiguity here when Rawls seems to consider "teleological view in the classical sense" what should probably be better defined as "modern individualistic ethical view".

into the impasse of neutrality and ethical relativism. Indeed, there is an increasing and widespread consensus over the need for such ethical foundation. However, not many people today are willing to revisit and seriously put into question those elements of modern doctrines that have slowly corroded the concepts of nature and authority due to an excessive exaltation of freedom as autonomy.

It is common to say—and I do not think that there are strong reasons to disagree—that the modern State was born out of the criticism to the organicist political model to the advantage of the individualist model.[22] The organicist model refers to the classical (Aristotelian) model that is usually exemplified by the metaphor of the all-encompassing individual: the State is like the body of a big man, and the citizens are its parts.[23] This model seems to be contrary to the idea of human rights because the part, as such, is conceptually instrumental to the good of the whole (of which it is part). If the individual is part of the political community he can be sacrificed to it—as a leg can be sacrificed to the overall good of the ill body of which it is part. Modern political doctrine's revolution, on the other hand, is about putting the individuals before the State. This is the meaning of contractualist theories: individuals exist with their rights (in the state of nature) before the political community, which is created afterward (through the social contract) in order to better protect them.

Although there are no serious reasons to disagree with the general features of this historiographical interpretation, it is surprising that the so-called organicist model seems to perfectly identify with the modern utilitarian model, in which individuals can indeed be instrumentalized to the good of the political community—i.e., to *the greater good of the greater number*. However, the concept of part does not imply the possibility of a total and indiscriminate sacrifice. Of every whole there are essential and non-essential parts, and even the non-essential ones cannot be unnecessarily sacrificed without damaging the good of the whole. The brain, for example, is no doubt a part of the human being, but it is a part so essential that it

---

22 See, for example, N. Bobbio, *The Age of Rights* (Polity Press: Cambridge, UK, 1991).

23 The obvious reference is to Aristotle's *Politics*, but also the Thomas Aquinas' *De Regno*.

could never be sacrificed without at the same time destroying the human being of which it is part. The leg, on the other hand, is not essential as the brain is, but if we amputate it when there is no need of doing it, then we are irreparably and foolishly damaging the whole of which it is part. Thomas Aquinas, among others, has certainly defended the political model today often called organicist, but he has also thought that the innocent man is an *essential* part of the political whole. There is no way to sacrifice the innocent man without damaging the political community. The innocent man is inviolable: this is the fundamental difference between the classical organicist model and utilitarianism.

I would add that authors like Aquinas cannot be criticized for restricting the concept of inviolability to the *innocent* man because this is still nowadays a basic principle of our public ethics and of our legal systems. Criminal law is entirely grounded on the principle that a guilty person is not anymore inviolable, and as a consequence can be punished in several ways (detention, pecuniary punishments, etc.) when the good of the community demands it. Of course, punishment should also tend to the good of the criminal, but if the common good were not at stake we would not have any reason/right to punish him. Every agent acts in view of his ultimate good or end, as does the political community, which has a common ultimate end. The State cannot act *only for the sake of the criminal's good*. Paternalism is a misunderstanding of classical political theory. The law enforcement system (police) is based on this same principle: any restriction to personal freedom, to privacy, etc., is only justified if (a) it is for the common good, and (b) in case of certain, presumable or suspect guilt. Even legitimate defense only makes sense in cases of aggression (materially of formally) describable as unjust. To criticize Aquinas' point that only the innocent person is *per se* absolutely inviolable is like trying to demolish our entire political society and our public moral conscience.

What I want to stress here is that in spite of its undeniable merits, the individualist model irreparably denies a concept that is essential to our moral political (common) sense: the concept of the common good as a good transcending the good(s) of individuals as such. I think it is an obvious truth that nobody is more important than all of us together or than the entire political community. This is why patriotism is the key (public) virtue of the good citizen. The hero who sacrifices himself for his country receives the highest honor and awards. What is conceptually difficult is to put this truth together with the other, that the innocent person is an essential part of the political community (the whole) and that he cannot be *violated* in any way. The debasement of the concept of common good brings with it the debasement of the political authority, which is the depositary of that common good and responsible for it. Political authority is the other side of patriotism. A strong political society recognizes itself in its authority, which, for its part, feels responsible for the pursuit of a higher good comprehensive of the goods of each individual member of the community. The individualist attitude takes cohesion away from the political community, and damages a responsible moral attitude in its leaders.

The philosophical political doctrines that lie at the origins of the modern liberal State are linked to a strong process of secularization of society and morality. The so-called "School of Natural Law," to which thinkers like Rousseau and Locke belong, flourishes under the auspices of the famous premise by Grotius that the natural law would remain valid *etsiamsi daremus non esse Deum*—even if God did not exist.[24]

From this school the American and French revolutions took their main impetus, and the first authentic bills of human universal rights emerge.[25] The modern tradition of natural law is no longer said to have a religious character, but is instead secular. It is said to be dominated not by a "*heteronomous* attitude of the spirit"[26] but by an *autonomous* one. In this tradition the moral law is only "set by that 'nature', that peculiar essence of man

---

24 U. Grotius, *De iure belli ac pacis*, (Paris: 1625, Prolegomena 11). On Grotius' role in the history of natural law theory, see A. P. D'Entrèves, *Natural Law: An Introduction to Legal Philosophy* (London: Hutchinson University Library, 1951); and H. Rommen, *The Natural Law. A Study in Legal and Social History and Philosophy*. Trans. T.R. Hanley (St. Louis: Herder Book, 1947). Unlike Rommen, Passerin D'Entrèves tends to highlight the centrality of Grotius' contribution.

25 See N. Bobbio, *The Age of Rights*. Hittinger highlights that modern American tradition, unlike the Europeans, continues to recognize the existence of a "higher law." See also, R. Hittinger, *The First Grace: Rediscovering the Natural Law in a Post-Christian World* (Wilmington, Delaware: ISI Books, 2003), p. xxv.

26 See G. Del Vecchio, *Storia della filosofia del diritto* (Milano: Giuffrè, 1948), p. 31.

which is his reason."[27] This path of modern thought can also be described as the history of the gradual removal of the concept of authority, and it has deep and subtle theoretical roots. In contractualist modern theories the state of nature is the place of natural rights, and it is a world without authority and law. Authority and law come into existence later, as the first fruit of a social agreement among human people. Modern natural rights conceptually precede authority, where legislative power resides.[28] Setting a limit to human authority is precisely the function assigned to those natural rights. However, this limit no longer comes from the law of a higher authority.

It is a *vexata quaestio* if it still make sense to talk about law in the state of nature, where there are no rules endowed with the power of authority, and where the limits to someone's action cannot but come from the mere power of someone else. The reduction of law to power and the loss of the semantics of justice is the *skeleton in the closet* of all contractualist doctrines.[29] It is also a *vexata quaestio* if the modern secularistic reaction to the concept of authority is truly a reaction not to the classical tradition—in which God's will is always an expression of his reason—but rather to the voluntaristic degeneration of classical thought initiated by Scotus and Ockham. This degeneration was carried on to the dawn of modernity by the famous dispute between nominalists and antinominalists.[30] What is certain is that the basic elements of modern contractualist ideology[31] are all linked to the negation of any principle of authority (whether theoretical or ethical) that is external to the autonomy of individual people.

In the state of nature, natural rights is synonymous with natural powers or absolute freedom. The only nature to which they refer is freedom itself.

---

27 See G. Fassò, *Storia della filosofia del diritto. Volume II: L'età moderna* (Bologna: Il Mulino, 1968), p. 113.

28 See R. Hittinger, *The First Grace: Rediscovering the Natural Law in a Post-Christian World*, op. cit., pp. 12–16.

29 See H. B. Veatch, *Human Rights: Fact or Fancy?* (Baton Rouge: Louisiana State University Press, 1985).

30 Concerning this issue, let me refer readers to my *God and the Natural Law*.

31 The idea of a social contract in and of itself is not modern as it was already present in classical authors like Aristotle, Augustine, and Aquinas. See Chapter VIII.

There is no nature that freedom ought to seek at and serve. Autonomy, as the *form* of freedom, is the only foundation and the only true substance of modern natural law theory. The social contract is a manifestation of the absolute power of individual freedom. If we put aside the Hobbesian hypothesis in which the contract's outcome is the complete submission to a despot, liberal society appears to be the society in which civic freedoms are grounded on the absolute autonomy of the majority of the individuals: that is to say, on the individuals' freedom to be their own law. It is an interesting historical irony that the political fiction of the majority's autonomy—or general will—turns into, first in Rousseau's theory and then in France's regime, a very convenient tool for despotic and totalitarian regimes.[32]

Untethered from a foundation in nature, human rights—the heirs of the natural rights proclaimed in the nineteenth-century declarations—become rights to pure or absolute choices, and everyone can invoke them for whatever he or she likes to do. Recent discussions on alleged human rights to abortion, euthanasia or to homosexual marriage show that the mere form of freedom is not sufficient to justify rights and to avoid social conflicts. Nowadays, the language of human rights suffers from demagogical abuse, which is progressively depriving it of meaning and is pouring itself out into the national and international courts of justice in an alarming way. It is becoming more and more apparent that the political community's *legitimacy* cannot simply depend, as Weber argues, on a democratic procedure, but it should also be grounded on objective and true contents and meanings.

3. From *Lex Naturalis* to *Ius Naturale*

The devaluation of the concept of nature implicit in modern natural law theories is particularly apparent in the transition from the early nineteenth-century declarations' linguistic use of natural rights to the twenty-century declarations' use of human rights. By itself, the transition does not involve

---

32 The conceptual transition from the mere concept of freedom to the concept of general will cannot be taken for granted. Rousseau has never explained why *I* should be or feel freer when the (general) will *of others* decides what rules *I* should be subjected to.

a substantial change in the role and function played by those rights. The devaluation of the concept of authority, on the other hand, is apparent in another linguistic change. In Latin European languages this change involves an increasing preference given to the expression *ius naturale* (usually translated with terms related to rights like "rights," "diritto," "derecho," "droits") at the expense of *lex naturalis* (usually translated into terms like "law," "legge," "loi," "ley").

Broadly speaking, *ius naturale* (natural right) does have more of an objective meaning, while *lex naturalis* (natural law) has more of a subjective meaning. *Ius naturale* points to the existence of an objective *ordo* (i.e., an organized whole which includes all things) in the universe, according to which something is due, or belongs, to something else as part of this something else's whole. *Lex naturalis*, on the other hand, refers this (natural) *ordo* to a divine source—namely to a legislator who wanted and arranged the *ordo* the way it objectively presents itself to the observers. By 'subjective' meaning, therefore, I only mean that the semantic area of *lex naturalis*—contrary to the semantic area of *ius naturale*—cannot do without reference to a legislating God—namely to the subject who is responsible for the existence of the natural *ordo*.

In English, this sketch is made more complicated by the fact that both *ius naturale* and *lex naturalis* are commonly translated as "natural law" (*ius naturale*, sometimes, also as "natural right"). This is why Hebert Hart could confidently affirm that natural law has not always been associated with the existence of a divine legislator, and that the success of this expression is due precisely to this conceptual independence from human and divine authorities.[33] As far as the two Latin expressions are concerned, this statement could partly hold true for *ius naturale*, but not for *lex naturalis*. So, what Hart is truly saying is that in his opinion natural law has been successful only for its meaning related to the translation of *ius naturale*.

Whatever one thinks of Hart's viewpoint on the matter, there is no doubt that *ius naturale* has been more successful in modern times than *lex naturalis*. It is also unquestionable that it recalls the idea of an ethical objectivity that precedes human-made law and that should somehow influence

---

33 See H. Hart, *The Concept of Law* (Oxford: Oxford University Press, 1961), Chapter IX.

it.[34] However, we do not reflect often and enough (certainly Hart did not) on the fact that *ius naturale* does not contain a semantic reference that is perfectly explicit in *lex naturalis*—namely, the reference to the authority and the legislator. Under this respect, the devaluation of the concept of authority and the secularization of ethics that goes along with the history of modernity coincide with a devaluation of the classical concept of law (*lex*) in favor of a generic and formalistic usage of the term *ius* in its several contemporary translations.

Those who undertake civil law studies today soon discover that the two most fundamental categories of the so-called "general theory of law" are objective law (or legal system) and subjective law (or rights claims). Studying law in an objective sense is equivalent to studying the legal system, or to studying the overall legal experience in an attempt to *delimit* and describe it. This delimitation and this description are the crucial problems that trouble all modern and contemporary legal theorists. This more or less started with John Austin who entitled his most famous work *The Province of Jurisprudence Determined and the Uses of the Study of Jurisprudence.*[35]

The terms "objective law" and "legal system" are as easy to use as they are vague and difficult to define. The traditional meaning of *lex* is very specific. It relates to the main act of political authority, which regulates the community and grounds or grants individual rights. Broadly speaking, *lex* is an act of the highest political authority (the legislator) which regulates people's action with reference to classes of people (universality of the law) and classes of cases (abstractness of law).

As we have seen in Chapters III and VII, Thomas Aquinas defines *lex* as "an ordinance of reason for the common good, made by him who has care of the community, and promulgated."[36] This concept is much broader than the one we usually employ. For Aquinas, *lex* can be general and abstract or particular and concrete, but above all it is always an act of the

---

34 When I use expressions like "ethical objectivity" or "duty" I assume that the reduction of natural law to mere factual limits to human action—as read in Hart—is a deterioration (or destruction) of the very idea of natural law. See Hart, *The Concept of Law.*

35 J. Austin, *The Province of Jurisprudence Determined and the Uses of the Study of Jurisprudence* (London: Weidenfeld and Nicolson, 1971 [1832]).

36 *ST,* I-II, q. 90, a. 4.

authority that *orders* the parts of the legal system (or the political community) to its (common) good. While doing this, it determines whether they belong to the system. In other words it determines their legal character as the character that defines their being part of a political community and a legal system.[37] Unlike Aquinas, contemporary legal theory tends to put the element that defines what is legal before the law (*lex*).

For Aquinas, *lex* is the first act of government and the principle of order of the community. What does not fit this government and order is not properly legal. It goes without saying that Aquinas' *lex* comes before the modern theory of the separation of powers. Many acts that we ordinarily attribute to the executive and judiciary powers would be legislative in the Thomistic framework. Norberto Bobbio repeatedly emphasizes that one of the key characteristics of modern legal positivism is the "theory of legislation as the preeminent source of law," or considering law "*sub specie legis.*"[38] Now, this is certainly true in the sense of the law's (*lex*) formal force or power, but not in the conceptual sense of its legal character. Modern legal science develops—both in the Anglo-Saxon sphere with Austin and in the German sphere with Merkel—in the direction of identifying, delimiting, and describing the essence of what is legal as something to which *lex* (even if the strongest) is only one of the elements.

The *lex* of our general theory loses its predominant, ordering role to become one source of law among others: one element in a system that transcends it. Since premodern law (*lex*) was the ordering act of a rational intelligence, this declassing coincides with the exclusion from the essence of law of order and finality to the advantage of formalism and power as defining traits of the law. The law of our general theory is not legal because of an end (a common good) to which the political authority aims but because of some formal descriptive element(s) that, allegedly, should be able to identify and define it as legal. Our law (the art of the good and equitable) has been increasingly separated by politics (the art of the good government).

Of course, the legal world includes many elements that do not belong as such to *lex* (for example customary rules), but this is only true if by law

---

37 For the meaning and implications of Aquinas' concept of law, see also my *God and the Natural Law.*

38 See N. Bobbio, *Il Positivismo Giuridico* (Torino: Giappichelli, 1996), p. 130.

we mean only human-made law. Aquinas' definition applies not only to human law but also to the act of government of an authority that transcends the human realm and that orders all of creation to its ultimate end or common good. This act of government is the eternal law, of which natural law is the part concerning human beings. What is included in the order of the eternal law is good, and in a certain sense *legal*. What is not included in it has lost something of the goodness or (legality) that it should have. Human law is just (fully and properly law) when it specifies and determines the natural law in relation to the concrete circumstances of a specific political community. When this happens, it arouses the right sense of justice and obedience in the citizens.

With these premises, it is possible to better frame the conceptual and semantic relationship between *lex naturalis* and *ius naturale*. For Aquinas, *ius naturale* exists as an ethical objectivity that precedes and grounds human law because it is the emanation of the rational creative act of God. *Ius naturale* is the way in which God's law exists in the creatures leading them at the same time—from the *inside*, by means of their own nature—to their specific good and to the ultimate end, or common (political) good, of the entire universe.[39]

The most important task that contemporary political theory has to face might just be finding solid foundations on which to build peace and happiness for our pluralistic and multicultural democratic societies. The value that we attribute to pluralism is already an ethical non-relativistic choice. There is an increasing and across-the-board agreement among different philosophical approaches regarding the fact that pluralism cannot be grounded on the relativism intrinsic to the classical liberal principle of neutrality. This relativism in turn lies on the modern exaltation of freedom as pure form or pure autonomy. The problem is that the same ethical relativism that characterized the main early modern political doctrines continues to characterize the most important and widespread contemporary political theories.

My discussion here focuses on the underlying reasons of such relativism, mainly by offering a critical reading of some aspects of Rawls' theory of justice and of key conceptual features of the eighteenth and nineteenth-

39 See *ST*, I-II, q. 90, a 1; q. 91, a. 1-2.

century contractualist doctrines from which the modern State originates. One of my premises (which I develop elsewhere[40]) is that the relativism of modern and post-modern political doctrines builds on the gradual devaluation of the concept of nature. This devaluation, both historically and conceptually, begins with the separation of nature from its Creator. If nature, with its meanings, is not important for God and is not the fruit of his intelligence, ultimately it is not important for anyone. It becomes intrinsically unintelligible and meaningless, or open to any contingent meaning that a person wants to give it.

The process opposite of relativism involves the search for an ethical foundation of pluralistic societies, and it must somehow go through a rediscovery of God and of nature as created. Good pluralism, so to speak, is that which—precisely because it is not relativistic—recognizes that nature can offer a common ground for dialogue. It also attributes intrinsic importance to nature because it remains open to a transcendental dimension which makes it important before, and independently of, human provisional agreements. Maybe this is utopian, or maybe it is utopian to imagine a peaceful pluralistic society grounded on mere autonomy, or on the mere agreement of its members. Then again, maybe it is utopian to take the very idea of human rights seriously when intentionally separated from the dimension of the sacred and the mystery. Other people's dignity and their fundamental rights will always appear as a limit to our freedom to do whatever we like whenever we do not see why we should not. There is a historical and common sense moral experience that says that people usually accept limitations to their freedom when they recognize a transcendent, and partly mysterious, foundation for the meanings of things—especially for the meaning of human dignity. This moral experience has too long been neglected.

---

40 See, for example, my *God and the Natural Law*.

INDEX